ELEMENTARY PRINCIPAL'S COMPLETE HANDBOOK

Practical Techniques & Materials for Inservice Administrators

FRED B. CHERNOW • CAROL CHERNOW

PRENTICE HALL
Englewood Cliffs, New Jersey 07632

Prentice-Hall International (UK) Limited, *London*
Prentice-Hall of Austrialia Pty. Limited, *Sydney*
Prentice-Hall Canada, Inc., *Toronto*
Prentice-Hall Hispanoamericana, S.A., *Mexico*
Prentice-Hall of India Private Limited, *New Delhi*
Prentice-Hall of Japan, Inc., *Tokyo*
Simon & Schuster Asia Pte. Ltd., *Singapore*
Editora Prentice-Hall do Brasil, *Rio de Janeiro*

© 1992 by

PRENTICE HALL

Englewood Cliffs, NJ

10 9 8 7 6 5 4 3 2

Library of Congress Cataloging-in-Publication Data

Chernow, Fred B., 1932–
    Elementary principal's complete handbook : practical techniques &
materials for inservice administrators / Fred Chernow, Carol
Chernow.
     p.   cm.
    Includes index.
    ISBN 0-13-253402-9
    1. Elementary school administration—United States—Handbooks,
manuals, etc. 2. Elementary school administration—United States—
Forms. I. Chernow, Carol, 1934–   . II. Title.
LB2822.5C4 1992
372.12′00973—dc20   92-4279
                                                          CIP

ISBN 0-13-253402-9

PRENTICE HALL
Professional Publishing
Englewood Cliffs, NJ 07632
Simon & Schuster. A Paramount Communications Company

Printed in the United States of America

About the Authors

FRED B. CHERNOW is a school principal on Staten Island, New York. He has served as an elementary school principal in both inner-city and suburban schools for more than twenty years. He has conducted courses for school administrators as well as for teachers aspiring to become principals. A frequent contributor to publications that provide inservice training for principals, he is an Adjunct Associate Professor at St. John's University and also City University of New York.

CAROL CHERNOW has taught in Anne Arundel County, Maryland, as well as New York City on a variety of grade levels. For many years she taught communication skills to adults for the federal government. She currently teaches language arts at the middle school level. She is also the coauthor of the best selling *Classroom Discipline and Control* as well as the *Elementary Principal's Model Letter Kit*.

Acknowledgments

The seed of this book was planted by Winfred A. Huppuch, Vice President/ Education Publishing with Prentice Hall's Business and Professional Books Division, who encouraged us to pull together current successful practices utilized by elementary school principals. "Win" provided wise counsel over several lunches while regaling us with his wit and charm.

The fleshing out of the book from its early skeletal, idea stage was provided by our remarkable and indefatigable editor, Sandra Hutchison, whose experience as both a teacher and an editor proved invaluable to us. Sandy's critical eye and detached oversight shaped this project into a labor of love.

Working with us in getting the manuscript through to publication was a perceptive production editor, Barbara O'Brien.

Many long nights found Jill Selman and Bernadette Kress typing from our handwritten notes. We are grateful to them for their prompt delivery of polished manuscript pages.

Most of all, we are indebted to the dozens of principals who submitted material, read rough drafts, and breathed fresh air into these pages.

Fred B. Chernow
Carol Chernow

New York
January 1992

About This Resource

Today's elementary school principal wears many hats: administrator, instructional leader, child advocate, disciplinarian, guidance counselor, to name just a few. As principal, you must fulfill your many roles while juggling the needs of pupils, parents, teachers, and the community. Your job has probably never been more challenging than it is today.

That is why the *Elementary Principal's Complete Handbook* offers you a comprehensive selection of proven strategies for successful administration, as well as time-saving forms and sample materials you can copy or adapt for immediate use. The authors have drawn on their many years as principal and classroom teacher—as well as the experiences of successful administrators across the country—to bring together this all-in-one resource. You will find practical guidelines and materials here for every area of your job, in chapters like the following:

"Developing Academic Goals": Provides information on improving pupil performance, improving teachers' techniques, building multicultural awareness into your curriculum, and assessing your own performance as an instructional leader.

"Improving Discipline": Discusses how to prevent discipline problems before they occur, help teachers assert themselves in the classroom, analyze behavior problems, and enlist parent support in discipline cases.

"Putting Shared Decision Making to Work for You": Provides down-to-earth advice about this challenging but rewarding structure, including a discussion of possible start-up problems and how to determine if your school is ready.

"Reducing the Impact of Society's Problems": Discusses guidelines for helping children of divorce, preventing alcohol and other drug abuse, building self-esteem in young black males, reporting child abuse and neglect, and more, with a special emphasis on keeping parents alert and informed.

"Getting the Most out of the School Budget": Provides advice on lobbying for your school's share of the district budget, providing effective fiscal safeguards, taking advantage of school-business partnerships, and using fund-raisers wisely.

"Working with the Power Structure": Provides tips and techniques for winning support from your superintendent, school board, elected officials—even the central office clerical staff—while avoiding political pitfalls.

In the *Elementary Principal's Complete Handbook*, you will also find suggestions and materials to help you meet your many responsibilities, in chapters like the following:

- Making School Meaningful for Your Pupils
- Improving the Climate of Your School
- Motivating Teachers to Do Their Best
- Working Successfully with Parents
- Reaching Out to Your Community
- Communicating Your School's Message
- Meeting Your Pupils' Special Needs
- Enhancing Your School's Guidance Program
- Improving Scheduling and Time Management
- Supervising and Evaluating Your Staff
- Growing as a Leader

As you already know, good intentions alone are not enough. To be successful, you need a wide range of skills and specific, concrete examples of how to organize and administer today's elementary school. We hope that the hundreds of sanity-saving tips and techniques in this resource will lighten your load, increase your effectiveness, and help you preserve your enjoyment of one of the most important jobs anyone can have.

Fred B. Chernow
Carol Chernow

Contents

REPRODUCIBLE FORMS AND SAMPLES

Chapter 1

Developing Academic Goals

Ms. Lee feels as if her years as a successful classroom teacher in no way prepared her for the job of principal. The instructional strategies and techniques of teaching that she perfected appear to be lost in her role as principal. She'd love to get into classrooms and help new teachers improve the learning situation for pupils. Her predecessor was deskbound and snowed under with paperwork and phone calls. She has followed this pattern. It seems that there aren't enough hours in the school day.

■FACILITATOR, CATALYST, cheerleader, oilcan, fulcrum, or hinge—pick the metaphor that you feel best describes the changing role of the principal as we approach the twenty-first century.

Your role as elementary school principal is not the same as it was in the past. The knowledge and skills which made a principal successful a decade ago are not enough today.

It is time to reexamine our leadership beliefs and practices regarding running today's elementary schools. Changes in society and in schools impose on principals' duties and obligations, far exceeding anything in days past. A partial list of new concerns includes

- Health problems, including AIDS
- Nontraditional family structures
- Changing economic status of the community
- Environmental problems
- Explosion in technology
- Movement toward parental choice of the school their children attend
- Movement toward national testing standards.

Principals have always had the job of making schools run and making them run efficiently. This includes

- Leading the faculty
- Training the staff
- Encouraging the pupils
- Creating a code of discipline
- Fostering an esprit de corps
- Coordinating resources
- Scheduling and developing programs
- Maintaining a safe and clean building
- Involving parents.

Difficult as these tasks may seem, they alone are not enough. The main job today is to see that students learn and that they learn at levels far exceeding the levels of the past. The shift is from keeping the school running to focusing on results. It is not enough to conduct schools as we did ten years ago. We must zero in on making sure that students learn.

Take the following test of your vital signs as a school academic leader.

How Are You Doing as an Academic Leader?

1. Are your students of average ability being challenged?
2. What is the quality of mainstreaming for your special-ed pupils?
3. How do you identify gifted and talented pupils?
4. To what extent do you talk with colleagues about ways to improve the level of instruction?
5. Regarding curriculum, are you content to leave alone the teacher who is a good disciplinarian?
6. How much encouragement do you give the teacher who tries out new instructional approaches?
7. Do you have a policy on lesson preparation and writing plans?
8. Do your teachers feel comfortable approaching you about improving their instructional expertise?
9. What is your philosophy regarding teaching pupils?
10. Do you set an example for growing professionally through graduate coursework, professional publications, and writing articles?
11. Is there a single approach to teaching reading in your school?
12. To what extent are parents "taught" skills in helping their children read, study, and do homework?

After reviewing your honest responses to these questions, you will be better able to lead your staff in developing and meeting high-level academic goals for your pupils.

1–1 CREATING A CLEAR VISION FOR YOUR SCHOOL

As an elementary school principal, you are both accountable and responsible for all that goes on in your building. Of course, you may choose to delegate some of your responsibilities. However, while you may appoint others to be responsible for many managerial tasks (such as standardized testing, curriculum materials, or the guidance program), you are responsible for setting objectives and goals.

Setting school goals or creating a clear vision for your school is one job that must not be delegated. Running your school cannot be a one-day-a-time operation in which teachers and pupils go from one day to another, looking forward to Fridays and the month of June.

Every staff member, pupil, and parent must participate, either directly or through democratically selected representatives, in creating a statement that spells out, in simple language, the goals or objectives for the current school year. The vision may be a three- or five-year master plan, and the goal or objective for the current year may be part of the larger vision.

For example, when Vincent DiLeo was appointed principal of his Illinois school, he met with pupils, parents, and teachers both informally and in large groups to assess their feelings about what areas needed the most improvement. Some of his techniques for assessing the perceived needs of each group included the following:

Pupils

- Visiting classrooms and asking opinions of older pupils
- Talking to individual pupils in his office and in hallways
- Discussing problems with small groups in the lunchroom and the schoolyard
- Questioning pupils in assembly

Parents

- Asking for opinions at PTA meetings
- Meeting with the executive board of the PTA
- Questioning parents who were transferring pupils into or out of the school
- Surveying parents via questionnaires in newsletters
- Speaking at parent guidance workshops

Teachers

- Meeting with grade leaders to elicit their perceptions
- Discussing problem areas with teacher union leadership
- Asking for opinions at faculty meetings
- Talking with individual teachers alone or in small groups during lunch hour or before and after school

The long-range vision that emerged from these discussions was the need to turn the school around, halting its downward slide in pupil performance, staff morale, and parent confidence. This clear vision was broken down into some specific goals for each of the next three years:

Year 1: Greater classroom control and improved school discipline

Year 2: Increasing minimum standards of class work, homework, and teacher expectations

Year 3: Greater parent involvement in school life

Although each year's goal was interrelated with the other two years, it became the focus of attention for that particular year.

The goals for each year were written out in clear, appropriate language for each of the three constituencies: parents, pupils, teachers. These goals were referred to in assemblies and meetings. Committees were set up to evaluate any progress toward meeting the year's goals at the end of each marking period. Goals were revised only after conferring with each of the three groups.

This formalized approach to management by objectives involved everyone in setting and then reaching for a common goal. It gave everyone a clear vision of what the school was about and what it wanted to achieve.

In schools we examined, the following objectives were often part of each school's vision:

1. To ensure the implementation of all curriculum areas by
   a. utilizing special abilities of staff
   b. expanding in-service teacher training
   c. creating parent awareness of needs
2. To intensify programs in skill development by
   a. developing sequential levels of grade requirements
   b. conducting periodic reviews of levels of achievement
   c. providing services for pupils with special needs
3. To raise the academic level of all pupils by
   a. evaluating the effectiveness of the teaching on a regular, planned basis
   b. improving the consistency of homework assignments, implementation, and homework's place in the total learning program

Reviewing these techniques and objectives will help you become ready to create a clear vision for your school.

1–2 STRENGTHENING YOUR INSTRUCTIONAL LEADERSHIP ROLE

As head of your school, you must become the leader in improving the instructional program. You must show clearly that you are concerned about the continuous improvement of instruction; otherwise, teachers, parents, and pupils will assume that you assign higher priority to areas other than learning. When you give visitors to your school a tour of the building, you should make clear to them your grasp of the curriculum offerings and of the instructional goals for each grade. As we have seen in our many visits to schools, this knowledge is not characteristic of every school principal. Some are preoccupied with school teams or bands. Others spend most of their energy cultivating parents and school board members. Some closet themselves in their office, spending most of their time on the telephone or reading mail. A few are custodians at heart and occupy their time with minor repairs to the school building.

The following questionnaire will help you measure yourself against principals who are leaders in improving the instructional program in their schools.

How Are You Doing as an Instructional Leader?

1. Describe the kindergarten program in your school. What kind of formal teaching is taking place?
2. How are children grouped for instruction in grades 1 through 5?
3. Which reading series is used in each grade? Do you favor a single basal reader throughout the school? Why or why not?
4. What other reading approaches are used?
5. What are your school's standards for homework?
6. Is there a sex education or family life program? Which classes are involved?
7. What are the social studies topics for each grade?
8. How are the needs of the average pupils being met?
9. What preparations are made for the standardized achievement tests in reading and math? How does the school make use of each year's results?
10. What services are available for pupils in need of remedial help?
11. Are you involved in helping teachers implement the course of study or syllabus?
12. How are new teachers helped in planning lessons and vitalizing instruction?

The answers to these questions should be at your fingertips. Incorporate them when you address parent or community groups and when you show visitors around your building.

There are other ways in which you can strengthen your instructional leadership role:

1. Visit every classroom every day. Let teachers and pupils know that you are not a remote figure and that you think what they are doing is important.

2. Ask teachers to send you every month a set of class papers from one of several areas: spelling tests, book reports, creative writing, math homework, etc. Write comments or put stickers on outstanding papers.

3. Have teachers send you pupil report cards a few days before they are to be distributed. Review them and give each class a pep talk as you return the report cards to each teacher.

4. Spend a few minutes at each of your PTA meetings discussing one area of the curriculum.

5. Talk to pupils in assemblies about your standards for excellence in school work.

6. Encourage pupils by conducting essay contests, spelling and math bees, a school newspaper, and other academic activities.

7. Allocate money for school and class libraries, maps, globes, and enrichment materials as well as basic textbooks.

8. Contact successful members of the community to speak to pupils about the importance of education in the work world.

9. Personalize instruction by recruiting reading volunteers and role models to work with individual pupils who need help or encouragement.

10. Make literacy a priority by giving pupils books as incentive awards, setting up reading programs for parents and other adults in your community, and scheduling schoolwide silent reading periods. Invite authors or local theater groups to read aloud to pupils. Promote pen pals or other letter-writing activities.

1–3 PROMOTING PROFICIENT TEACHING TECHNIQUES

Certain effective teaching strategies are common to schools in which academic goals are met. As the supervisor of instruction, you should frequently and informally observe your teachers as they teach. The occasional formal observation of a planned lesson is not enough.

As you visit classrooms, keep in mind the ten-point checklist provided here.

Classroom Visit Checklist

☐ **1.** Are teachers allocating enough learning time? Is a minimum amount of time spent on noninstructional activities, such as announcements, clerical chores, and money collection? Is the school administration helping to accomplish this goal?

☐ **2.** Do teachers establish reasonable criteria for success? Are appropriate academic challenges set and achieved? Do teachers consider individual student strengths and weaknesses in setting goals?

☐ **3.** Do teachers evaluate prior experience of pupils to reinforce relevancy of instruction? Is there a continuing spiral of teaching and learning through the grades?

☐ **4.** Do you see the use of varied teaching activities to enhance learning? Are teachers using computers, cable TV, etc., when appropriate?

☐ **5.** Do teachers teach not only "what to learn" but "how to learn"? Are pupils able to apply learning to different real-life contexts, such as completing an application, ordering materials, or reading a train schedule?

☐ **6.** Do teachers provide clear, concise directions and monitor pupils' comprehension of directions? Do they often stop, check for understanding, and then repeat directions if necessary?

☐ **7.** Are teachers using brisk-paced instruction to assure high levels of content coverage?

☐ **8.** Do teachers use good questioning techniques? Do they call on pupils who have not volunteered an answer? Do they ask a balance of factual and thought-provoking questions?

☐ **9.** Do teachers use a variety of learning materials? Are teachers overly dependent on duplicated worksheets and workbooks requiring one-word or short-phrase answers? Are teachers assigning, correcting, and returning sustained written work from pupils?

☐ **10.** Do pupils seem truly engaged in the learning process? Are they raising their hands to answer or volunteer? Are they in front of the room sharing experiences? Do they write at the board and move about the room?

Take notes on what you see as you go around your school building, using this ten-point checklist as a guide. A simple technique is to keep a pack of index cards wrapped in a rubber band in your pocket. Use one card for each teacher, and make brief notes after you leave the room. By referring to these cards, you will see patterns of teacher growth. Do not do any writing while in the room, however; it would intimidate the teacher.

1–4 CONDUCTING STAFF MEETINGS THAT IMPROVE LEARNING

Monthly faculty or staff meetings are frequently overlooked opportunities for improving the level of instruction. Meetings devoted to sharing successful teaching practices would certainly be a welcome relief from the boredom of meetings where the typical agenda consists of announcements and admonishments. Announcements are important, of course, but most of them can be made in a weekly printed bulletin. Admonishments are best made in private and in a problem-solving atmosphere.

Faculty meetings are a legitimate part of the in-service growth of each staff member. Successful meetings do not happen by accident. They require planning and organization. One approach to topic selection is to poll the staff. Another is for you to select a curriculum area that needs improvement. Or, you may want to present a variety of successful teaching practices you have observed during classroom visits. Individual teachers can present their particular strategies and techniques.

A sample polling device is provided on the next page.

There are two conditions that influence the success or failure of faculty conferences: physical and psychological. The physical conditions include tangibles such as lighting, ventilation, space, seating, etc. You can't ask teachers to sit in furniture designed for second graders and participate enthusiastically.

The psychological conditions are frequently overlooked. These intangibles are just as important but less obvious than the physical conditions. They include the extent to which teachers

- Feel safe in presenting ideas
- Are encouraged to try new approaches to teaching and sharing
- Feel that you value their contributions to the meeting
- Feel that their investment in time and effort is worthwhile
- Are committed to improving instruction.

The principal who is aware of the importance of both environments will conduct staff meetings that improve instruction.

Staff Meeting Questionnaire

To assist the planning committee in setting up a program of staff meetings that will be of value, we need your help in scheduling the meetings for October 4, November 6, and December 8. They will begin at 3:10 P.M. in the school library.

Please check the three areas that interest you the most. Rank them as 1, 2, and 3. Add any other subjects that interest you.

☐ **1.** Constructing teaching units

☐ **2.** Writing lesson plans

☐ **3.** The art of questioning

☐ **4.** Teaching creative writing

☐ **5.** Using big books

☐ **6.** Teaching reading in the content areas

☐ **7.** The whole language approach

☐ **8.** Helping pupils solve verbal problems in math

☐ **9.** Including AIDS instruction in the health curriculum

☐ **10.** Using drug abuse materials

☐ **11.** _____

☐ **12.** _____

☐ **13.** Are you in favor of serving refreshments? _____

☐ **14.** Do you have any suggestions for improving our staff meetings? _____

_____

_____

Please place your completed questionnaire in my letter box by September 26.

1–5 BUILDING MULTICULTURAL AWARENESS INTO THE CURRICULUM

In reaching for excellence in education, you have a responsibility to increase multicultural awareness. By understanding the similarities and differences of various cultural groups, your pupils will learn that all people have the same basic needs, though they may meet them in different ways.

Stereotypes can be perpetuated in school by unquestioned acceptance of traditionally "appropriate" sex roles, as well as teaching materials and bulletin boards that reinforce social bias. For example, a learning environment that does not represent a wide spectrum of races, physically disabled people, and senior citizens in effect denies the existence of these individuals. Urge your teachers to consider this when selecting teaching materials. Help them review their use of language and methods of teaching.

The elementary school program should provide many experiences to help pupils develop a positive self-image and realize their full potential. By your own example and through administrative action, be sure to take these steps:

- Order teaching materials that depict both males and females in nurturing roles.
- When appropriate, order books in the predominant language that the pupils hear at home.
- Encourage pupils to choose from a variety of toys and games at recess.
- Avoid sexism in assigning monitors (e.g., have girls serving on the audiovisual squad and boys as kindergarten monitors).
- Avoid sexist language by using such titles as these:
  firefighter   mail carrier
  police officer   sanitation worker
- Allow boys and girls to participate in all physical activities they enjoy (i.e., boys jumping rope and girls playing basketball).
- Arrange trips or classroom visits that will expose pupils to role models engaged in nontraditional jobs.
- Extend awareness of the handicapped through stories, films, classroom visitors, and other appropriate activities.

Help your teachers understand the basic elements of their pupils' culture and language. For example, teachers may observe the following characteristics in children from diverse backgrounds:

- In traditional Hispanic cultures, little or no eye contact when speaking to elders is a sign of respect.

- In traditional Asian cultures, the head is considered holy and should not be touched or patted.
- In Haitian culture, using the given or family name is not as great a sign of respect as using title, such as "teacher."
- In Indo-Chinese cultures, gesturing with a crooked finger pointing upward, to indicate "come here," is used only for animals. The gesture to people is with four fingers pointing downward.

In upper grades, pupils should use materials that show the contributions of non-Western cultures to our country's greatness: Arabic numbers, African music, Japanese technology, etc.

1–6 ASSESSING YOUR PERFORMANCE AS AN INSTRUCTIONAL LEADER

With all the demands on the principal as disciplinarian, public relations director, bookkeeper, and letter writer, there seems to be less and less time to be spent as a teacher of teachers, or instructional leader. Some principals are occupied by other duties and cheerfully relinquish their role in improving instruction. In today's schools, it is foolhardy to do so. Your success as a principal depends on how well your pupils are learning. You cannot afford to abdicate this awesome responsibility.

Look over the "Instructional Leader Checklist" and see how many tasks you are performing every day. Each one is geared toward instructional improvement. Try to look at this checklist whenever you have a free moment. The time you spend on these tasks will yield greater results than time spent on the telephone or reading mail.

If you can say "yes, I do" to twelve or more items on this checklist, you can be proud of yourself for putting instruction first. A score of 8 through 11 means that your heart is in the right place, but you need some help with time management. A positive response to seven or fewer items indicates that you need to examine your priorities carefully.

1–7 IMPROVING PUPIL ACHIEVEMENT

A child's education begins at birth. If a child is deprived of physical and emotional nourishment and intellectual stimulation during the preschool years, his or her teachers will have to play catch-up. However, in some schools, low pupil achievement has been halted and even reversed.

Researchers have found out what makes effective schools different from noneffective schools. Effective schools are defined as those where pupils score well above the district mean on standardized achievement

Instructional Leader Checklist

☐ **1.** Visit classrooms on a daily basis.

☐ **2.** Meet with teachers individually to discuss teaching strategies.

☐ **3.** Conduct in-service courses or invite others to do so at your school.

☐ **4.** Review sample texts and other learning materials for possible adoption.

☐ **5.** Assist new teachers in adopting the course of study to the needs of their pupils.

☐ **6.** Orient substitute teachers to school procedures, goals, and teaching styles.

☐ **7.** Help vitalize instruction by introducing audiovisual aids, such as computer software, cable TV, etc.

☐ **8.** Review procedures for report cards and parent-teacher conferences to ensure accurate reporting of actual pupil progress.

☐ **9.** Check teachers' lesson planning.

☐ **10.** Conduct periodic formal observation of lessons, complete with postobservation conferences and written reports.

☐ **11.** Anticipate standardized test schedules and check to see that pupils are being prepared for such tests.

☐ **12.** Make periodic checks of pupils' classwork, test papers, homework, and creative writing samples.

☐ **13.** Meet with teachers to get their feedback on books and materials in use as well as their requests for new books and materials.

☐ **14.** Evaluate the current program with a group of teachers to see if school academic goals are being met. Formulate revised instructional objectives when needed.

☐ **15.** Capitalize on skills and expertise of successful teachers and pair them as mentors to new teachers.

tests. The data reveals that when the following characteristics are present, low pupil achievement can be improved dramatically:

1. The principal is a strong instructional leader. The principal has definite plans for attaining achievement gains. Nothing is left to chance. The school's academic goals are stated, and teachers, parents, and pupils have participated in wording them. These three constituents are constantly reminded of their goals.

2. There is emphasis on basic skills instruction. Reading and math lessons take precedence over all other school activities. Pupil and teacher attendance is carefully monitored to ensure achievement in basic skills, which is seen as a primary goal of the school.

3. Pupil progress is monitored frequently. Teachers use weekly classroom tests to monitor pupil progress toward instructional objectives. The school has a standardized, objective means of measuring student progress. Parents are regularly informed of their children's scores on class and achievement tests.

4. School staff has a positive expectation for all students. The teachers believe that a common standard of instruction applies to all children. No students are excluded from instruction. In-school suspension for disruptive pupils is preferred to out-of-school suspension. The principal instills in teachers an optimistic attitude about teacher impact on pupil achievement.

5. The school's climate is safe, orderly, and businesslike. It is neither rigid nor loose. Accepted standards of behavior are known to pupils, teachers, and parents. The pupils know that the adults are in charge.

Does this mean that if you do all these things your pupils' scores will go up? We can't say for sure. It's tempting to believe that we could increase achievement this way, especially since adhering to these characteristics would not cost a lot of money—it depends primarily on a strong principal. All the research tells us is that these characteristics are found in effective schools. We don't know for sure if these characteristics cause schools to be effective. Those principals who have followed these five basic characteristics report improved pupil achievement. Why not try it in your school?

Chapter 2

Improving Discipline

Ms. R. is principal of K–5 school just outside of Philadelphia. She feels that she has assumed the role of pupil disciplinarian. Most of her time is spent responding to SOS calls from teachers who can't or won't solve their own classroom behavior problems. She doesn't mind sharing some of her expertise in this area with her teachers. She *does* resent having to clean up after them when they don't take preventive steps or assert themselves in the classroom. Ms. R. wants to help her teachers become more accountable for classroom management.

■IN EVERY SCHOOL there are some teachers who pride themselves on solving their own classroom management problems. There are others who throw up their hands and complain, "I'm not here to be a police officer; I want to teach and not discipline all the time."

The reality is that no teaching can take place until classroom control has been established and the teacher is in charge. Everyone's a winner when you help your teachers improve their discipline survival skills.

2–1 TEN STEPS TOWARD ESTABLISHING GOOD DISCIPLINE

The primary concern of teachers when they face a class for the first time is, Will I be able to maintain discipline? Will the pupils follow my directions?

As the head of the school, there is much that you can do to establish an orderly, well-run school in which good discipline is the rule and not the exception. Let's face it: Unless your teachers can maintain discipline and control, very little instruction will take place.

Good classroom discipline starts at the top, but it requires the support of the foot soldiers as well as the captain. Study the following proven strategies and put them to work tomorrow morning.

1. *Make discipline a priority.* Talk about the need for order at every faculty conference, at PTA meetings, and at pupil assemblies. Let the teachers, parents, and pupils know that you consider it important.

2. *Support your teachers.* By your deeds as well as your words, show your staff that you are behind them in their efforts at maintaining discipline. Respond promptly to notes about a misbehaving pupil. Call parents to your office. Remove pupils for short periods of time. Discuss with teachers a variety of classroom management techniques.

3. *Establish a ladder of referral.* Work out a discipline referral system with your staff that involves the parent, teacher, guidance counselor, yourself, and any clinical help available (social worker, psychologist, nurse). Avoid confusion and duplication of service by establishing steps or rungs for each infraction.

4. *Be available.* Make yourself available to talk with individual teachers who are having behavior problems with particular pupils. See them before class, at lunch, or at any mutually convenient time. Be supportive—do not blame the teacher. Instead, make positive sugges-

tions. Follow up on weak teachers. Make sure new teachers have a potential for control before you make them tenured staff members.

5. *Provide escape hatches.* There comes a time when even the most skillful teacher needs some time out. Make it possible for a teacher to send a disruptive child to the office for an hour. Establish procedures for in-school suspension when necessary. Review district policy with teachers for suspension or expulsion from school.

6. *Work with parents.* Let parents know what will and what will not be tolerated in school. Let them know the school policy regarding class-room disruption, foul language, fighting, cheating, vandalism, etc. Point out what the school is prepared to do and what parent responsibilities are.

7. *Post rules and regulations.* Together with teachers, work out a list of behavior rules that pupils must follow throughout the school. These are in addition to classroom responsibilities that individual teachers may establish regarding homework, classwork, etc.

8. *Refer to rules when talking to groups of pupils.* Clarify and illustrate these schoolwide behavior rules when talking to groups of pupils in the lunchroom, at assemblies, etc. If a pupil is suspended, let the others hear from you the reason why and the punishment for each infraction.

9. *Avoid corporal punishment.* Paddling or other forms of corporal punishment does not change pupil behavior for the better. It does foster resentment and further misbehavior. Let your teachers know how you feel about this subject. District or state laws may also prohibit teachers from using corporal punishment.

10. *Practice preventive discipline.* Identify situations that are likely to promote misbehavior, and stop problems before they take place. Make yourself highly visible during morning line-up, lunch time, and bus dismissal. Be alert to particular pupils who may try to take advantage of large-group situations or an absent teacher. You may want to remove a volatile pupil from his or her class when the regular teacher is absent.

2–2 HELPING TEACHERS WIN PUPIL COOPERATION

Your teachers look to you as a resource in helping them with discipline problems. The best approach you can use is to help them prevent problems before they occur. (Of course, many teachers want to use you as a purveyor of punishment for individual offenders.)

What are some positive steps you can take to make your classrooms a calmer place? After talking to hundreds of teachers with good control, we have come up with some things that they do in common—steps that they take to enlist student cooperation. We have distilled them into this list of ten steps that you can help your teachers put to work—right away.

Ten Commandments for Pupil Cooperation

1. *Confront your students.* Make the misbehaving pupil aware of his or her specific misdeed. Focus on what is happening here and now. Don't talk about "last time" or "you always"; instead, talk about right now. The point is not to make the student ashamed or defensive; it is to make the student aware of what he or she is doing and why it is wrong.

2. *Look at the consequences.* Make the pupil evaluate the consequences of his or her behavior—not so much in terms of good or bad, but rather in terms of its effects. It is better to say, "Could you tell me what happened here?" rather than "Why did you . . .?" Notice how the second question invites the pupil to rationalize his or her action. Try not to evaluate the behavior yourself. Evaluation by others invites defensiveness. Ask the pupil to evaluate his or her behavior. Since the pupil is responsible for his or her deeds, let the pupil evaluate the effects of it.

3. *Make room for a choice.* The pupil must recognize that he or she is not locked into previous misbehavior. The choice or alternative behavior must be such that the pupil can put it into operation. The pupil, with teacher direction, develops a plan that will work. The plan must outline a choice in very specific terms. For example, "When Jody says something about my mother, I will walk away." Notice how specific that is. It's much more effective than a vague, "I will try to . . . ." That is too easily excused. The "will try" is too weak and indefinite.

4. *Restate the plan.* Paraphrase or restate the alternative behavior that you have agreed on. Make sure the pupil and teacher know and agree to the details. For example, "As I understand it, you are going to bring your notebook to class every day next week." Note the mention of time. Don't expect the pupil to commit to the plan forever. Limit plans to three or four days. You can easily extend the period after the pupil has built up a feeling of success.

5. *Have the pupil say it out loud.* Don't fall into the trap of being the one to state the plan of action and merely have the pupil say, "OK." It's relatively easy for a pupil to bow his or her head and say, "OK, I'll try" when the teacher lists the expected behaviors. It's much more of a commitment when the pupil explicitly states in the form of a contract just what he or she will or will not do. When the pupil makes the statement it becomes more binding.

6. *Mend broken promises.* Sometimes the promise of positive behavior falls flat. If that happens, don't punish or accept excuses. Accept the explanation, acknowledge the failure at face value, and repeat steps 1 through 5. The failure may be because the original plan was too ambitious (e.g., "I will think before I speak" instead of "I won't call out in class.") It's best to put the emphasis on the plan rather than fault the pupil.

7. *Provide support.* Give some encouragement when you see that the pupil is obviously trying. Let the pupil know you are on his or her side. Congratulating appropriate behavior takes less time and works better than reprimanding undesired behavior. It can be as simple as saying, "Maria, your written work is looking much better."

8. *Keep at it.* Don't give up. You are changing long-established attitudes, both yours and the pupil's. Try and try again. In the beginning, you may only be able to focus on partial success. For example, "You were fine last week. Let's see how it goes tomorrow."

9. *Give some space.* Frequently the pupil needs some time to think through what the two of you have been talking about. Provide some thinking time in a quiet, out-of-the-way place. Recognize that it sometimes takes a little time to let off steam, to get over feeling abused, or to think of alternatives.

10. *Take class time.* Most of us are so aware of the need to teach a body of subject matter that we are loathe to take a few minutes of class time to elicit pupil cooperation. Encourage your pupils to voice their opinions concerning how the class is conducted, the amount of work required, the approach to the topic, and so on. No one should fault another person's perception. A caring, cooperative atmosphere should be emphasized.

These ten suggestions will make a significant difference in the classroom if applied regularly and consistently. They are rules your teachers can live with and can't work without. Teachers must be able to assert themselves and take control.

We've heard a great deal in recent years about assertiveness training. Long before this term came into vogue, good disciplinarians in the classroom were practicing the tenets of assertion.

What kind of person is a good disciplinarian? First and foremost, the disciplinarian is assertive. The assertive teacher clearly communicates what he or she wants and feels, why he or she feels that way, and what he or she will do. The assertive teacher makes sure that students understand his or her communication. The assertive teacher also strives to encourage and listen to student-expressed needs and takes care to support their rights. A shortened form of assertiveness is the old adage, "Say what you mean and mean what you say, but do not be mean."

You can help your teachers become more successful as disciplinarians if you give them these nine steps to follow.

Nine Ways to Be Assertive and Not Mean

1. Establish what you want and need and why this is important.
2. Back up what you want with action. Tell your class in advance what you will do if your directions are not carried out.
3. Set limits clearly and explicitly by indicating what you want pupils to do.
4. Recognize student manipulation and resist it.
5. Respond positively to those pupils who have behaved appropriately.
6. Do not blame pupils for their errant behavior.
7. Listen to pupils. Make it clear that you hear them and that you understand the situation.
8. Be consistent without being rigid.
9. Be corrective without being punitive. Do not seek retribution, merely correction.

The assertive teacher is not rigid. Sometimes he or she must alter or revise rules to accommodate realistic counterconditions. Yet most of the time, these good disciplinarians are explicit, fair, firm, and consistent.

In addition to being assertive, you must show your teachers how to analyze pupil misbehavior and how to write it up.

2–3 HELPING TEACHERS ANALYZE BEHAVIOR PROBLEMS

Too often, principals don't write up the specific infractions that occur in their school. On the day of the incident, we are aware of every detail. However, in a week or two we have forgotten the details and remember only the hurt feelings. When these infractions become a pattern, it is important for the sake of the pupil and ourselves to keep a running record of what is going on.

You may wish to jot down in a notebook the date, the participants, and the time and place of the infraction. If you see a pattern developing, you may want a more detailed summary of the misbehaviors.

Some school systems have an actual assessment tool that assists the teacher in analyzing the behavior of the acting-out student. Such tools help the teacher and principal think through not only the misbehavior but also a plan of action for dealing with it. On the next page is a representative

BEHAVIOR ANALYSIS SUMMARY

1. Describe the undesirable behavior. Be descriptive, not judgmental.

   _____

   _____

2. How often does this occur? _____

3. What is usually happening before the undesirable behavior occurs? _____

   _____

4. What in the classroom environment may trigger this behavior? _____

   _____

5. When this behavior occurs, what does the teacher do? What consequences or punishment usually follow the undesired behavior? Is it ignored?

   _____

   _____

6. What do the student's peers do? _____

   _____

7. What is the effect on the student's work? _____

   _____

8. What behavior would you desire to take the place of the undesired behavior?

   _____

9. Who else in the school can assist in helping the student with this problem (principal, parent, counselor, nurse, etc.)?

   _____

10. What curriculum modifications might help to change this student's behavior?

   _____

   _____

11. Describe suitable consequences that are to follow the undesirable behavior. Be sure to state these consequences so that both pupil and teacher can agree on what they are; be specific.

   _____

   _____

sample of the various assessment tools we have surveyed. There are many benefits to using this form or one like it. First, it is therapeutic for the teacher to take pen in hand and write. It relieves pent-up anxiety and hostility. You will notice that the teacher is pressing harder on the pen and probably writing at a faster pace. Some say the pen is mightier than the sword. The teacher may feel like slaying the student with a real sword, but since that is not possible, the teacher can release some tension by writing down his or her feelings on the subject.

Second, other professional members of the school staff will find these observations very helpful. The guidance counselor, school administrators, clinical staff, medical staff, and other agency people will find these notations useful in working out a strategy for the pupil.

Finally, it will help structure your plan of action in working with the pupil. Since you must continue to work with this pupil, you might as well have a written course of action to follow. By filling out this behavior analysis summary, you are forcing the teacher to put on paper the things you are going to look for the next time. The summary helps you structure a course of action to prevent such problems in the future.

2–4 HOLDING TEACHERS MORE ACCOUNTABLE FOR CLASSROOM MANAGEMENT

Teachers themselves often create disruptive situations. Too often, misbehavior is viewed as a student problem and solvable only by home environment, peers, or significant others in the pupil's life. Your teachers have a great deal to do with the way students behave. An important first step is for them to accept responsibility for much of their students' behavior.

Many teachers have set ways of trying to control their classes. They use the same approach regardless of the level of the class or background of the pupils. You can help them assume greater responsibility for good discipline by having them apply the teacher-tested strategies provided on the next page. By making your teachers more accountable, you are helping them prevent discipline problems *before* they occur.

On the next page are some other devices and strategies.

2–5 PREVENTING DISCIPLINE PROBLEMS

It's better to *prevent* discipline problems than to deal with them after they occur. Early in the school year, you will know which pupils are likely to be disruptive or uninterested. The techniques listed on page 24 will help you "turn on" the disaffected pupils so they can make a positive connection to their school and their teacher.

TEACHER ACCOUNTABILITY STRATEGIES
FOR BETTER CLASSROOM MANAGEMENT

1. Embarrassing a student as punishment causes resentment and future problems. Example: "You were supposed to be writing a letter, but Judy decided to write Tom a note instead. Would you all like to hear what Judy wrote to Tom?" Embarrassing Judy might give you some momentary satisfaction, but in the long run you will be the one to suffer.

2. Punishing an entire class because one student broke a rule is counterproductive. Example: "No one goes to the assembly until the person who took the chalkboard eraser stands up." Group pressure may be used to enforce rules, but it is futile to hold up the whole class in the hope that one pupil will own up to his or her misdeed in public.

3. Carrying a grudge against a student for an extended period of time demonstrates a lack of maturity. Example: "No, you may not leave for the rehearsal ten minutes early. I remember the tone of voice you used yesterday."

4. Being prepared for class is a must. Pupils can tell when the teacher is just "winging it." They sense a lack of concern on your part if you come to class unprepared. It conveys a sense of uncaring on your part. So why should they care?

5. Misbehaving students are not attacking you personally. While this may happen occasionally, you are not the target in most cases of pupil misbehavior. Most children are displaying self-hatred when they do contemptible things in the classroom. As the adult, you should spend your energies redirecting pupil actions rather than medicating your bruised ego.

6. Rewarding misbehavior will beget more misbehavior. For example, you make the class clown sit in front of the class. This is socially rewarding for many students who suffer from some ego deficit. The only way they know to get attention from their peers is to act in a clownish manner. If you give them notoriety for their actions, they construe this as a reward and try to perpetuate it. Instead, seat the class clown in the back of the room.

7. Pronouncing a student's name correctly shows the student that you respect him or her as a person, and the student will return that respect. Get to know the names of your pupils very quickly. Anonymity breeds disruption, especially for pupils who arrive mid-year.

8. Being alert to your students' moods is an asset. After a few weeks, you will get to know the students in your classes. There will be times when you will sense that it is best to ignore a pupil or at least not call on him or her this time. The pupil will appreciate your understanding.

9. Use common courtesy. Teachers want their pupils to act politely in class. Haven't you overheard colleagues say things to pupils that you find embarrassing? Be on guard not to fall into that trap yourself. Treat your classes with respect, and they will live up to your expectations.

10. Showing pupils that you care about their performance in class will build their feelings of confidence and trust. Say things like, "I knew you could do it." Or "You really are good in math." Pupils who sense that their teacher "likes" them are not likely to become discipline problems.

Steps to Reach At-Risk Pupils

1. Every child has a birthday, and most children have their birthday while school is in session. With a computer (or manually), you can add the names of birthday boys and girls to your desk calendar. By making a point of congratulating these pupils at some time during the day, you build rapport with pupils. The more volatile, aggressive children are soothed by such a positive stroke initiated by the principal.

2. Set aside five minutes each day to call parents at work or at home to report *good* conduct. If the teacher reports any improvement in behavior, do not hesitate to let the parents know. Parents are grateful for the good news, and this positive reinforcement goes a long way in helping pupils develop good conduct patterns.

3. Use videotapes to reward pupils who have turned in homework on a regular basis after being deficient in this area. Principal Brent Wendling of Kenton, Ohio, rents comedy classics once a month and shows them during the lunch hour to pupils who have shown a dramatic improvement in work or conduct.

4. Keep minor infractions from escalating. When a pupil is first sent to the office for poor behavior, make the most of the opportunity. Don't let the child just sit there—a common practice. Instead, find out the pupil's weak subject and give him or her some individual tutorial help. This builds a bridge between a vulnerable pupil and the caring principal. Let the pupil see that you are human, interested, and concerned.

5. Get a written account of what happened. Use the following "What Happened?" form, which the accused youngster fills out. Keep a file on children reported. Check to see if a pattern of misbehavior is emerging. Photocopy the sheet and mail one home when you think it is appropriate. Share these reports with the guidance counselor or agency staff members such as social workers, psychologist, etc.

"What Happened?"

Pupil's name _____ Class _____ Date _____

1. Why did the teacher send you to me? _____

_____

2. Was any other pupil involved? Who? _____

_____ What did they do? _____

_____

3. What did the teacher say or do? _____

_____

4. What can you do to make sure this does not happen again? ____

_____

_____

_____

Pupil's Signature

What else can you do when a teacher sends a disrespectful pupil to the office?

After the usual attempts at home contact and a lecture on the need for self-control, the principal is frequently at a loss for what to do with the young offender. If you send the pupil back to class after just a few minutes, the teacher will be disappointed and the rest of the class may feel that the offense went unpunished.

A pragmatic approach that can turn this into a learning situation for the pupil is to make it a writing experience. The old-fashioned approach which asks the pupil to write "I will behave in class" one hundred times is nonproductive. At best it teaches the youngster how to write in columns. (The pupil is likely to fill the page with "I, I, I" followed by "will, will, will," etc.)

STUDENT RESPONSE FORM
DISTURBING THE CLASS

Name _____ Class _____ Date _____

You have been reported for _____

by _____ . In this school, students may not do that.

    Read the following questions. Answer them in complete sentences. Use your best handwriting. You may practice on a piece of scrap paper.

    The way you do this will show me, your teacher, and your parents whether you have learned your lesson.

1. Tell us what you did that disturbed the class. Tell the whole story. If you need more room,

ask for another sheet of paper. _____

_____

_____

_____

_____

_____

_____

_____

2. Why did you behave this way? _____

_____

_____

3. How can you improve your behavior? _____

_____

_____

_____

A better idea is to hand the pupil a preprinted form that you have photocopied. You can compose five or six variations and have your secretary keep a file of them ready at all times. They begin with a brief preamble followed by three or four questions that require full-sentence answers. The language is kept simple. For young pupils or nonreaders, you can read the sheet aloud and have the pupils dictate their answers. They then draw a "before" and "after" picture on the back of the page. These show the "wrong" (before) and "correct" (after) behavior.

The sample provided will give you a good idea of how this student response form works. Some suggested topics include

- Disturbing the class
- Getting along with others
- Using bad language
- Fighting in school
- Running in the hall
- Bus or lunchroom behavior.

2–6 REDUCING PUPIL ACCIDENTS

One important reason for maintaining good discipline in your school is to provide a safe environment for your pupils. Pupils who misbehave are likely to be accident prone and are likely to cause other pupils to become injured in school. The "Pupil Safety Rules" on page 28 are subtitled "To Read, Sign, and Obey."

Have your teachers read these rules with the pupils as a class lesson. Insist that pupils *and* parents sign the sheet. A folder of the signed safety rules sheets should be kept for each class in your office. When you must speak to a pupil or parent about a behavior problem, it is an effective technique to pull out and refer to the signed form.

2–7 ENLISTING PARENT SUPPORT IN DISCIPLINE CASES

To enlist parent support in discipline cases, you must first recognize the basic need of all parents regarding their child's school: their desire to be important. You are the principal. Society says that you are important in the child's life. You can recommend that the pupil pass or fail, be promoted or left back, be graduated or held over. Parents, on the other hand, often feel important and that the cards are stacked against them. The most they can do is withdraw their child from school. But few parents have the money or inclination to register their child in private school.

PUPIL SAFETY RULES
To Read, Sign, and Obey

1. I will not shove or touch other pupils on the class line.
2. I will not run around corners, tables, desks, or through the halls.
3. I will not accept candy, gum, any treats, or rides from people I have never met before.
4. I will not throw papers, pencils, crayons, books, etc. on the classroom floor, in the halls, or in the auditorium.
5. I will keep my lunch table and floor very clean, as if I were eating in my own house.
6. I know the best route from my house to the school. I know the basic street safety rules and follow them all the time.
7. I know the safest ways to get out of my house in case of a fire. I know how to prevent fires.
8. I have heard and follow the rules of safety and fire prevention as explained to me by my teacher.
9. I do not call other pupils names, tease them, or hide their belongings.
10. I do not hit other pupils or swing book bags, belts, or lunch boxes.
11. I will listen to my teacher's instructions on fire drills and other emergencies.
12. I will behave quietly on the bus lines and on the bus, and get on and off the bus without running or pushing.
13. I will be on my best behavior in the auditorium during assembly programs.
14. I will use a quiet voice in the lunch room.
15. I will follow the red and green traffic markers painted on the doors.
16. I will be careful in the bathroom and not swing on the doors.
17. I will watch my fingers when opening and closing doors.
18. I will not abuse any property either in the neighborhood or in the school.
19. I will wait INSIDE if taking the school bus home. If I am a walker, I will wait for my parent in the school yard.

Please save this notice for future use.

TEAR OFF

_____   _____
Parent's signature   Date

_____   _____
Pupil's signature   Date

Successful principals begin by making parents feel important. Just knowing that parents want to feel important is not enough. You must show them a certain respect. One way to do this is to give your whole-hearted attention when they speak. You can do that if you follow these steps:

1. Become genuinely interested in them and their situation.
2. Always think in terms of what the parents are feeling.
3. Learn to listen. Do not interrupt.
4. Practice patience. You may feel that they are being foolish, but hear them out.
5. Never take parents for granted. Don't diminish them as human beings.
6. Be concerned about your pupil. Keep the pupil your main focus of attention.

When you practice these techniques to give parents your whole-hearted attention, you'll give them a feeling of importance. We all yearn for respectful attention. We want our ideas and our opinions to be heard. Have you ever been snubbed by a haughty waiter, left standing on a corner by an independent bus driver, or completely ignored by some store clerk? You know that feeling, don't you?

Learning to listen to parents with everything you've got means putting aside your own interests and preoccupations, at least for a few minutes. You must concentrate on what the other person is saying. You must focus all your attention on him or her.

You can often learn more from what parents don't say than from what they do. Learn to listen between the spoken words. Watch for changes in voice tone and volume. Sometimes you will find a meaning that's in direct contrast to spoken words. And watch facial expressions, mannerisms, gestures, and body movements. To be a good listener and to listen with everything you've got, you'll have to use your eyes as well as your ears.

When you listen in this way, you'll gain these benefits:

- You'll get support from parents.
- Difficult situations will be eased.
- Hard-to-reach parents will seek you out.
- Parents of antisocial students will work with you.
- You'll gain the respect of the parents you meet.

This is not really a secret—except that so few principals put it into practice. Those that do don't talk about it.

The checklist on page 30 will help you discuss serious infractions with parents.

CHECKLIST FOR DISCUSSING DISCIPLINE PROBLEMS WITH PARENTS

☐ **1.** Give the parents a chance to ventilate their feelings. Be sure to let the parents state their position first. Do not interrupt until they are finished. They may be overly sensitive about being interrupted. Pent-up emotions have a tendency to cloud objectivity.

☐ **2.** Highlight the objective data. Realize that most of the information a parent has comes from the pupil's highly subjective reports. Bring to the meeting all the hard data you can: test papers, attendance records, statements from eyewitnesses, examples of vandalism or theft, and so on.

☐ **3.** Stay on track. Keep the conference focused on the pupil and his or her ultimate goals. Parents frequently prefer to concentrate on what they, the parents, expect of the pupil. Stay with the here and now. Emphasize what the pupil is doing in class. Don't make comparisons between siblings.

☐ **4.** Keep the conference aligned with your theme: how the parent and the teacher can work together for the welfare of the child.

☐ **5.** Hold up the image of the total picture rather than getting bogged down on the immediate problem. This is not to say you should avoid the immediate problem; it is why the parent is with you. But don't bypass the valuable opportunity to create a partnership out of misunderstanding. Settle the issue and place it in its true perspective.

☐ **6.** Be positive. No matter how grave the situation, there must be something good you can say about the pupil. Say it. Then move on to positive recommendations rather than dwell on only shortcomings. The hard facts you have supplied on the negative aspects of the pupil will speak for themselves.

☐ **7.** Use props. Use the evidence you brought to the meeting with the skill of a courtroom lawyer. Don't tip your hand all at once. When you are ready to present your evidence, keep it in a folder or large envelope. Unveil each piece of hard data one at a time. Build your case by presenting the most damaging evidence *last*. When you are ready to terminate the interview, or you feel you have gained the parents' support, put all the negative material back in the folder and, with some flair, move it to one side.

☐ **8.** Let a smile be your umbrella. When you have sensed that the parent is ready to forge a partnership with the school, give one of your sunniest smiles. This will cement the deal more than a notarized signature on a contract.

Most parent-teacher conferences are pleasant when there is no major problem to be resolved. But life is not always so easy. Increasingly, principals face ugly situations that cannot be overlooked. On these occasions, it is imperative that you involve the nurse, counselor, or other professional staff member when meeting with parents.

The checklist on page 30 gives some proven, common-sense approaches to working with a hostile parent, or a parent facing a difficult situation.

Use these eight approaches and you will win parent support even when discussing serious infractions.

2–8 DEALING WITH SUSPENSIONS

There are times when informal conferences and letters to parents fail to solve the problem behavior. The next alternative is a brief suspension from school—usually no more than five school days.

This is helpful in several ways:

1. Suspension provides "shock therapy" to acting-out pupils who think that nothing will happen to them no matter how bad their behavior.
2. Suspension makes parents realize that the misbehavior of their child is indeed serious and not just a series of childish pranks.
3. Suspension informs the other students, including the victim, if any, that the school means business and that serious offenses do not go unpunished.
4. Suspension speeds up the process of getting a pupil referred for help from an outside agency or other Board of Education unit.

The suspension process begins with a written notification to parents of a child's misbehavior. It's a good idea to hold a presuspension conference as a last step before a formal suspension. This gives the pupil a second chance and prepares the parents for the possibility that their child will have to stay home for up to five days if there is another untoward incident.

At the presuspension meeting, present all the available documentation leading up to the meeting:

- Anecdotal material written by the teacher
- Notes on previous meetings with the parents
- Specific incident reports of past misconduct
- Any reports from outside agencies.

SUMMARY OF PRINCIPAL'S SUSPENSION HEARING

Name of pupil _____

Address _____

Dates of principal's

_____ suspensions _____

Date of birth _____

Date of principal's

Tel no.   Home _____ Business _____ suspension conference _____

Date pupil returned

Grade _____ to class _____

Current attendance for this school year to date

Present _____ Absent _____ Lateness _____

Agency, if any, to which pupil is known:

_____

_____

Who was contacted at the agency? _____

Result of agency contact: _____

_____

Reason(s) (specific) for suspension:

1. _____

2. _____

3. _____

Efforts of school personnel prior to suspension:

1. _____

2. _____

3. _____

Suspension Hearing Summary, *continued*

Action(s) to be taken as a result of the hearing:

1. By school personnel: _____

_____

2. By the pupil: _____

_____

3. By the pupil's parent(s): _____

_____

Additional comments:

_____

_____

_____

_____

_____

_____

At this meeting, give the parents and pupil a chance to speak before you give the school's perception of the problem. Give them a chance to respond to the complaints that the school has filed. Allow the parents to ventilate any hostile feelings or attitudes. Encourage the pupil to state in his or her own words what the problem is and why the behavior took place.

Involve the pupil in ways to change the specific actions that are causing the problem. Together with the parents, design a plan using the pupil's suggestions and the school's rules and regulations. The pupil must understand and agree to comply with the plan that is finally worked out. Write it out and have the pupil, parents, and principal sign it.

Keep a summary of the suspension hearing. (A summary form has been provided here.) This summary gives you, on two pages, a handy recap of what went on during the suspension hearing. You may need this information later in the year. A copy should be part of the pupil's record as long as he or she is in your school.

The ideas in this chapter should help you and your teachers take control of each classroom and thus the school. Classroom management is the necessary prerequisite to meaningful instruction.

Chapter 3

Putting Shared Decision Making to Work for You

Jane S. has read a great deal about shared decision making and school-based management. She would love to get her staff involved in these innovative programs. By learning these skills and strategies, Jane S. hopes to move her teachers out of the comfortable rut many of them have dug for themselves. She would like to know some of the things to look out for and some of the precautions she can take.

■SCHOOL-BASED MANAGEMENT is a reform effort currently sweeping across the country. The initiative is injecting new energy into the administration of our country's public schools and new creativity into the classroom. This approach is tapping the creative energies of dedicated school professionals to grapple with and solve the many difficult problems our public education system faces as we head into the next century.

In education, as well as in business and even foreign affairs, we are learning that working in a group, learning from others, taking risks, and developing new problem-solving strategies are necessary for success.

Recent studies have affirmed that in more effective schools, the educational community within the school has involved teams of teachers, support staff, parents, and even pupil leaders in the decision-making process.

A basic goal of shared decision making is to get everyone involved in schoolwide decisions without sacrificing efficiency or ignoring accountability. Team building and communication skills are key components of the process. Usually five to eight team members are chosen across grade and job title lines, and they, in turn, ensure that the whole staff continues to be informed and involved. Much depends on the team members' communication skills in exchanging information with the rest of the staff. Each school has its own customized plan in which the staff and parents need to be fully invested. By *investment* we mean a sense of commitment to improvement in the school's climate, progress, and morale.

An important first step is to keep the staff informed through discussion so that they can make more enlightened decisions about teaching practices, curriculum, in-service training, content, and instructional strategies for the benefit of the pupils.

Decision making includes, but is not limited to, the following:

- How the school budget is spent
- Priorities of support services
- Scheduling within the school day
- Space allocation
- Ladders of pupil referral
- Curriculum design
- Textbook selection.

36

3-1 FIVE BASIC CORNERSTONES OF THE PRINCIPAL'S ROLE

1. School-based decision making means that the principal, who is responsible for everything that happens in the building, will solicit input from teachers, pupils, and parents. The principal will not make unilateral decisions without consulting with the school's constituencies, but will actively seek out the judgment of concerned parties on all significant issues. Everyone for whom the destiny of the school has importance is invited to contribute to the school-based decision-making process.

2. With shared decision making, the whole management team and, in turn, the whole school community, is responsible for the success or failure of a given strategy or decision. The ultimate responsibility for the school rests with the principal, but this wider ownership can often mean the difference between success and failure of a particular initiative (e.g., a new curriculum, new grading system, student leadership initiative, or textbook selection).

3. School-based decision making means that committees of educators and parents will work with the principal to set goals and to develop strategies for achieving them that apply to their individual schools.

4. The principal helps build support or acceptance for especially difficult decisions or endeavors. If a person is involved in the decision making that leads to a specific program or adoption, he or she is more inclined to work hard to make that idea succeed.

5. In school-based decision making, the principal strives for consensus. When dedicated people do the necessary research and have access to all of the available information, they will generally agree on a decision. However, each participant in the process must realize that from time to time his or her judgment will not prevail. Despite this, they must continue to work for what is best for the pupils and make their voices heard when the next issue comes before the group.

The shared decision-making model embraces the old saying, "Two heads are better than one." With shared decision making, teams of people from different positions in the school community—the classroom, the cafeteria, the guidance office, the security desk, *and* the principal's office—work together to devise solutions to problems that any one of those constituencies alone couldn't possibly solve.

3–2 WHEN IS A SCHOOL READY TO BEGIN?

In a school where the principal has assumed the role of parent, grand-parent, or godparent to the staff—for years—and has made unilateral decisions, there cannot be an abrupt change to shared decision making overnight.

The advantages of such a move must be explained at a staff meeting or meetings. Some advantages include

- A sense of ownership
- Professional dignity
- A chance to exchange ideas
- An opportunity to work collaboratively
- Less bureaucracy
- Reduced isolation
- Room for changes to occur
- Parent involvement.

Teachers who have taken part in shared decision making have commented as follows:

- "[It was] a shot in the arm after years of sameness."
- "[It provided] a recognition of the fact that all segments of the staff have something to contribute to the whole school: teachers, administrators, aides, paraprofessionals, cooks, etc."
- "I no longer feel isolated in Room 107—let out only when the bell rings."
- "I enjoy the interchange of ideas on school improvement with teachers from other grades and departments."
- "It's nice to know that the administration acknowledges the fact that a kindergarten teacher has something to contribute toward the achievement of schoolwide goals."

After this concept is presented in your school, you can seek staff volunteers for a committee to explore schoolwide participation. This exploration can take many forms, including the following:

1. The principal discussing the idea with the central or district office to assess their support (this must come first)
2. Reading the growing literature on this topic in professional publications

3. Visiting a nearby school that has implemented shared decision making
4. Inviting a speaker on the topic from a local college or teacher's organization
5. Discussing the idea with leadership of the parents' association to determine their interest.

When these steps have been taken, the committee should meet again to discuss members' feelings and the various constituencies' level of commitment to the concept. It is then the committee's job to present the concept to the entire staff. This can best be done in small-group meetings, such as grade and subject area meetings, lunch groups, car pools, etc. When sufficient time has been spent talking to every staff member, a vote is taken. At least two thirds of the staff must be in favor of the idea. A means for evaluation and discussion must be built into the commitment. A one-year trial period is common.

For shared decision making to take place as a schoolwide practice, the following traits must be present. You will know your school is ready to begin when

1. You are ready to take suggestions from parents, nonteaching staff members, and even pupil leaders.
2. You are willing to spend time discussing many school decisions that you formerly made by yourself.
3. The committee is prepared to report back to the rest of the staff and pledges to reflect the feelings of the staff at future meetings.
4. All the participants recognize the importance of the project as a contribution to the success and effectiveness of the school as a whole.
5. All participants recognize their freedom to try new ideas and understand that they are free to take risks.
6. All participants recognize that the ultimate decision, after considering all facets of school-based decision making, rests with the principal.

When these factors are present, you are ready to begin. A common technique of successful transitions to shared decision making is to rotate the leadership of the team meetings. It is important for the principal not to be the automatic committee meeting chairperson.

3–3 DEVELOPING GOALS AND OBJECTIVES

Shared decision making and school-based management both depend on setting goals and objectives. Every school needs them, just as a ship needs a rudder. When you observe an outstanding lesson in a teacher's classroom, he or she undoubtedly has a stated goal or objective for the lesson. Similarly, effective school leadership is based on good planning.

You and your staff can better focus your energies and have clear direction if you first agree on your goals for the year. When you agree on common purposes, priorities become more self-evident and day-to-day activities become part of an overall meaningful pattern.

Many school staffs are not accustomed to goal setting as a shared activity between administration and faculty. To be a creative leader, you must influence the staff's thinking by presenting your vision for the school and then elicit their ideas and suggestions. Goal setting must tap into the hopes and desires of your staff to reflect their visionary thinking.

One way to stimulate their thinking is as follows:

The Goal-Setting Process

1. Devote time at the June or September faculty conference for developing goals.
2. Pose the question, "What would you like to see happening at our school one year from now?"
3. Ask the teachers to visualize concrete events that could take place. They should be specific in relation to teachers, pupils, and parents.
4. Break up into grade levels and have each small group list its goals on a large sheet of paper.
5. After each small group has finished summarizing its goals, post the sheets of paper in front of the room. Together with the staff, pull out common elements and transcribe them onto a single sheet of paper. These become your school goals.

Some sample goals include the following:

- "Pupils will have alternatives for conflict resolution, and fighting will decrease."
- "Teachers will be more directly involved in purchasing textbooks, supplies, and equipment."
- "Parents will be encouraged to become more involved in school projects and their children's learning."

While *goals* are broad statements of fairly long-range duration, *objectives* are statements that define measurable behavior that leads toward a goal. Objectives give concrete reality to the vague hopes of a goal. A well-stated objective will state specific steps toward reaching a goal. Good objectives include these four elements:

1. WHAT action is to be taken?
2. WHO is expected to do what?
3. WHEN is each step to be taken?
4. HOW MUCH must be done to satisfy the objective?

The following are examples of educational objectives and the four elements they satisfy:

- The number of incidents of fighting   WHAT
  among fourth and fifth graders   WHO
  will be cut in half   HOW MUCH
  by June of this school year.   WHEN

- Eighty percent of the third-grade pupils   WHO
  will score above grade level   HOW MUCH
  on the standardized math test   WHAT
  administered in May.   WHEN

Have your teachers brainstorm about goals and objectives. The total staff should review the ideas generated for clarity and reasonableness, making any adjustments required. You will then have a staff that knows where it's going and has a sense of ownership in reaching its goals.

3-4 WHAT ARE SOME START-UP PROBLEMS?

As in any new program, the first year will generate a number of problems. Most will be start-up problems that can be anticipated by looking at the experience of other school districts. We discuss nine of them here.

These initial problems are worth noting. Not only have schools experienced similar problems, but they have tended to find similar solutions. The common solutions are important because they seem to work in a variety of school settings.

1. *Asking too much.* Some pilot schools undertook too many projects and procedural changes in the first year. Eventually, these schools realized that their enthusiasm had led to long "wish lists." By the end of the year, the schools had discarded their unrealistic wish lists and were concentrating on a few high-priority items.

2. *Tunnel vision.* Some teacher representatives on the decision-making teams were unprepared to deal with schoolwide problems. Their job experiences had given them a limited view of school operations. Once exposed to discussions in the team meetings, they developed broader perspectives. But that led to a second problem: Changes in the rep-

resentatives' views were often regarded with suspicion by their constituents. Some teachers said that their representatives now "sounded like the principal." To alleviate this problem, many schools opened the meetings to any staff members who wished to observe the discussions firsthand.

3. *Handling new roles.* Some teacher representatives lacked training to deal with administrative issues that the teams addressed. The solution: Give the teacher representatives in-service training in the more technical areas of school operations.

4. *Problems conducting meetings.* Some teams learned quickly that they were unprepared to conduct productive meetings. Without clear agendas, meetings often continued for hours as new issues or problems came up; without proper rules of order, discussions often digressed. The pilot schools resolved this problem by training team members in the rules of order and by initiating procedures for setting agendas.

5. *Increased workload.* Decisions that once took only minutes of the principal's time now took much longer and involved more people. Any issue in question had to be placed on the agenda for a scheduled meeting. The team might direct the issue to an ancillary committee for fact finding, which would require the group to reschedule the issue for consideration. The process could take weeks. This problem, unfortunately, appears to be inherent in shared decision making but can save time later.

6. *Burnout.* Considering the increased workload, it is not surprising that staff members active in the program tended to burn out. Adding to the problem was that other staff members had chosen not to participate actively. In some pilot schools, the dual problem of burnout and nonparticipation raised doubts about whether the program could continue. Try to involve as many staff members as possible by rotating committee memberships.

7. *Conflicts.* Shared decision making can aggravate an existing conflict between teachers and a principal. The staff members in some pilot schools welcomed shared decision making as a means of challenging the principal. This attitude tends to escalate the conflict. Training in conflict resolution can help staff members. In situations of extreme conflict, however, training might not be enough. Such cases emphasize the importance of carefully deciding on a school's readiness. A survey you can use to determine your school's readiness has been provided here.

8. *Pressure on the principal.* Some of the principals felt that if a team decision resulted in a major blunder, it would be the principal who would be held accountable, not the team. Yet one of the clear benefits of working with a management team is the support one can gain from

the team when it comes to taking risks or making tough decisions. Many of the solo decisions principals make every day are educated guesses about what we think will work. The truth is that sometimes our best efforts fail, and we have to try new approaches.

9. *Problems of size.* The severity of some of the problems seems to be directly related to the size of the school. Larger schools tend to have more representatives, larger committees, longer meetings, and so on. These conditions can aggravate problems such as narrow perspectives, difficulty in conducting meetings, and increased workloads. This can be helped by narrowing the list of projects undertaken or breaking down into mini-schools.

Compiling your own list of common problems and solutions may prove valuable to you. Because such a list consists of workable ideas for circumventing start-up problems, it should prove valuable to any school contemplating school-based decision making.

PRINCIPAL'S SURVEY FOR DETERMINING STAFF READINESS FOR CHANGE

1. Have any staff members expressed an interest in experimentation or innovation? Who are they?
2. List those staff members likely to be counted on to spearhead shared decision making or school-based management once it is launched.
3. Who in the central office would you need to contact before beginning any program for change? Which central office staff members can be utilized as resource people?
4. What would be the single most important outcome for change that you would like to accomplish?
5. List those teachers or parent leaders you would need to convince if any project for change were to occur.
6. What are some areas of school life that you think would be a good starting point for shared decision making?
7. What are some potential impediments for change in your school at this time? What can you do about them?
8. How would you assess the level of staff morale at this time?
9. What would you identify as the teachers' main area of concern?
10. Is your parent association ready to participate in a major undertaking like shared decision making?

3–5 WHAT PRECAUTIONS SHOULD YOU TAKE?

For shared decision making to work, you must take several precautions.

Precautions for the Principal

1. Don't forget to demonstrate at all times that the participation of teachers is needed and wanted and that the results of group and individual efforts will be used.
2. Don't force participation. The basic choice of whether an individual teacher will or will not participate should be his or her own. For participation to be worthwhile, the teacher must be willing.
3. Don't exclude anyone. The decision-making plan should make possible the continuous participation of all members of the staff who care to take part.
4. Don't limit participation. Opportunities for teacher participation should be provided at every stage of an activity, from the time the purposes are determined and a plan of action is mapped out, to the time when the plan has been carried out and the results evaluated.
5. Don't squeeze. If you insist on limiting the areas in which teachers are to participate, the limitations should be as few as possible. Everyone should understand the areas in which teacher participation is to occur.
6. Don't usurp the board of education. It should be recognized as the final authority for the adoption of school policies, not only because the board possesses the legal right but also because it represents the public, which is a larger democracy than the school personnel.

3–6 IS IT WORTH IT?

Despite all the complaints about shared decision making, most principals believe that teacher participation in decision making is worth all the extra effort. Jack Bloomfield of the National Association of Elementary School Principals sums it up: "Leadership in today's schools is not only a matter of what a leader does, but how he makes people feel."

Shared decision making makes teachers feel involved and important. It even makes them appreciate *your* job more. The secure principal can open the doors of shared decision making without fear.

It's human to resist change; and it's human to fear a change in which you feel you will lose something, especially power. But school administrators can't hold on to their traditional roles, because the public is demanding changes. Like everyone else, administrators have a choice: Embrace change, or you will find that you have no power left to fight for.

It is worth the trouble to encourage teachers to share in decision making. Here are some representative techniques and outcomes:

1. Build ownership by including teachers in hiring. It is flattering for a senior teacher to be asked by the principal to sit in on an interview of a prospective teacher, aide, or other staff member. The senior teacher may have a special insight into the needs of the school. He or she will certainly want to help the new employee succeed. Including teachers in the hiring process builds a sense of belonging in the school.

2. Improve staff morale. A Nevada principal swears that shared decision making can be just the thing to turn a negative faculty around. "I felt like Darth Vader—the evil lord," he reports. "When we switched to team decision making, it really boosted staff morale. The teachers began to feel a sense of ownership in the school. Not all decisions were made 'on high.' A lot of ideas percolated up from the classrooms."

3. Generate innovative solutions through teacher involvement. A Pennsylvania principal was agonizing over a crowded situation in the pupil lunch room. He turned the problem over to his school management team. Soon they suggested a workable solution—two lunch periods. They volunteered to assist in monitoring the lunch period. In return, the teachers now had a common meeting time for planning lessons and sharing ideas.

4. Build a closer staff. By becoming involved in mutual planning and decision making, teachers become a more cohesive organization. Many petty grievances and cliques start to disappear. Regular education teachers begin to appreciate the unique problems that special-ed teachers face. Upper-grade teachers see the special nature of early childhood classes.

5. Diminish resentment of administration. When teachers are involved in parent councils, community organizations, and staff complaints, they see the many-faceted pressures on the school administration. Many remark, "I wouldn't want your job for all the tea in China," yet they offer suggestions that help smooth things out.

Shared decision making has been effective in schools for several years, but the experience has varied from place to place. To give you an accurate picture, we quote a variety of sources here. Through reading what's going on in other places, you will know what you can or cannot expect in your own situation.

1. Robert J. Holzmiller, principal of Hopi Elementary School in Scottsdale, Arizona, is not ashamed to admit that his school's foray into site-based decision making has left him feeling scared. He reports that the district has provided few guidelines on how teams in its five pilot schools are to go about the process of changing school governance.

2. The skills needed to be effective in working with a team of teachers, community members, parents, and students are different from the skills most principals were taught, notes Dale Mann, a professor at Teachers College, Columbia University. "All the bets are off," Mr. Mann says. "They can no longer be oldstyle [chief executive officers]. Is their new role clear? Not at all."

3. Even principals who are enthusiastic say that watching a team make mistakes is difficult. "My whole problem now is I'm starting to get concerned that if they don't follow through, do they fall on their faces or do I pick them up and scramble?" asks one principal.

4. In Los Angeles, principals are concerned that the concept of shared decision making was negotiated without their input. They don't feel that their opinions were sufficiently solicited. The Los Angeles teacher contract established "school leadership councils"; half of those members are teachers. The principal has one vote on the council and no power to veto its decisions.

5. In contrast to the experiences of principals in large urban areas, principals in Prince William County, Virginia, have been given significantly more authority under the suburban district's new site-based decision-making program. The school board approved a sweeping plan that will allocate a lump sum to each school based on calculations of how much it costs to educate each student. Teams of faculty members, parents, and students at each school will determine how best to spend the money, with the superintendent's approval.

Even principals and teachers who are in agreement about shared decision making must struggle to find ways to release teachers from the classroom for committee work. There are no simple solutions to this problem. Changing the school schedule to create blocks of time in which teachers could meet would be a step toward real restructuring, but is not always possible.

Shared decision making calls not for one leader, but for a group of leaders. This group must be able and willing to share among its members the authority and power that come with leadership. Fundamentally, then, shared decision making requires a rethinking of traditional definitions of leadership.

This new leadership model and decision-making process can seem difficult and even scary to all team participants. Principals may feel that it is particularly awkward, since we are accustomed to a very different role and decision-making process. Imagine, though, how overwhelming those same decisions could seem to someone who has never had the authority to make them.

To make the school-based management initiative work, you must set the tone and facilitate the transition of other team members to their new responsibilities. Even though you become a part of a team, by the nature of the principal's traditional role as leader, the whole school community will look to you for their cues. Given your training and experience, you are in a position to lead the team and the whole school community in the right direction. Experience has shown if the principal is enthusiastic and demonstrates a spirit of cooperation, teachers will follow.

Chapter 4

Making School Meaningful for Your Pupils

Roger M. is trying to boost the rate of pupil attendance at his K–5 elementary school in Illinois. Awards and incentives have helped, but Roger is certain that pupils don't see school as meaningful. Many of them don't see any point in the lessons presented, the books they use, the assignments they're asked to complete, or school in general. Roger wants to exercise his instructional leadership role and improve the environment of his pupils. He's looking for ways to make school relevant.

■As PRINCIPAL, YOU should be concerned with how your pupils view their school. Do they feel safe? Do they ever have fun in school? Do they see a purpose in the activities they participate in? Are their subjects and lessons meaningful? Is homework a direct outgrowth of the day's lessons?

The world is changing. Our schools must change, too. As heads of schools, we can be agents of change. Of course, we must follow the mandates of school boards and superintendents. But let's not kid ourselves— each day there are many opportunities for us to prod pupils and staff into more relevant, meaningful activities—activities that make school meaningful for our pupils.

Keep your eyes and ears open to what works in other schools, and incorporate the successful methods and programs that will make a difference. Various nostrums have been trumpeted in recent years for school improvement: open classrooms, multicultural education, team teaching, etc. While all of these have a place, none of them alone can make school a relevant place for your pupils.

Instead, in the following sections we discuss four concrete approaches that successful principals have used in the 1990s.

4-1 BUILDING STUDENT COMMITMENT TO LEARNING

The most important hat that you wear each day is that of instructional leader.

Four Shirt-Sleeve Solutions to Ensure Pupil Commitment to Learning

1. *Expect more from your pupils.* Insist that your teachers focus on results. Check that they are assigning homework and reviewing it to see that it is done. Meet with teachers to point out the need for essay writing and not just workbook activities in which pupils fill in the blanks and never write a complete sentence. The province of Ontario, Canada, has long expected pupils to be critical thinkers and problem solvers— not merely worksheet completers. Ontario pupils regularly outperform U.S. pupils on international assessments of math and science.

2. *Know pupils as individuals.* Encourage your teachers to spend a few minutes each day talking to individual pupils—alone. They should

get to know each pupil's strengths and weaknesses, likes and dislikes, family and peer pressures. This will help the teacher plan meaningful lessons, and it will help the pupil bond with a caring adult. In the same way, you, as principal, can get to know more pupils by inviting a small group for lunch once a week or by having teachers recommend different pupils with special needs to serve as your office monitor to run errands.

3. *Utilize pupil-tutors as role models.* Rhode Island has introduced a plan to tutor every interested third grader, using older pupils and people from the community. The cost to the school is minimal. The older pupils look forward to helping the third graders and gain insight into the teaching and learning process. In San Antonio, the middle school and high school students have mentored elementary pupils in a six-year program in which grades showed marked improvement for both groups.

4. *Involve parents directly in school projects.* Work conducted by James Comer, a Yale University psychiatrist, in seven school districts has shown that intense parent and community involvement in schools can dramatically improve the learning of poor, urban minority youngsters. The state of Missouri has created a "parents and teachers" project. It works because it involves parents in education from the very beginning and trains them to be their children's first and best teachers.

To change the ways we do things means risk. To conduct business as usual has not always worked. Assume your instructional leadership role and see the difference!

4–2 STRATEGIES FOR SELECTING TEXTBOOKS

Your school budget probably includes textbooks as a large slice of the pie. In some schools the ordering of textbooks has become a clerical chore, and little is done to involve the consumers—the teachers and pupils—in the process. You don't want that to happen in your school.

In some areas, textbooks have received a bad rap—without justification. The fact is that textbooks do not teach, teachers teach, and textbooks are merely a major tool in that process. Textbooks are also a powerful means for transmitting a core of shared cultural knowledge.

The pupils and teachers in your school should be involved in examining sample books, making choices, and evaluating the textbook at the end of the year.

Here are some tips for selecting textbooks that will bring out the best in your teachers' lessons and motivate your pupils:

Down-to-Earth Tips for Selecting Textbooks

1. Set up a textbook selection committee that includes teachers from various grade levels, some pupils, and some parents.

2. Elicit from the committee which textbooks they feel should be replaced and which ones they want to reorder. Have them determine reasons for their choices.

3. Make available shelf space for sample textbooks from different publishers on different subject and grade levels. Devote one or two file drawers to catalogs and ancillary materials such as study guides, copy masters, and answer keys.

4. Encourage committee members to review sample copies throughout the year and to write down their comments, which will also be kept in the file cabinet.

5. Determine the amount of money you have available for books. With your committee, set up a list of priorities for this money in descending order. Keep a record of "wish list" books that will be ordered only after higher priorities are taken care of.

6. Cultivate the various sales representatives that call on you throughout the year. Ask them to mail you sample books and teachers' guides for subject and grade levels high on your list. Keep their business cards for future reference. Volunteer to "pilot" a new book that a publisher is promoting. This can bring you a substantial number of free books.

7. Insist that teacher members of the committee truly get feedback from other teachers so various staff views are represented. Likewise, parent members should present the views of the PTA regarding the level of difficulty, quality of homework assignments, and level of questions contained in the texts. Pupils selected should be representative of the school as a whole.

8. Decide whether supplementary materials, such as workbooks, blackline masters, or other learning materials available from the publisher, should be purchased.

9. Place your order early enough for delivery before the start of the school year. Teachers are frustrated when they don't have enough books for each pupil on the first day of school.

10. Prepare an evaluation form so pupils, teachers, and parents can react to new books after they have been in use.

As the principal, you are responsible for ordering textbooks that will interest your pupils. The preceding tips will help you set up a viable selection process. But as the instructional leader, you must be aware of the following eight guidelines for textbook selection.

Guidelines for Textbook Selection

Look for the following qualities in the textbooks you review:

1. Activities that integrate writing into all curriculum areas
2. Multiethnic, multicultural readings relevant to pupils' lives
3. Open-ended questions that stimulate the imagination and call for analysis and evaluation skills
4. Controversial topics presented from more than one viewpoint
5. Activities that involve forming hypotheses and making recommendations
6. Math programs that incorporate the use of manipulatives and calculators
7. Teachers' editions that suggest stimulating activities and not just answers to questions
8. The cost of paperback editions versus hardback editions of the same book. Will it save money in the long run to get the hardback book now?

Utilize these strategies when it's time to order textbooks.

4–3 BOOSTING THE LITERACY LEVEL OF YOUR SCHOOL

According to *Becoming a Nation of Readers: What Principals Can Do* (published by the U.S. Department of Education), school principals continue to play the critical role in fostering good reading practices and a love of reading.

Acting as literacy promoter remains one of the most important parts of the elementary principal's job description. While this may be no surprise to you, many principals miss the opportunity to raise the level of reading and writing among pupils in their schools. Review the "Literacy Checklist" to see how many of these literacy boosters you have tried this year.

Begin to keep a log of the various activities in your school that promote literacy. Share it with the central office staff. They will put it to good use in assisting other principals. (And send a copy to us, in care of the publisher. We'd love to give you credit for some unusual ideas in our next book.)

LITERACY CHECKLIST

☐ **1.** Do you have a school library that is accessible to pupils, parents, and teachers?

☐ **2.** Does every classroom have a class library with books that circulate?

☐ **3.** Is there a campaign each year to sign up pupils as members of the town or branch library?

☐ **4.** Is at least one PTA meeting devoted to reading and writing instruction, including activities for parents to foster reading skills at home?

☐ **5.** Does your school order magazines geared to elementary school pupils, such as *Ranger Rick*, *The Electric Company*, *Cricket*, *Sesame Street*, or *National Geographic World*?

☐ **6.** Do you encourage storytelling as an activity? Do you and your teachers read aloud to pupils on a regular basis? Do your pupils participate in a schoolwide storytelling contest?

☐ **7.** Are there other special events in your school that encourage reading, such as read-a-thons, book fairs, book swaps, or writing contests on a particular topic (fire prevention, women in history, Black History Week)?

☐ **8.** Do you invite pupils to your office to read aloud to you? (This is a great motivator for English as a Second Language pupils.)

☐ **9.** Is there a coordinated reading instruction program in your school that proceeds from grade to grade with one basal reading series?

☐ **10.** Are your pupils encouraged to write letters to pen pals, elected officials, celebrities, and shut-ins? Are the responses displayed on bulletin boards?

☐ **11.** Do you maintain a valid assessment program to determine the success of your teachers in teaching reading and writing?

☐ **12.** Are you involving your school community by inviting and training reading volunteers? Do teachers take pupils on class trips to newspapers, libraries, or bookstores?

☐ **13.** Do you offer incentives to pupils who have improved in reading or who have read a great many books? (Incentives can be buttons, ribbons, bookmarks, or class pizza parties.)

☐ **14.** Is your school involved in national programs, such as Reading Is Fundamental or Book-It?

☐ **15.** Are there times during the day when every pupil is engaged in uninterrupted, sustained, silent reading (USSR)?

If you can answer yes to ten or more of these questions, you are indeed a literacy promoter.

4–4 SIX LEADERSHIP BEHAVIORS THAT BUILD STUDENT ACHIEVEMENT

"I really want to make my school meaningful for my pupils," you say. Much of what your school does to promote a positive learning environment *is* within your power to influence and control.

After distilling what we have seen and read about from all over the country, we have determined that the following six traits are common to all successful schools.

Practical Ways to Help Pupils Achieve

1. *Provide an orderly atmosphere.* Do what is necessary to make sure your building is quiet, pleasant, and well maintained.

2. *Support teachers.* Develop your goals and aims with your teachers. Then stand behind them and insist that they carry out the school's mission.

3. *Coordinate instructional programs.* Make sure there is an agreed-on scope and sequence through the grades. Provide teachers with courses of study for every subject they teach.

4. *Emphasize achievement.* Be visible and involved in what goes on in every classroom. Reward academic excellence and stay on top of pupils who don't do their homework or disturb the teachers' lessons.

5. *Demonstrate instructional strategies.* Get involved in lesson planning, selection of learning materials, and teacher training.

6. *Monitor pupil achievement.* Set expectations for the entire school and check to see that those expectations are being met. Collect class test papers on a weekly basis.

Practice these leadership behaviors, and academic achievement levels at your school will improve.

4–5 DIFFERENT STROKES FOR DIFFERENT YOUNG FOLKS

To motivate all the pupils in your school, you must be aware of their various learning styles and which of those styles may be dominant. According to Harvard University psychologist Howard Gardner, all normal pupils are capable of at least seven forms of intellectual accomplishment. One or more may be stronger than others, or dominant, in a given child.

You can help your teachers put Gardner's research to work in their classrooms by making them aware of what to look for. They can encourage students who show promise in a particular learning style and provide intervention for those at risk, helping each pupil find his or her niche in learning.

Here's how to recognize the characteristics of each learning style and how to supply the materials, activities, and experiences that will reinforce these strengths in your pupils.

The Seven Styles of Learning

1. *The Wordsmith*
   Traits: Loves to read, write, and tell stories. Good memory for facts and trivia.
   Materials: Typewriter, tape recorder, word processor, alphabet games, books, magazines, etc.
   Activities: Joke telling, oral reading, storytelling, taping, writing reports.
   Trips: Libraries, book stores, newspaper office. Book talk with author.

2. *The Reasoner*
   Traits: Good at math. Strong problem-solving and reasoning skills. Asks logical questions.
   Materials: Collects objects; likes mechanical toys and games requiring thinking.
   Activities: Classifying, experimenting, exploring. Constructing riddles and puzzles for others to solve.
   Trips: Museums; science and computer fairs.

3. *The Imager*
   Traits: Needs a mental or actual picture to process new information. Enjoys maps, charts, diagrams. Good imagination; can draw, design, and create things. Frequently daydreams.
   Materials: Films, maps, charts, illustrations, mazes, puzzles, construction toys, colorful objects.
   Activities: Media presentations, chart construction, original class plays, TV commercials, short stories, poetry.
   Trips: Theaters, art museums, planetariums, science fiction films.

4. *The Music Lover*
   Traits: Responds to music, remembers tunes. Aware of sounds: birds, clocks, etc.
   Materials: Musical instruments, sound systems, tapes, CDs.
   Activities: Rhythm band, memorizing lyrics, learning an instrument. Learns best when new material is set to music.
   Trips: Concerts, operas, performances, music stores.

5. *The Mover*
   Traits: Good at physical activities. Likes to move around, touch things, tap feet and fingers.

Materials: Hands-on crafts. Utilize gym equipment and manipulative objects.
Activities: Expression through dance, drama, and movement. Making things.
Trips: Attend sports and dance events. Participate in physical activities and crafts.

6. *The Socializer*
Traits: Leadership skills; enjoys people; skilled at organizing, communicating, negotiating.
Materials: People to talk with. Furniture that can be clustered in groups. Tape recorders.
Activities: Opportunities to share a skill or recall an experience. Discussions, interviews, debates. Group work, committee reports, etc.

7. *The Loner*
Traits: Strong sense of self. Dreamer. Prefers working alone. Follows through. Shy with strangers.
Materials: Space for solitude. Biographies of individualists. Solo games.
Activities: Independent research activities. Diaries, journals. Poetry, artwork, collections.
Trips: Quiet walks through public gardens, museums, churches. Libraries for browsing.

When we recognize and foster our pupils' different interests and styles, we let them know that they have valuable contributions to make to their own lives and to our world.

Determine what kinds of materials, activities, and trips will "stroke" each of your young folks. Be sure they get to experience them.

4–6 EXTENDING THE SCHOOL DAY AND SCHOOL SERVICES

The prevalence of poverty, drugs, single-parent families, and two-career couples has transformed the task of schools. Teachers and principals are overwhelmed trying to be surrogate parents, social workers, and psychologists.

The traditional 8:30 A.M. to 3:00 P.M. school day is being extended at both ends to meet the needs of working or impaired parents. Breakfast programs before the start of school and latchkey or after-school programs make it possible for some pupils to attend school from 8:00 A.M. to 6:00 P.M.

As principal, you must provide security for children and staff at these times, instruct the custodian to maintain the school building at a comfortable temperature, arrange for transportation, and make sure that teachers are providing meaningful supervision of the pupils during these extended hours.

In addition to the longer school day, many schools are extending their services to reach troubled families whose problems are crippling their children's ability to learn. They are trying to connect these families with social services they need. These "one-stop shopping" schools, as educators and social service professionals call them, are trying to bridge the gap between the society American schools were intended for and the one that exists today.

One-stop schools come in dozens of forms. Of course, you cannot start such a program alone. But you should become familiar with similar programs around the country so you can adapt a program to meet your school's needs.

- In Owensboro, Kentucky, one teacher functions as a link to social agencies for such services as health screenings, psychological counseling, welfare, and housing.
- In Plainfield, New Jersey, the schools offer services in health, counseling, employment, substance abuse, family counseling, and recreational programs. In addition to the school administration, the New Jersey Department of Human Services is involved. After the first three years of the program's existence, the schools noticed improved attendance and grades.
- In St. Louis, Missouri, the "Caring Communities" program serves preschoolers through fifth graders at the Walbridge Elementary School. The program includes tutoring, after-school childcare, parent skills training, and home visits for families in crisis.
- In San Diego, California, the "New Beginnings" program guides families through the maze of city and county services. Social service workers are placed at elementary schools. They get to know high-risk families. Teachers refer children and families with problems to workers called "family service advocates," who guide them through the supermarket of services.

The approaches vary, but each principal is aware that trouble at home usually means trouble at school. Savvy principals look for ways of teaming their parents with the often bewildering array of social services.

There are some built-in hurdles you should be aware of before you plan your program.

1. *Teacher avoidance.* Many teachers feel they are in school to teach pupils and not to function as social workers.
2. *Parent apathy.* Some parents have been frustrated in the past with unsuccessful efforts on the part of "do-gooders" and so are wary of the school's efforts.

3. *Turf battles.* The school and the social agency may have to compete for tax dollars. The program may or may not be housed in the school building. The social workers may not want to take direction from the principal.

4. *Confidentiality rules.* Many social service agencies and schools have trouble sharing information with each other because of rules of confidentiality. Case workers may want to keep their cases out of official school files. Principals may not want to release test scores to case workers.

5. *Red tape.* Rules and codes may strangle a principal who wants to work informally with a social agency. Disputes can break out on transporting children from the school to the center. For instance, must it be in a school bus, or can it be a van?

If you are prepared, you can anticipate many problems. If you demonstrate a cooperative, flexible spirit, you will promote similar feelings from the agencies; then the children and their families will benefit.

4–7 MEETING THE HEALTH NEEDS OF YOUR PUPILS

Helping your pupils achieve a state of well-being which enables them to function at their best is an important part of your job. This usually takes three forms: health services, health education, and safe and healthful school living.

State and local health regulations affect the school health program. You can improve your school's delivery of health services by looking at the "Health Needs Assessment" provided here.

HEALTH NEEDS ASSESSMENT

Part One: Health Services

1. *Appraisal*
Teacher's daily inspection of children
Vision and hearing testing
Height and weight measurement
Teacher-nurse conferences
Dental examination requirements
Comprehensive physical report

2. *Prevention*
Immunization updates
Communicable disease control
Safety checks
Emergency care
First aid materials

3. *Remedial*
Clinic appointments
Follow-up services
Correction of defects
Practitioner visits

Part Two: Health Instruction
Hygiene and health education lessons
Audiovisual materials on health
Sex education curriculum
AIDS instruction for teachers
Lessons on nutrition and sound health practices
Instruction in the dangers of substance abuse
Antidrug assemblies
Visits to child health stations
Participation in community health fairs, walkathons, etc.
Physical fitness activities
Team sports

Part Three: Healthful Living

1. *Physical environment*
Heating, lighting, and ventilation needs
Lunch room sanitation
Rest room appearance and sanitation

2. *Emotional climate*
Noise level in various school areas
Pupil-teacher ratio
Provision for individual differences
Curriculum adaptation for pupil needs
Class placement of pupils

3. *Health and Safety Practices*
Realistic scheduling
Fire protection and drills
Asbestos inspection
Inventory of irritating chemicals
Insect and pest control
Sound custodial practices

Review the experiences of your pupils using this rather extensive list. No principal should take this as a personal report card. However, it can serve as a useful reminder of the varied and complex issues affecting the delivery of health services. Invite two teachers and two parents to review it with you.

There are many occasions when you will need to communicate with parents about a health problem. Few are as annoying as the need to tell a parent that his or her child has head lice. We have included a sample letter for your use on page 62.

Allison's mother couldn't believe her ears. The school nurse must have made some kind of mistake. Surely Allison couldn't have lice!

Allison is a happy first grader. Her parents live in a nice part of town and are fussy about personal cleanliness. Allison gets a bath every evening.

The very idea of the principal telling her that Allison had to stay home until all signs of the infestation were gone! What's going on in that school, anyway? These were some of Allison's mother's thoughts on the way home.

Allison could have caught lice in a lot of different ways. She might have borrowed one of her friends' combs, barrettes, or hair ribbons. She might have hung up her coat alongside the coat of an infected classmate. The lice could easily get from one coat collar to another. When she let a friend listen to her cassette player, the headphones could have easily trapped and transmitted lice.

Parents frequently direct their rage at the principal when their child is sent home to be treated and not allowed to return until all eggs or nits have been removed. These measures are appropriate, and mandated in most places, in stopping the spread of this annoying but not dangerous parasite.

4–8 HANDLING AIDS PREVENTION INSTRUCTION

Even the youngest pupils in your school have heard of AIDS—some may even know an AIDS victim who has died. Your concern as the head of the school is how to provide nonthreatening, age-appropriate material and instruction on the prevention of this disease.

Because of the sensitive nature of this topic, it is important that you involve parents, teachers, and community members before you launch a teaching program. If your school already has a family life or sex education program, then AIDS prevention is a natural outgrowth of other instruction on sexually transmitted diseases.

Pediculosis Letter

PS 6
Park Avenue
Anytown, U.S.A.

, 19___

Dear _____ :

There has been some incidence of pediculosis (head lice) among the children in our school. We are examining the hair of each pupil and will be excluding from school for treatment those who are found to be affected. It is expected that a temporary exclusion coupled with home treatment will be successful in ending any cases.

Excluded pupils will be returned to school after treatment and inspection of the hair and scalp show elimination of the lice.

Your child, _____ , of Class _____ has been found to be infected. He/She must stay home until all nits (eggs) are gone. See your pharmacist for a suitable product. Follow the manufacturer's instructions.

Please understand that we have found only a few cases among our children. This is no reflection in any way on a person's personal hygiene or cleanliness. This condition is found especially among school children and can be picked up anyplace on contact with a person with nits or lice.

Thank you for your cooperation. If you have any questions, you can reach me at 876-5432.

Sincerely,

Alice Lindane
Principal

You must be concerned with the comfort level of your teachers in discussing this topic as well as the feelings of the parents. A successful program can be started with a committee of teacher representatives from different grade levels, an equal number of parents, and a health professional from a local hospital or clinic. Some of the items this group should explore include

- The grades to be involved
- The topics to be covered
- The materials to be used
- The training of teachers
- The involvement of health professionals.

From time to time, the committee should be called together to determine progress, identify problems, and focus on long-range goals. They should conduct an evaluation at the end of the year. By utilizing a committee approach, you can gauge the feelings of staff and parents before setting off on a program that does not have the support of either group.

Some nuts-and-bolts suggestions that have been used in successful programs include the following:

1. Pictorial representation may help pupils to comprehend how the body's immune system works. Diagrams used to identify or distinguish between healthy or different immune systems should be clearly drawn and labeled.
2. Assistance should be given in identifying, pronouncing, and understanding the necessary technical terms used in the lessons: virus, immune system, opportunistic infection, etc.
3. Provide information that debunks myths about casual contact and AIDS.
4. Try using a question box in which pupils can deposit anonymous questions to be answered in class.
5. Check that current approved videotapes on AIDS are available to teachers. Some are suitable for circulation among interested parents.

The subject of AIDS may be too abstract for some children. Using current events articles is one way to help pupils see the topic more concretely.

Convey a positive, nonthreatening attitude toward this topic. Teachers and pupils will sense your attitude.

4–9 PROVIDING PUPILS WITH A SAFE ENVIRONMENT

If school is to be meaningful for your pupils, they must feel safe. Yet a recently released study conducted by Texas A&M University reveals that in Central Texas half the boys and 20 percent of the girls had been involved in at least one fight during the past school year. A fifth of the pupils said that they thought carrying weapons was an effective way to prevent fights.

Parents measure a school and its leadership by how safe their children feel in class, in the school yard, in rest rooms, and in other areas.

By promoting safety, you can gain the support of the community and school staff as well as the confidence of pupils and parents.

The following steps will promote pupil safety as well as a school environment conducive to learning.

School Safety Steps

1. Pupils should be aware of the consequences of misbehavior.
2. A behavior code should be posted in classrooms and reviewed periodically.
3. Posters around the school, articles in the principal's newsletter, and meetings of the PTA and school assembly are excellent avenues for detailing expected pupil behavior.
4. Periodic loudspeaker announcements should provide reminders concerning expected pupil behavior.
5. Require pupil spectators to leave a fight scene. Insist that failure to disperse immediately may result in disciplinary action.
6. Follow up every fight by appropriately punishing the assailant. This can be the best deterrent. Punishment may include parent contact, in-school suspension, or pupil expulsion.
7. Emphasize positive steps regarding good behavior in a variety of situations (especially the lunch room, school bus, play yard, and hallways).

Sometimes a distraught teacher will summon you to the classroom to deal with an angry pupil who is out of control. The following hints will help you deal with such a situation.

Handling Classroom Conflicts

1. Use a steady, controlled voice. Avoid a shrill or raised voice.
2. Appear steady, unruffled, and calm. The pupil will probably be none of these.

3. Do not touch an agitated or angry pupil. Use nonverbal commands whenever possible (such as an extended index finger).

4. Encourage the pupil to leave the room with you. This will remove the pupil from an "audience" and will help him or her save face.

5. Be reassuring to the offending pupil as well as the rest of the class. This will let them know that you are "cool" and not hysterical.

6. After the incident is over, document everything that happened. Include names, a brief description of events, and the teacher's statement. Be sure to inform the pupil's parent.

Handle any disturbance in or around your school as an opportunity for creating an even more positive school climate. By reassuring the rule-abiding pupils that you are serious about enforcing rules you give them a sense of confidence in the school and its principal.

Communication with pupils, parents, and staff is the key to maintaining a tension-free, safe environment. It is important to discuss behavior at faculty meetings. You should feel comfortable discussing school safety topics at pupil assemblies and parent meetings. Your school community needs to feel confident that safety matters are discussed openly and that guidelines and procedures are in place for promoting pupil safety.

4–10 STEPS TOWARD MORE MEANINGFUL PUPIL ASSESSMENT

How many times have you tried to explain to a parent a reading score on a standardized test? We've all had pupils whose test performances did not reflect their actual classroom work.

There is a movement to supplement and even replace standardized tests in reading and math with portfolios of pupils' actual work. Vermont is doing this statewide, and many school districts around the country have moved in this direction.

Why not try this in your school as a supplement to the more formal testing? You can use the results to help place pupils in next year's class, identify gifted and talented pupils, recognize the need for special education, and select pupils for individualized instruction.

Educators' and parents' concerns about dependence on bubble sheets and multiple choice questions have brought some reform:

- Passages on reading tests have been lengthened to approximate real-life reading materials.

- Math tests go further than merely testing computation skills. They now include tests of reasoning ability as well as problem-solving skills.

- Many tests now have essay-writing sections.

Here are some ways to include portfolios and performance assessments in your schoolwide testing program:

Selected Portfolio Ideas

1. Have pupils fill language arts portfolio folders with poems, essays, short stories, and scripts.

2. Fill mathematics portfolios with solutions to homework problems, geometric string designs, scale drawings or maps, and pupil-made graphs. Include pupil-written explanations of solutions to verbal problems.

3. Provide pupils with journal-writing experiences. Collect samples of these in a folder.

4. Require pupils to take a science performance test. Have them perform an actual experiment. Test younger pupils with magnets and balance scales. Rate pupils on accuracy, use of instruments, and ability to form generalizations.

5. Have a team of teachers evaluate portfolios of a grade other than their own. This will help provide teacher objectivity.

While you cannot eliminate multiple choice tests, you can personalize and supplement your pupils' testing to make it more meaningful.

You will encounter some problems. It's difficult to get teachers and parents to accept evaluation tools that are not packaged, objective, validated, etc. It's also difficult to develop authentic assessments that consistently measure similar skills from pupil to pupil.

Performance assessment is also more time-consuming than traditional paper and pencil tests. But supporters argue that the benefits outweigh the drawbacks.

Start by using portfolios and performance assessments as an adjunct to regular tests. If enough of your colleagues follow your lead, you may be able to supplant standardized testing in your district—if that's what you want. Remember, it doesn't make sense to test violin playing or softball prowess with written, multiple choice questions—so why use answer sheets for higher-order skills like the ability to think and communicate?

Chapter 5

Improving the Climate of Your School

PS 5 is having trouble getting substitutes to cover teacher absences. It's a fairly new building with a mix of pupils from middle-class backgrounds. Yet substitute teachers would rather work at PS 3, an inner-city school, or PS 8, a sixty-year-old, overcrowded building. When questioned about PS 5, the substitute teachers reply, "It's such a cold place," "Nobody seems happy there," or "They don't make me feel welcome."

The principal is concerned. He wants to do a good job. Each teacher seems concerned—yet the staff's overall impression of the school is negative.

■For seven or more hours each day, you and your teachers are together in an enclosed community. This can be tiresome unless you make it a pleasant experience.

Working with staff members, you can make your school a warm, positive place where parents, staff, and pupils come willingly to work together on reaching common goals. This chapter shows you how.

5–1 TAKING A LOOK AT YOUR SCHOOL'S CLIMATE

In identifying more effective schools from the standpoint of academic achievement, standardized test scores, and pupil behavior, the public always refers to the school's climate or tone. This is more difficult to measure than a reading score or grade average, yet it is a vital component of any assessment.

What are some characteristics of a positive school climate? They will vary from place to place, but the following factors are common:

Factors in Measuring a School's Climate

1. There is a general feeling of well-being throughout the building.
2. Pupils appear to be living and learning in a relaxed, tension-free atmosphere.
3. Teachers are cheerful and nonthreatening.
4. Parents feel welcome and frequently attend special events as well as regular meetings.
5. The building is clean, well-ventilated, and inviting.
6. Staff expectations about pupil achievement are high.
7. There is a sense of order throughout, and discipline problems are kept to a minimum.
8. An overall plan or sense of direction appears to be evident to all staff members.
9. Attention is given to pupils with special needs, whether they are gifted or special-ed youngsters.
10. There is strong administrative leadership and direction.

Take a look at your school's climate. Pretend you have never visited your building before, and look at it with fresh eyes. Use this checklist.

School Climate Checklist

☐ **1.** Can you park a car near your school? What is the condition of the parking area?

☐ **2.** What is the first thing you see as you approach the school? Is there any graffiti or litter?

☐ **3.** Where is the play area? Is it inviting to children?

☐ **4.** What do you see when you enter the building? There should be a sign-in book or a security guard. Does a sign direct you to the principal's office?

☐ **5.** Does anyone greet you when you reach the office? Does the office appear chaotic, sterile, or neat?

☐ **6.** Is there evidence of pupil work on display in the halls or office? Is the work current?

☐ **7.** What is the condition of the bulletin boards? Are items commercially prepared or done by pupils? Are items frayed or fresh looking?

☐ **8.** What does the school smell like? Is it well ventilated, or are you overwhelmed by disinfectant, lunch room, or locker room odors?

☐ **9.** Are the halls quiet, with orderly pupil movement, or are there stragglers sauntering about without any direction? Do pupils carry room passes?

☐ **10.** What does the school sound like? Can you hear teachers scolding pupils in the classroom? Do pupils run in the hall?

☐ **11.** Where is the principal most likely to be found—in his or her office, in the halls, in classrooms?

☐ **12.** How do your staff members greet visitors? Are they generally friendly, hostile, suspicious, or threatened?

☐ **13.** What is the attitude of nonteaching employees (secretary, custodial and lunch room workers, security guard, school aides) toward visitors? Is it indifference, abruptness, or helpfulness?

☐ **14.** Do the pupils seem happy? Do very young children wave and smile at visitors? Do older pupils treat each other with respect? Do the pupils seem involved in what they are doing?

☐ **15.** Is there evidence of pupil participation in cocurricular activities—science fair winners, poster contests, sport or athletic events, photographs of class trips, peer tutoring?

☐ **16.** Do you see any interaction between faculty members, such as team teaching, assembly programs, small-group instruction, and cooperative planning?

☐ **17.** How do the teachers look? Are they neatly dressed; do they take pride in their appearance? Do they appear happy and involved or bored and glassy-eyed?

☐ **18.** Is there an overdependence on the public address system for announcements throughout the day?

☐ **19.** Are rules or goals posted in halls or classrooms?

☐ **20.** Is recess time safe and organized or frantic and haphazard?

This is a rather detailed checklist of factors that contribute to a positive school climate. Like any subjective measure, it depends on forthright, honest answers. If you really want to get a feel for the kind of public image your school gives, try making some photocopies of this checklist. Hand one to the custodian, parent association president, teachers' union representative, and the newest teacher in your school. You'll be amazed at their responses. Virtually everyone sees the school differently. Some really brave principals have involved pupils and itinerant personnel, such as social workers, in their evaluations.

5–2 MAKING YOUR SCHOOL LOOK MORE ATTRACTIVE

Children who spend their school day in an attractive environment are more likely to keep it clean, feel secure, and take pride in their work. Each of your teachers has a different standard for what they consider an attractive classroom. You can encourage teachers to make their rooms an attractive learning environment, and most teachers will respond. There are always a few teachers who seem to thrive on clutter and are too busy "teaching" to pay attention to appearances. Encourage all teachers to provide a clean, neat learning environment, and let each teacher's creative sense reign.

There are ways in which you, as the principal, can provide an attractive school environment for all your pupils—both in general areas, such as hallways, and in individual classrooms. Let's begin with the more difficult task: How can you get teachers to make their classrooms more attractive? This inventory of ideas will help.

Improving the Appearance of Classrooms

1. Review with the custodian a schedule for sweeping classrooms as well as cleaning (floor mopping and waxing, window washing, etc.).

2. Check that each classroom has adequate closet space and bookshelves for storage of materials. Are there adequate bulletin boards?

3. Order supplies teachers can use to spruce up their rooms: large sheets of colored construction paper, staplers, alphabet charts, large tablet charts, oak tag, felt-tip pens, etc.

4. Discuss learning environments at your first faculty conference. Let the staff know that you consider an attractive classroom a priority.

5. Write a note to teachers who have mounted a particularly attractive display in their classroom.

6. Visit classrooms informally and regularly. Comment on items of room decor or areas that need improvement.

7. Hand out memos containing suggestions for classroom organization, such as a science corner, library corner, media center, and art, reading, or other interest centers.

8. Include classroom appearance when you write up formal observations of teachers' lessons.

9. Hold grade or lunch-time meetings in the classroom of a teacher who has done a particularly good job of organizing the classroom. This will encourage others to do the same and will compliment the teacher whose room has been selected.

10. Help teachers with bare, untidy, or disorganized classrooms. Take a few minutes to help these teachers get organized. Some teachers really don't know how to get started. No one ever showed them. You can make the difference.

When you are satisfied that your teachers are committed to improving the appearance of their classrooms, you must make the common areas look good—the lobby, halls, lunch room, bulletin boards, and outside areas.

This list will help you get started.

Making Your School Look More Inviting

1. Don't try to do everything yourself. This project requires monthly changes and can't be a one-person job. Set up a committee that includes a teacher from the lower grades and another from the upper grades, a member of the custodial staff, a school aide, and yourself. It will be the committee's responsibility to gather display material from each class and change hall bulletin boards. The committee can draw up a schedule of responsibility.

2. Label every hall bulletin board unobtrusively (1, 2, 3, etc.). Set up a monthly schedule of teacher responsibility for each bulletin board.

If you have twenty teachers and ten hall bulletin boards, each teacher will be responsible on alternate months of the year for a seasonal display of pupil work.

3. Set up a permanent display case or bulletin board in the lobby or entrance hall where most people enter the building. This can remain unchanged for two months or longer. Welcome visitors with a large poster; list key people and their location as well as each teacher and his or her classroom. Arrange for a sign-in book if no security personnel or parent volunteers are available.

4. Encourage teachers and/or parents to take candid photos of pupils engaged in a variety of seasonal activities and school events. Display these in hallways where there is the most traffic. Change them monthly.

5. Don't allow any one grade or class to dominate the display material. The purpose of the schedule is to let every class shine at different times in different locations.

6. Don't encourage destruction of bulletin boards. Cover some boards with sheets of clear plastic. Don't put up any items that would encourage fingering or marking by pupils.

7. Encourage teachers to display a pupil-made welcome sign or poster on their classroom door. This is especially inviting during open house.

8. Hold poster contests throughout the school year. Pupils love them; they are instructional and will provide you with many attractive posters to display. Some example themes include Women in History, Black History Month, Team Up to Clean Up, and UNICEF campaigns.

9. Place posters in community store windows, announcing school events and inviting visitors (e.g., for the science fair, Grandparents Day, band concerts, etc.).

10. Pick up candy wrappers or other litter dropped in the halls, and in this way encourage pupils and teachers to do the same.

The most important component of an attractive school is the appearance of its pupils. Remind your teachers to encourage pupils to practice personal hygiene and to take pride in their appearance. At P.T.A. meetings and through flyers help parents to distinguish between school clothes and play clothes. Set up occasional dress-up days for special assemblies. Compliment pupils on their attractive appearance, and watch the contagion spread!

5-3 REDUCING THE NOISE LEVEL

One of the best indicators of a well-run school is the noise level as you walk through the building. The less effective the school, the higher the decibel level of sound.

Although we recognize that human beings have varying levels of voice volume and that larger, more crowded schools are likely to be noisier, there are steps that you can take to reduce the noise level of your school.

Different parts of the building generate different kinds of sound. An exciting volleyball game in the gym produces one kind of happy sound. A couple of hundred pupils eating lunch on a rainy day when they can't go outside will produce another kind of sound.

A variety of sounds are generated from different classrooms at different times of day. The movement of a class through the hall going from their classroom to another activity will depend on the class, the activity, and especially the teacher. Some teachers pride themselves on orderly, quiet hall movements, while others resemble camp counselors taking their charges for a swim.

As the head of the school, you must set the tone regarding the level of noise that is tolerable. A hum of activity is positive, but unproductive noise is a form of pollution and should be stopped before it gets out of control.

You will find the following hints helpful in improving your school's climate.

Guide to Reducing Noise Pollution

1. Keep public address announcements to a minimum. Whenever possible, cluster the day's announcements into one broadcast at the start of the day. Conscientious teachers find it disconcerting when their lessons are interrupted for an announcement about an increase in the price of lunch milk.

2. Insist that teachers keep their classroom doors closed. This is an important security precaution. It also eliminates distraction caused by pupils in the hallway. In addition to aiding classroom management and discipline, it reduces hallway noise.

3. Set up a system of out-of-room passes. If a teacher excuses a pupil to use the washroom or go to the office, the pupil should have a pass. The pupil should record the date and time he or she is out of the room in an "Out-of-Room Book." Teachers will have to do this for kindergarteners and first graders. This will reduce excessive movement of pupils in the halls.

4. Meet with the school aides and teachers in charge of the lunch room to devise rules and regulations that will ensure a tension-free lunch period with a minimal noise level. Try different seating and serving patterns until you have a system that works.

5. Train pupils to observe silence at certain times and in certain areas. Absolute silence should be mandated for fire drills, standardized test sessions, and the library.

6. Eliminate unnecessary bells, gongs, and buzzers during the school day. Meet with a group of teachers to see which of these signals are necessary and which can be discarded.

7. Tour the building with your custodian to investigate what kinds of acoustical materials can be used to reduce noise. If space permits, an empty room between the band room and a classroom can be a big help.

8. Enforce some basic rules for pupils, such as no running in the halls, no talking in stairways, etc. Discourage whistling or singing in hallways.

9. Set a good example by using a well-modulated voice and courtesy when talking to teachers, parents, and pupils. Avoid shouting instructions to a teacher three doors down the hall.

10. When modernizing your building, consider sound-absorbing drapes, acoustical ceiling tiles, and carpeted areas as important instructional enhancements, not just cosmetic touches.

5–4 MAKING SCHOOL MORE CONDUCIVE TO LEARNING

In some schools there is so much focus on keeping pupils and parents happy that there is little focus on the main mission of the school—education. In other schools, so much of the teachers' time is focused on discipline problems or administrative details that little instruction takes place.

Although parent involvement, pupil events, discipline problems, and administrative directives are all part of a school's climate, it is important to make learning the first priority.

The items listed on page 75 can serve as an outline for planning faculty conferences or as a survey for assessing your school's priorities.

5–5 YOUR ROLE IN IMPROVING SCHOOL CLIMATE

There is no question about it: Your attitude and personality leave an imprint on the general tone or climate of the school. The way in which you assert your leadership affects the functioning of the school staff more than any other quality.

The effective principal must be concerned with improving instruction. Even veteran teachers must be observed and given suggestions.

In all of your dealings with teachers and other personnel in your school, be mindful of their egos and feelings of self-worth. This is perhaps the most important element in any program of teacher training or staff development. You may be *right* about something (pedagogical, philosophical, logical, etc.), but if you present your correction in a manner that demeans the staff member, you may as well be wrong. Staff members will

LEARNING PRIORITY SURVEY

Beside each statement are five numbers. Decide how much you agree or disagree with each statement. Circle one of the following as your answer.

1—strongly disagree
2—disagree
3—not sure
4—agree
5—strongly agree

Statement	Response				
1. Goals are clear.	1	2	3	4	5
2. Academic achievement is rewarded.	1	2	3	4	5
3. Communication is open.	1	2	3	4	5
4. Instructional time is used well.	1	2	3	4	5
5. Rules are enforced with consistency.	1	2	3	4	5
6. Administrative leadership is strong.	1	2	3	4	5
7. Discipline policies are agreed on.	1	2	3	4	5
8. Teacher attendance is good.	1	2	3	4	5
9. Teachers are involved in decision making.	1	2	3	4	5
10. Pupils participate in school activities.	1	2	3	4	5
11. Parents get frequent feedback on pupil achievement.	1	2	3	4	5
12. Parents are invited to workshops and meetings.	1	2	3	4	5
13. Textbooks and learning materials are appropriate.	1	2	3	4	5
14. There is general agreement about the curriculum.	1	2	3	4	5
15. Evaluation is carried out fairly and regularly.	1	2	3	4	5

pay no attention to your suggestion or correction if they have been hurt. They will be thinking about their bruised ego and not about how right you are. As an administrator, you are responsible for seeing that things go smoothly. Sometimes you must criticize. When you do bring something negative to an employee's attention, do it in a way that is instructive and not destructive.

Your management of classroom teachers will improve if you remember the following when you must criticize. (Also remember that sometimes not to criticize is far worse for the teacher. A tactful reminder from you is better than a reprimand from someone else. This is especially true for new teachers.)

1. Leave out all personal remarks. It is better to ask, "What happened?" instead of "Who did it?"
2. Focus on the mistake itself and not on the personality.
3. If formal criticism is necessary, choose the right time and a private place.
4. Never lose your temper with a teacher.
5. Begin with something positive.
6. Allow sufficient time for a response.
7. Follow up by praising any improvement that you have noted.
8. Set a good example for your teachers to follow.
9. Never put in writing your unfavorable comments about a teacher unless you have thought about it for seventy-two hours.
10. Make it a practice to return to the teacher all copies of a letter of criticism at the end of the school year if there has been an improvement or no reoccurrence.

Teachers can be trained to improve their daily performance if you approach them in the right way. The best in-service training programs may look good on paper but will not be worth much if the wrong person is in charge of implementing them. As the leader of the school, you must set an example of concern for self-improvement. You must show your teachers that you care about their feelings before you can get them to care about refining their techniques.

5–6 HANDLING CLIQUES AND POWER PLAYS

In almost every school you will find informal groups of teachers who have banded together because, for one reason or another, they find themselves congenial. These groups can have considerable influence over the behavior and job attitudes of other individuals, especially new teachers. Whether a clique is disruptive or cooperative depends a great deal on how you decide to meet the challenge.

In every group there is someone who is the most popular and who is the acknowledged leader. In most cases, the problem of dealing with cliques becomes a question of recognizing the popular leader and finding a way to ensure his or her cooperation.

Teacher cliques present no cause for alarm as long as they continue to perform up to your standards and cooperate. Yet many such groups are anything but productive. If you find any of the following characteristics in some of your staff, it's time to intensify your efforts to gain their cooperation.

Danger Signal Checklist

☐ **1.** They keep their performance to a level that's far below their capacity but equal to their past performance.

☐ **2.** If one or two teachers consistently volunteer for extra assignments, they are rejected by the rest of the group.

☐ **3.** Newcomers to the staff, no matter how well you train them, quickly adjust their performance to the group's normal low level.

☐ **4.** If teachers do something extra, they make it clear that they are doing you a favor and you shouldn't expect it to last.

If you take the following steps, you'll be able to gain the cooperation of any teacher clique.

1. Recognize the group's leader as well as all the members, and encourage their cooperation instead of fighting the clique's existence.

2. Show your interest in the group's goals and back them up when their requests are reasonable.

3. Look for signs of boredom among your teachers, and discourage the tendency to slack off by setting a good example at all times.

4. Develop the group's interest in the overall program, and treat your workers as you like to be treated.

5. Look for factors that the group considers important, and show your understanding of their problems.

Successful administrators learn to work with the informal leaders among their staff to develop a mutual understanding of the school's objectives.

You will find teachers who relish a certain degree of power. Sometimes they feel they have earned it because of their seniority. Other teachers feel that the nature of their assignment (graduating class, gifted pupils) entitles them to a certain dominion over other teachers. By massaging the egos of such teachers, you may buy a temporary peace. But the rest of the staff will resent it and you will emerge as the loser. A better idea is to channel the energies and talents of these people into a positive path that will benefit the entire school.

The best solution is to give every teacher a sense of empowerment. Many of your tasks can be done better by teachers, followed by your review:

- Ordering textbooks
- Distributing supplies
- Planning conference agendas
- Scheduling assembly programs
- Arranging class trips
- Making curriculum adjustments.

Encourage one of your power-hungry teachers to chair a committee, or put him or her in charge of one of these projects. You will be harnessing the energy of an active staff member, and you will also be fostering school-based management.

5–7 ENCOURAGING A CLIMATE FOR CREATIVITY

The best strategy for improving the general tone or climate of your school is to put your teachers' ideas into action. This will give your staff a sense of ownership in running the school. They will not feel that they are being managed with a factory-style approach. Teachers resent a top-down organizational pattern. They have ideas of their own about how the school can be improved. Give them a chance to try out their ideas.

New ideas are cropping up everywhere. Pick up any professional journal or magazine, and you will read about new ideas in education. Some really work! Some look like remakes of old, established practices. But better ways of doing things are always welcome. Where do these ideas come from? They frequently start in the classroom. It takes a wise principal to capitalize on these ideas. Some may need alterations; others need amplification—but the basic idea comes from a concerned teacher who has found a better way of teaching something.

You can establish a climate that will encourage and stimulate new ideas and successful practices. *You set the tone in your building.* Your school can become an arid wasteland of tired practices repeated each year, or it can become a fertile ground for new and fresh ideas. Your teachers will be loathe to try new methods unless you encourage them. Here are eight steps that will help you establish a creative climate.

Creative Climate Game Plan

1. *Point out which areas need improvement.* Be specific. What kind of idea do you need? Give your teachers some sort of target. Exactly what needs improvement? Don't say, "Reading needs improvement." Say, "We need to improve students' comprehension of a selection's main idea." Be as concrete as you can. Plant the seed and step back as the teacher gets it growing.

2. *State the facts.* Collate all the available data and pertinent information, and pass this along to the teacher. Let the teacher know the unsuccessful methods that you have tried. Don't waste his or her time with dead ends and blind alleys. Trial and error works, but trying what has already failed is time-consuming in most cases.

3. *Try the obvious first.* Being close to a situation sometimes makes the solution to routine problems more difficult to find. Encourage your staff members to try an obvious solution before going on to the more esoteric. For instance, if pupils are not doing their homework, ask teachers if their parents have been told and if their help has been requested.

4. *Inspire teachers through brainstorming.* Encourage your staff to use their imagination in more creative ventures. When trying to think of innovative ideas, you must depart from routine solutions. Tackle the problem from every angle, whether it makes sense or not. For instance, if pupils avoid creative writing assignments, perhaps encouraging them to enter essay contests with prizes that appeal to them would help.

5. *Bear down.* Encourage your staff to concentrate on the task at hand. Get them to think about it intensely. They should stick with it until they come up with a new idea. Never let them give up until they reach their frustration point.

6. *Take time out.* When teachers have done all that they can, forget it for a while. They've done their part. They've planted the creative seeds. Now let their subconscious minds (and yours) harvest the crop.

7. *Await the answer.* No one knows how long that subconscious mind will simmer away. Sooner or later, the thought, the idea—the answer—will bubble to the top. When it does, it usually surfaces with lightning speed. Be ready for it, no matter what you may be doing at the time. Be sure to write down the details when the idea does emerge.

Good ideas are elusive. Encourage your teachers to write down the details of their ideas.

8. *Do something about it.* Put the idea to work at once. Try it out. You may have to modify it to make it work. Eventually, you might have to discard it, but you'll have enough ideas to keep you going if you follow these steps. Only by implementing teachers' ideas will you encourage others to think of new ideas. Some ideas may sound impractical to you, but it is important not to react with scorn or impatience. There's no surer way to discourage your staff's original thinking than to ridicule an idea.

Another strategy that will work wonders in turning your school around is to plan ahead for how you give orders or direction. A frequent complaint in many schools is that the teachers don't know what the principal wants. The following steps will help you train new teachers as well as your more experienced staff members.

A Daily Dozen for Climate Control

1. Make sure all your instructions are detailed and that they anticipate any questions your staff may have.

2. Tell your staff the reasons for any order.

3. Carefully describe the standards that you expect.

4. Allow sufficient time for completing any task.

5. Plan intervisitation of staff members.

6. Help teachers evaluate their own performance through closed circuit TV or written evaluations.

7. Demonstrate how you would like something taught.

8. Supervise and inspect closely and constantly.

9. Help staff members set goals and objectives.

10. Be patient. Encourage a new employee with praise when earned.

11. Set up buddy teachers. Everyone has something to offer a colleague.

12. Smile. Punctuate your suggestions with a smile that says you are not angry, just concerned.

Good luck. This chapter will put you on your way to improving the climate or tone of your school.

Chapter 6

Motivating Teachers to Do Their Best

Sometimes Jim feels as if he would like to use a cattle prod on about half the teachers in his school. They enter the building as if they were zombies and sleepwalk through the day. Virtually nothing excites or enthuses them. Their pupils have caught this sense of lethargy. Although the classrooms are orderly, the lessons are dull. The senior teachers are taking more sick days, and two of his newest, most enthusiastic teachers are talking about a career change. The union chapter leader is busy with complaints. Overall, Jim feels that the pupils are being shortchanged.

■IN SOME SCHOOLS the principal and teachers maintain an adversarial relationship. The principal feels compelled to stay on the teachers' backs so they don't goof off. He or she feels compelled to check up on the staff constantly to make sure they are carrying out their responsibilities. The teachers, on the other hand, view the principal as a martinet—as a distrusting, cold, detached, overseer.

Successful principals view their teachers as partners and share with them positive feelings of mutual respect. In this chapter you will learn techniques for motivating your staff.

6-1 REVITALIZING YOUR SENIOR TEACHERS

Teaching is a complex, draining, isolating activity for many teachers as they approach their fifteenth year. Today's curriculum demands make planning more complex. Meeting the needs of more diverse pupil populations is emotionally draining. Being locked up in a self-contained classroom is socially isolating. Mid-career can be a time of crystallization—some teachers get frozen in place and increasingly fragile. Yet for many others it continues to be a satisfying, challenging, ongoing vocation. The teachers on your staff, no doubt, fall somewhere in the middle of this continuum.

Your role as principal is to maintain the positive growth of your staff. You want to provide opportunities that avoid premature resignation or complacency and instead open up options for growth and revitalization.

To continue in a positive, satisfying career, your teachers need a work environment that provides recognition, growth, variety, and sharing.

Recognition

Veteran teachers need *more* recognition than beginners, not less. That is a mistake many principals make. They tend to take their senior staff for granted. Instead, help restore senior teachers' feelings of success by recognizing their accomplishments and their struggles. For example,

- Send personalized letters of commendation for class performances.
- Display a plaque in the lobby recognizing teachers with fifteen years of service.

- Remember significant milestones in a teacher's life. Send cards on special anniversaries, graduations of children, or births of grandchildren.

Growth

Stimulate your senior teachers' awareness of choice and exploration. Emphasize their potential for growth and influence. Involve them in cultural and life enrichment activities that may or may not directly affect their teaching. Talk to individual teachers or small groups about some of your own life-expanding activities. For example,

- Arrange a theater party or invite a group of teachers to attend a concert together.
- Begin a book club in which staff members exchange current books or magazines.
- Start an annual picnic or barbeque to bring the staff together in a social setting.

Variety

Encourage teachers to change a grade or subject that they teach. Institute measures that create job variety and enrichment for staff. Enable teachers to use their unique skills, develop new competencies, and expand their professional autonomy. Give them room to experiment with their teaching techniques. For example,

- Have teachers in each grade select their own textbooks from a fixed dollar allocation.
- Encourage team teaching or other alternative teaching styles.
- Set up an after-school enrichment center in which teachers are paid on a self-sustaining basis to offer pupils instruction in art, crafts, music, dance, or sports.

Sharing

Develop opportunities for collegiality. Let teachers get together to discuss strategies, select materials of instruction, and plan activities. Develop a support system among your staff members. Make them feel that they need to come to school to be with their peers. Such measures will enhance mutual trust and collaboration and reduce feelings of isolation. For example,

- Set up a committee of teachers on a grade level or subject area. Let them choose their own agenda.

- Enhance the teachers' lunch hour by revitalizing their lunch room or lounge. Involve them in refurbishing the room. Get some money from the PTA or a fund-raiser to buy a microwave oven, coffee machine, comfortable chairs, etc.
- Encourage the formation of an active social committee that plans school parties: Welcome Back, Christmas/Channukah, Valentine's Day, Spring Break, End of Term, etc.

Above all, make your teachers, especially the senior staff members, feel that you see their work as important and worthwhile. Ask their advice. Involve them in decisions that affect them directly (e.g., those about scheduling, trips, enrichment activities, etc.). Give your teachers chances for more responsibility. Let them put to work greater varieties of skills and abilities. Enhance their professional lives by setting up a career ladder, shared decision making, school-based management, peer review, or something else that enhances their professional lives. Make opportunities available as part of the regular contract day and year for teachers to work on curriculum development, staff development, and enrichment activities. Establish a small grant program that allows teachers to develop instructional materials or experiment with new teaching methods (e.g., "big books," computer-assisted instruction, etc.). In addition,

- Make available, and post prominently, announcements for promotional opportunities.
- Whenever possible, ask the central office to promote from within your school. Recommend your teachers for central office or after-school positions.
- Utilize assembly programs to free a few teachers to work on school-wide or professional projects.

You will find that some teachers have no desire for varied roles. For them, provide enrichment opportunities in their classrooms. Ask them to act as resource teachers for peers or as mentors for new teachers. Assign them a student teacher from a local college.

In short, revitalize your mid-career teachers by enriching their personal as well as professional lives. Make them want to come to work in the morning. Help them make friends in school: Change the location of their classroom; if you have more than one lunch period, let them eat with colleagues of their choice; put up a bulletin board in the teachers' lounge where they can display photos of their grandchildren. Get a local travel agent to publicize a ski weekend that single teachers in your school can go to as a group. Help newly widowed or divorced teachers establish a lunchtime support group with your school social worker. Set up a network of local repair people, medical providers, restaurants, and retail stores that will provide promotions or discounts to your staff members. Give your teachers a sense of belonging to a special group of people and not just being automatons who work in a plant that turns out pupils with an acceptable reading level.

Your senior teachers have a great deal of expertise to offer your school. Make them feel that they have something to offer—and they will!

6–2 REACHING OUT TO THE BEGINNING TEACHER

As a principal, you sometimes feel like a firefighter—moving about putting out small blazes that occur first in one part of the building and then in another. These "blazes" may be pupils fighting, teachers in need of support, or irate parents waiting to see you. They sometimes occur all at once and all seem to need your personal attention.

The group of people that's most easily forgotten, primarily because of their timidity, is beginning teachers. In most cases they are thrown into a classroom situation with little preparation or supervision from you. It's like being tossed into the deep end of a pool before learning to swim—while the lifeguard is legitimately busy helping others.

This list of ten ways to reach out to the new teacher will help you assist your most vulnerable staff members.

Ten Ways to Help the Beginning Teacher

1. Acquaint beginning teachers with other staff members who are available to assist them: guidance counselors, school nurse, grade leader, other administrator, etc. Tell them when these people are available and where they can be found.

2. Provide them with as much information as you can about the class they are teaching: test scores, report card grades, attendance data, parent involvement, behavior profiles, referrals made, evaluations by the previous teacher, health records, etc.

3. Distribute books and materials fairly. Make sure these beginning teachers get their fair share of the school's instructional materials, books, supplies, and audiovisual equipment. Give them pointers on using nonbook items, such as video players, tape recorders, etc.

4. Assign a buddy teacher or other experienced professional to work with each beginning teacher. This peer-to-peer guidance is less threatening than principal-teacher supervision. Your assistance will be more effective a little later in the year.

5. Tell beginning teachers something about the school community, local mores, ethnic make-up, socioeconomic level, etc. This is especially helpful in schools that serve a mixed pupil population.

6. Make beginning teachers feel welcome by introducing them to their peers at the first faculty conference and to individual staff members as you meet them. Encourage staff members to make the new teachers feel welcome. Personally assist beginning teachers with some of the school amenities—make sure they have a parking pass, washroom key, sign-in or time sheets, etc.

7. Be available for quick questions and/or guidance. Beginning teachers have many insecurities based on a lack of accurate information. Be supportive and patient in answering their questions. Provide them with a listening post. Let them "talk out" their problems, and cooperatively arrive at solutions.

8. Take care of their administrative and payroll needs. Make certain that all the paperwork has been done to ensure that they are paid on time—and at the appropriate salary step. Few things are more frustrating for beginning teachers than having to wait several pay periods for their first check and then find that they did not get credit for prior service or training.

9. Give beginning teachers some pointers on discipline and classroom management. Describe schoolwide procedures that they can use. Is there a detention room? Are form letters to parents available? Is there a dean or other person who metes out punishment? What is the school policy about calling parents?

10. Help beginning teachers organize their classrooms. Are there enough chairs and desks of the right size to accommodate their pupils? Are there enough bookcases? Does the teacher's closet have a working lock? Encourage new teachers to set up an attractive classroom environment: bulletin boards, interest centers, plants, class library, etc.

6–3 INSPIRING YOUR TEACHERS

If you can structure a job enrichment program, you will get your classroom teachers motivated. Job enrichment involves offering increased levels of responsibility and giving teachers the opportunity to use greater varieties of skills and abilities. For instance, have each grade elect a grade leader. Make this person your conduit for textbook samples that the grade can examine and recommend for adoption. Encourage the grade leader to become part of the school's curriculum committee. Publicize grade leaders' names in the PTA newsletter. Assign student teachers and beginning teachers to them so the new people can profit from the experience of the veterans.

Create a part-time position for a dean of discipline. This person can follow up on behavior problems, help new teachers prevent discipline incidents, and set up a code of behavior for all pupils to follow. You can provide time for this teacher each week by excusing him or her from an assembly period, hall patrol, or by offering his or her class an enrichment period with another teacher.

Talk to your teachers individually. Understanding what makes an individual teacher want to teach gives you the key to keeping your best teachers and inspiring those who are falling into ruts and routines.

Become involved in your teachers' plans. Take it as a compliment if one of your teachers asks you to help plan a unit of work. Classroom teachers are the loneliest people in the world. They frequently see themselves as being locked up with a group of pupils and not released until the bell rings. They are delighted to see another adult human being—even if it is the principal. Make yourself welcome by bringing them something—some instructional material, motivational device, or just a cartoon on a school subject.

We asked some principals who had energized their staffs to identify the effective behaviors that seemed to motivate their teachers. Here is the list they came up with. How do *you* measure up?

Teacher Motivators

1. Help a teacher move on to a new grade or subject.

2. Show a teacher how to reorganize class routines.

3. Order special learning materials that a teacher requested.

4. Ask about teacher preferences before assigning classes for next year

5. Discuss lesson plans with a teacher.

6. Give a demonstration lesson.

7. Arrange for a teacher to observe other classes.

8. Make it possible for a teacher to represent your school at a district meeting.

9. Pair an experienced teacher with a new teacher.

10. Encourage a teacher to take courses, attend seminars, etc.

Another way to inspire your teachers is to make sure they see you throughout the day. Even if they don't talk to you, they should see you.

This helps them feel connected. The more omnipresent you are, the more successful you will be. Your teachers should see you at least once in the morning and again in the afternoon. They must be aware of your presence in the line-up area, study halls, and the lunch room. Your "aura" must pervade the entire school. Just as insecure children like to know that their parents are home just in case they need them, your teachers should feel that you are always around. They are on the firing line, all day and every day. It's comforting to know that their back-up person is near if needed.

Be realistic. Expect a certain degree of resistance. Sadly, many teachers, especially in difficult schools, have lost interest in teaching. They have settled for the relative comfort of powerlessness. "There's nothing I can do, so I can't be held responsible." They often mistrust and reject sincere efforts by the principal. They have become suspicious. The best way to win them over is to be nonthreatening and to persevere. Just keep making yourself available in a friendly, nonauthoritative way and you will win them over—eventually.

6–4 DEVELOPING THE LEADERSHIP POTENTIAL OF YOUR STAFF

Effective principals are those who can challenge, stimulate, and free the people around them to perform at their highest level of competence. Only mutual respect and sharing between you and your teachers can create such a productive performance climate. The checklist on the next page will help you identify potential school leaders.

Try to bring each member of the staff into some leadership role on at least one occasion. Shared leadership involves pooling the skills and abilities of the entire group. This promotes a sense of group unity. Giving every member of your staff a sense of ownership will help your teachers enjoy coming to work each day.

6–5 IMPROVING TEACHER ATTENDANCE AND MORALE

Teachers' attitudes toward absenteeism have changed a great deal during the last fifteen years. Your veteran teachers probably never stayed out of school unless they were seriously ill. Many of the new teachers feel it is their duty to use up each year's allotment of sick days whether they are ill or not.

The level of morale is often reflected in teacher attendance. There are several steps you can take to improve teacher attendance. Following these steps will enable you to start the entire school on the way to a better attendance record:

DIMENSIONS OF LEADERSHIP BEHAVIOR

Circle whether your teachers do this always (A), sometimes (S), or never (N).

	A	S	N
1. *Listening*—Does the teacher draw others out? Can he hear and interpret communications from the sender's point of view?	A	S	N
2. *Expressing Ideas*—Does she come across clearly to both individuals and groups?	A	S	N
3. *Decision Making*—Does he involve others in the process? Does he consider the school objectives more important than making people happy?	A	S	N
4. *Relationships*—Does she harmonize and find compromise solutions in the group? Is she sensitive to the feelings of others?	A	S	N
5. *Task Orientation*—Can he prioritize, or does he work equally hard on important and unimportant tasks?	A	S	N
6. *Handling Conflict*—Can she use and work through conflict openly and honestly without a tendency to smooth or gloss over conflicts?	A	S	N
7. *Willingness to Change*—Is he willing to try new things, or does he defend his ideas against all others?	A	S	N
8. *Problem Solving*—Can she consider all pertinent information and not just her own ideas? Can she utilize the resources of others?	A	S	N
9. *Staff Development*—Does he encourage comments on his own mistakes or shortcomings? Can he take suggestions?	A	S	N
10. *Expressing Emotions*—Can she show empathy toward others? Does she appear open and honest in discussing feelings and situations?	A	S	N

Six Proven Ways to Improve Teacher Attendance

1. *Never neglect an absence.* Talk to staff members every time they are absent. Find out why they didn't come to school. You needn't be harsh or abrasive—just interested. You can tell them that you're sorry about the difficulty that prevented their coming to school. Then you can put their pride and sense of responsibility on the line by showing how the class was upset and other teachers had to work harder to cover their class or take some of their pupils.

2. *Show the cost.* You know that absences cost money. Money is something everyone can understand. Use it to show an absentee just how much staying out means to the children, to fellow teachers, and to the whole school. It's easy to understand that substitute teachers cost everyone something. Show how much could be purchased in the way of teacher materials for each absence. This is frequently the best way to convince a teacher that he or she should want to be on the job every day.

3. *Keep your own records.* A simple card file will show you which teachers take Mondays and Fridays off. By keeping the file up to date, you will be able to spot trouble coming. Talk to teachers about frequent weekend absences. Do the same for teachers who extend winter and spring holidays.

4. *Find out the truth.* Remember, as an administrator you are entitled to the truth about an absence. Don't think that you'll seem nosey by digging for the real reason. By doing this, you'll show that you're not easy to fool and that you consider excessive absenteeism to be a serious offense. Do the same for lateness.

5. *Put it in writing.* If you haven't been able to convince a teacher by talking to him or her about the seriousness of poor attendance, issue a warning. This shows that the administrator considers absenteeism to be a serious matter. It frequently shocks a chronic offender into a better attitude.

6. *Provide an example.* Make certain that your own attendance pattern is exemplary. Avoid staying out on a Monday or a Friday. If you are out for a principal's meeting or mandated conference, be sure to post an agenda or find other ways to let the teachers know why you are out.

Occasionally you have to look for the less obvious reasons why a perfectly healthy teacher chooses to stay out. Often you can see the reasons in the attitudes of teachers of the same grade level. If you have one or two who just don't like their colleagues and don't care how their absence affects the group, you have a potential attendance problem. Whenever there are frequent disagreements among teachers, or between you and the staff, you will have absences for the following two reasons: First, teachers sometimes react emotionally to unpleasant incidents and call in sick the next day. Emotions can make people genuinely sick. This can be alleviated if you take care of such matters before the teacher leaves for the day. Give the teacher a chance to ventilate his or her feelings before leaving the building.

Second, a teacher may feel that he or she can get revenge and punish you by staying out of school. The idea is that you'll appreciate the teacher more when you see how tough it is to struggle along without him or her. A good strategy here is to place your very best substitute in this teacher's room. In addition, find something positive to praise in this classroom when the teacher is out. Leave some evidence of the class's progress that the teacher will find when he or she returns to school.

There is probably no single cure for this type of absenteeism. Occasionally you can correct the situation by moving the teacher to another grade the following year. To be successful in raising the teacher's morale, this move would have to be mutually agreed on.

By looking at your school calendar, you can anticipate certain doldrums in the level of your staff's enthusiasm. The weeks before the spring break are frequently when most teachers complain. You can anticipate these low times in staff morale and try not to assign more onerous tasks at such a time. You may find it advisable to announce less pleasant tasks (due the following week) on a Friday. No matter what the assignment, few teachers lose their euphoria on a Friday. Or you might want to take advantage of the quiet, almost tranquil air that exists in most schools on a Monday morning.

6–6 FOUR PROVEN WAYS TO MOTIVATE TEACHERS

The principal's role is constantly changing. In recent years it has been more difficult to motivate teachers to take or accept a course of action merely because the principal would like it to happen. Yet every day, principals all over the country are motivating teachers to do what they ask. Here are some successful strategies that have worked for others, over and over again:

1. *Point out the logic of your request.* Teachers are reasonable people— otherwise they couldn't survive in the classroom! Instead of presenting a mandate or a request from a central office, *explain* the reasoning for the request. Explain both the long- and short-range effects of the action. Show teachers how you arrived at your decision. Elicit their support in carrying out the policy change. *Ask* them how this can be done. Let the action component come from them. Make teachers feel

that they are part of the solution, and they will be more likely to carry out the task.

2. *Encourage parent support of your teachers.* Too many teachers feel that pupils' parents do not appreciate their struggles in the classroom. Many teachers feel that they are taken for granted. Some teachers believe that the only time a parent writes a note or makes a visit is to complain. The wise principal helps shape parent attitudes toward the teaching staff in a positive way. Tell teachers every time a parent makes a positive comment about their child's progress or their child's teacher. Be effusive in reporting this. Don't make it sound as if you were surprised that the parent found something commendable to comment on. When talking to groups of parents, always praise the professionalism of your staff. Give parents the definite message that you like your staff. This will rub off on teachers' attitudes. Ask parents who tell you something nice about a teacher to take a moment to jot a note to the teacher and share the favorable comment. Photocopy letters and notes sent to you that are complimentary, and place them in the personnel files after showing them to the teacher. It doesn't hurt to help shape teacher attitudes toward parents, either.

3. *Celebrate Teacher Recognition Day.* Every school calendar has a day or week set aside to recognize or appreciate teachers. Make a big deal of it at your school. Encourage the parent association to sponsor a luncheon. If this is not feasible, have them serve coffee and cake in the morning as teachers clock in. One principal we know sends each teacher a long-stemmed artificial rose with a card of thanks. These are available for less than fifty cents in many Valentine's Day catalogs. In another school the principal decorates the teachers' lounge with helium balloons commemorating the great job the teachers have done. Let the teachers "find out" that you have orchestrated these festivities.

4. *Present teachers with free materials.* Everyone loves to receive a gift of some kind. Teachers always appreciate something they can use in the classroom. Resourceful principals are adept at getting sample materials that their teachers can use and enjoy. Don't let a book salesperson leave your office without getting some samples that some of your teachers can use. At conventions and meetings, fill a shopping bag with some "goodies" that some of your teachers can put to use. Be alert to mailings that cross your desk that offer free or low-cost teaching aids. Try to play Santa at least once every month and bring your teachers a learning aid or two. It's not uncommon to find a retiring teacher who, when emptying his or her classroom for the last time, comes upon the Book of Presidents or ruler that the principal gave him or her twenty years earlier, and remembers that day fondly. These little tokens are always appreciated. They also help to bond the teacher and principal as a team that works together.

6–7 SUPPORTING TEACHERS WITH DIFFICULT CLASSES

The teachers who need the most support frequently get the least attention in a school. It's natural for you to want to visit the gifted or bright class. It's rare that you want to visit the teacher with the worst-behaved kids. A frequent rationale is, "She has such a difficult class, I wouldn't want to get in her way or interrupt what she is doing." Yet it is the teacher with the difficult class who most needs the support. While it is important to minimize the number of interruptions and disruptions for such teachers, they could use a visit from another adult.

Why not assign your student teachers to these classes? They will learn a great deal that will help them when they become regular teachers. The pupils in these classes will gain much from the additional individualized help. The classroom teacher will be grateful for the extra pair of hands. The same is true if you have school aides without a regular assignment. Why not utilize them to help out in the more difficult classrooms? (For a small percentage of student teachers, this experience may test their true feelings about teaching as a career.)

Listening is an important skill you can use to provide these teachers with some extra support. Giving them a chance to ventilate their feelings about individual pupils away from the class is very therapeutic. Good listening requires three behaviors:

- Face the teacher. Don't look over the teacher's head or around the room.
- Maintain eye contact with the teacher throughout the conversation.
- Don't interrupt or correct the teacher while he or she is talking.

These three behaviors will encourage genuine communication. Never make corrections or engage in confrontations in front of pupils.

In addition, try to agree with at least some of the teacher's points, and emphasize your agreement. Restate the teacher's position accurately in the course of discussion. Avoid flat statements of disagreement, and concentrate instead on probing questions. Most of all, back up your viewpoint with reason and facts, not with emotion.

Be aware that the frustrations of working with hyperactive children sometimes bring out the worst in both the principal and the teacher. As the head of the school, you must review the situation and see the children through the eyes of the teacher, who faces them every day, all day.

6–8 DEALING WITH THE TEACHERS' UNION

Principals in large school systems have to work with a variety of unions: teachers', custodians', lunch room workers', bus drivers', security guards,' etc. The one union that virtually all principals are concerned with is the teachers' union. This may be a chapter of a larger national or state union or association. In recent years these unions have grown both in size and in power. In many parts of the country they are involved in improving education in general and so have won the support of parent groups and political leaders.

Because of their independent nature, teachers' unions cannot be controlled by the administration and certainly won't go away. It is in your best interest to learn to live with them. Successful school administrators have learned to work with the chapter chairperson in achieving a better school.

Your district superintendent may be concerned about the union's ultimate weapon: a strike. In your school, you will be concerned about union leadership filing violations of the contract. These formal complaints are sometimes referred to as grievances. When the union files a grievance, it is processed through a series of levels until it comes before an arbitrator. This may vary somewhat according to the contract and/or state law.

Principals are often confused about the function of the arbitrator. Arbitrators are not seeking truth, justice, and the American way. They are searching for what the parties meant when they signed a contract. An arbitrator is searching for a solution that will satisfy both parties. Sometimes it is impossible.

Besides trying to persuade the arbitrator, you should be concerned with two things: the efficient running of the school and the morale of the staff. There is no advantage in winning grievances and losing the support of your staff. As long as you are aware of this and don't take every complaint personally, you will avoid unnecessary skirmishing.

If things are generally quiet in your school and you have not angered the teachers, the union leadership will go along without a cause until you give them one. The "enemy" of school principals is not the union itself. When teachers make grievances, it's because of administration miscalculations that set off a chain reaction of union countermeasures. Unions thrive on adversity. They can't rally too much support or justify their grievance machinery if there is total harmony.

Be aware of another pitfall: When union leadership is not strong, you may be tempted to ignore it. Do so at your own risk. If you ignore or discredit the union leadership, it will be replaced. Then you will be facing a stronger, not a weaker, adversary. So if you've got a pliable and positive union, it's to your benefit to let the union leadership win a round or two now and then so they can keep face with their own rank and file. Knock out the leadership and the next group may be real guerilla warriors.

Remember, winning does not mean being all powerful and getting your way all the time. If you don't grasp this basic fact, you will make every teacher a foe. Unions are here to stay. Stop worrying about them and learn to work with them. Neither should you look for a love affair. Seek out a marriage of convenience and mutual trust.

Another caveat: Union loyalty is always issue specific and has nothing to do with you. You are not the target unless you choose to be. Whenever possible, seek out education issues that you and your teachers' union leadership can work together on. These can involve bond issues, small class size, more textbook and supply money, increased school security, and so on.

6–9 PROMOTING TEACHER CREATIVITY

Traditionally, principals use one of two approaches to promote creativity among teachers. The first and more common is the principal's direct involvement with a committee of teachers who are meeting to solve some specific problem or develop a new approach. Each person has an itemized agenda for this brainstorming session. The principal sees his or her role as a timekeeper who makes sure that the group remains on task. The principal is also concerned about the practicality of the suggestions.

In an increasing number of schools, the principal uses a hands-off technique for encouraging teachers to be creative. The principal starts the group off by stating the objective of the session, outlines the parameters to be observed, and then leaves the meeting. He or she checks in occasionally to answer questions and see if any help is needed.

In most schools, some combination of the hands-on and the hands-off techniques is best for encouraging teacher creativity. As you formulate the best approach for your school, consider these recommendations:

1. *Decide if you really want your teachers to be creative.* If you run a very structured, tightly organized school, creativity is less likely to be rewarded, so it may not flourish. You must determine how open you are to the changes that can flow from creative approaches. Studies of creativity suggest that the biggest single variable in whether a teacher will be creative is the teacher's perception of permission. Is it evident that creative behavior is welcomed, or do you want polite, predictable behavior that doesn't rock the boat?

2. *Identify the creative teachers.* Which teachers have demonstrated novel, original approaches to the curriculum? Use these more creative teachers as leavening to school committees.

3. *Channel teachers' creativity.* Creativity is only useful if it is directed. Focus on your schoolwide objectives without compromising creativity. Encourage unique approaches to standard situations, such as open classrooms, a studio in the school, partnerships with businesses, or nontraditional approaches to curriculum. Make sure the ideas can be implemented. Your role is to channel or guide the fresh approaches into practical applications.

4. *Avoid deterrents to creativity.* Don't build rigid systems that force teachers to conform. For example, get teachers' ideas on teaching reading. Must every class use the same basal reader? Ideas come from individuals, but implementation requires a team, so everyone must work together. Spend more time on dialogue. Everyone's ideas are OK, but work together to develop the best one. For example, encourage teachers of the same grade level to plan lessons together. Make your teachers feel that taking risks is acceptable. Make it less painful to fail—build safety nets for softer landings. For example, if teachers are trying a new approach to math, make sure pupils have basic number facts before they begin.

5. *Reward the creative teacher.* What motivates creative teachers? They often are not motivated by the things that typically motivate other creative people. Creative teachers aren't necessarily motivated by money or titles. They often do not want more responsibility or an administrative position. Teachers need positive recognition. This is especially true of creative teachers. Their self-esteem requires that their performance and ideas are recognized. As principal, you must provide that recognition. This becomes a balancing act because you don't want to hurt the feelings of the less creative teachers. They are likely to disparage the unorthodox ideas of their more creative colleagues.

   One strategy is to group teachers together on projects so the less talented, as well as the talented, achieve a sense of ownership of the final report or plan. This way, the less creative teachers are less likely to downplay the contributions of the more talented staff members and less tempted to sabotage them beforehand.

6. *Provide autonomy as well as clear limits.* Creative teachers need a degree of independence. You should not constantly interrupt them in the middle of a project to check on their progress. But they also need to know what the rules are. What are the objectives and how far will the principal let them go? Are there any dollar or time restraints? How much time is the principal willing to let teachers devote to this task? Will any time be provided, or must the teachers do all of this on their own time?

Your job as principal is similar to the job of an orchestra conductor. You must get everyone together to make the best sound (do the best job) while allowing individual members to do their own part as best they can. As the conductor, you know if the strings need a little more attention or if the woodwinds need extra help. This chapter discussed techniques for motivating your teachers to do their best work. Together, you can make beautiful music.

Chapter 7

Working Successfully With Parents

John W., principal of a K–5 school, is concerned about the attitude of many of his pupils' parents. They always seem to be griping about class placement, teachers, and even each other. Some parents feel that the school does little to involve them; that the administration does not care about parent opinions. Parents of at-risk pupils and parents who do not speak fluent English feel particularly alienated. John W. is a caring principal and would really like to reach out to the parents and get them involved. However, some of his earlier efforts fell on deaf ears.

■ IN RECENT YEARS, parents have become an increasingly important variable in the successful school equation. To omit them completely or to minimize their importance is to court failure.

You must maintain your leadership role in guiding the school while encouraging parent participation. This chapter provides you with suggestions and strategies for walking this tightrope with grace and security.

7–1 HOW WELL DO YOU INVOLVE PARENTS?

You have probably noticed that school programs and policies are only worthwhile if put into practice. The most successful parent program or open house can be negated by one seemingly insignificant oversight by a well-intentioned staff member. You may be guilty of some oversight or slight yourself. We have prepared this quiz to help you rate yourself in the area of parent relations.

Parent Relations Checklist

☐ **1.** What is your manner when greeting parents in the hallway? Does your demeanor say, "What are you doing here?" while your voice says, "Can I help you?"

☐ **2.** Does your building have helpful signs? Every building has signs telling visitors that they must report to the office, but are there signs telling them where the principal's office is? the nurse's? the guidance counselors'?

☐ **3.** How is the visitor greeted in the office? Is there a steel barrier of file cabinets? Has this been softened by pupil art work? Are there chairs for waiting?

☐ **4.** What do you do to welcome new parents when they register incoming pupils? Do you make an effort to greet them and tell them something about the school? Do you try to take them around the building or introduce them to their child's teacher?

☐ **5.** How do you report a child's successes? Do the child's parents have to settle for a computerized report card three times each year? Are your teachers encouraged to send home little congratulatory notes? A note from the principal may sound trite, but parents have been known to carry them around in their wallets for months.

☐ **6.** How do you report bad news to parents? Do you have a system of interim warnings or deficiency reports? Have you tried the telephone instead of the typewriter?

☐ **7.** What about the average student? Do you make an effort to remind the parents of these students that you know that their child is alive? Have you tried improvement cards or attendance banners?

☐ **8.** Is there a parent handbook to familiarize your parents with your school's philosophy? Is it genuinely helpful or just an amateur attempt at public relations? Were parents invited to participate in its preparations?

☐ **9.** Are parents involved in the day-to-day life of the school? Are they used as reading volunteers, lunch room aides, or advisory committee members?

☐ **10.** Do you circulate during parent-teacher conferences, or do you use this time for paperwork? Do parents see you each time they come into the building? Do you train your teachers to conduct positive parent-teacher conferences?

☐ **11.** What happens when a family moves away? Farewell questionnaires can be real eye-openers. Pay some attention to the parting comments of parents.

There are many ways to involve parents that are within your ability and that don't take more money, just more sensitivity.

7–2 TAKING THE FIRST STEP IN INVOLVING PARENTS

Most parents visit their child's early grades often but seldom get involved in the upper grades. This is a pity because their participation is equally or more important at the upper levels due to the serious challenges their children face. Sadly, some older pupils encourage nonparticipation.

In addition, teachers of grades 4 through 6 tend to be subject-area minded and do not always share the concern of the lower-grade teacher for each child's emotional development.

The following ideas for involving parents were developed by participants in a parent workshop in Toledo, Ohio. In each case, the principal initiated the program.

Six Ideas to Promote Parent Participation

1. Have school buses pick up parents and bring them to school for visits or special events. This may bring parents who have never been in the school before. Some parents have no car and can't take public transportation.

2. Invite parent volunteers to teach students in small groups, sharing any specialized knowledge the parents may have.

3. Hold mini-sessions to help parents understand curriculum areas. This is particularly important as students confront new subjects and teaching techniques. Some parents have never seen the lastest multimedia materials in use.

4. Arrange events in which parents and pupils can take part—an after-school art class, sports event, family living and sex education class, or typing practice.

5. Seek out parent volunteers for remedial tutoring, lunch room duty, field trip chaperoning, special education tutoring, making learning materials under the direction of a teacher, and helping out in the school office.

6. Invite parents to serve as judges for science fairs, spelling bees, art shows, and talent shows.

As professional educators, we assume that every parent knows of our availability. Because a few parents come into school, we frequently assume that every parent knows how to contact us. Parents do *not* automatically know how to contact the principal or guidance counselor. They do not know how to analyze their child's report card or how to find out his or her lastest reading score. They don't know whether you would welcome phone calls from them. And if they are new to your school, they don't know the many kinds of activities in which you welcome their involvement. Early in the school year, send home a letter urging parents to do the following:

- Call the school to check out facts when they hear a rumor either from their child or from a neighbor.
- Bring any special talent or skill they may have to their child's classroom.
- Call you when a problem arises or when a crisis occurs at home.
- Arrange a meeting with the guidance counselor to go over their child's report card or find out his or her latest achievement test scores.
- Let you know when their child is enthusiastic about a class project or seems to be having unusual difficulty with one.

- Offer their services as a volunteer.
- Join a parent-teacher study committee devoted to school security, concert planning, or community action.

Be certain to include the school phone number and also the phone numbers of resource people at the district office. Some schools use printed cards listing vital community services, the fire department, school, lunch room, guidance office, police department, ambulance service, and local hospital.

Have you thought about positive ways of building a bridge between your office and the homes of your pupils? Why not send home "Happy Grams"? These are pads of yellow paper approximately 5½ by 8½ inches with the words "Happy Gram" lettered across the top, accompanied by a smiling face. Appropriate messages might include "I was caught being good," "Student of the Week," or "Improvement Award."

Try getting parents to help you write a parent handbook. Such a brochure can give parents all kinds of important information on topics such as

- Before- and after-school programs
- Lunch procedures and money collections

- Time schedules
- Homework policy
- Registration of new pupils
- Calendar for the year
- Emergency procedures and drills
- Expected behavior in school
- Field trips
- Vacation day camp.

7–3 ASKING PARENTS TO GRADE YOUR SCHOOL

January is a good time to get some feedback from parents on how they view your school and its program. Since parents are accustomed to getting report cards that measure pupil progress, it is a good idea to encourage their participation by asking them to measure the school's progress toward its goals. The Parents' School Report Card on the next page illustrates this.

7–4 MAKING THE MOST OF PARENT-TEACHER CONFERENCES

Many school districts are using parent-teacher conferences to replace written report cards. Other schools are scheduling additional conferences in the afternoon as well as at night. Yet unless you and your teachers use these opportunities wisely, parents may be alienated by them. This section is a guide to more successful parent-teacher conferences.

Some parents come to school wearing many different expressions and disguises. The better you understand their attitudes and see through their protective ploys, the easier it will be to cope with them. Here are some of the games parents play:

1. *It's not my job!* Some parents place the blame for Johnny's failure on a working mother or absent father or last year's teacher. They come across as harried, hard-working single parents who are barely surviving the rat race. They imply that it is the teacher's job to motivate and encourage Johnny. The experienced teacher or principal listens quietly to the excuses and then firmly suggests one or two things the parent can do right now to bring about a desired result.

2. *The surprised innocent.* Parents may be tired of hearing year after year that their child has trouble making friends. After a while, they begin to show disbelief and will even assume a puzzled look and express surprise as they exclaim, "Jane has always been such a popular child!" The alert principal replies, "What can we do to help her make friends in this class?"

PARENTS' SCHOOL REPORT CARD

Parents: Please rate our school in the categories below by checking off the appropriate box on the right.

	EXCEL-LENT	GOOD	AVERAGE	UNSATIS-FACTORY	NO OPINION
CURRICULUM & INSTRUCTION					
Course of study in relation to your child's needs					
Learning materials in relation to your child's needs					
Teaching staff in meeting your child's needs					
Methods in meeting your child's needs					
The manner in which classes are organized					
Pupil-teacher ratio					
PROGRESS REPORTS					
Pupil report card					
Parent-teacher conferences					
Interpretation of standardized test scores					
GUIDANCE & COUNSELING					
Individual guidance					
Group guidance					
Support groups					
DISCIPLINE					
Classroom rules, routines, and management					
Playground rules, routines, and management					
Punishment meted out					
COMMUNICATION					
Exchange of information between school and home					
Newsletter					
ADMINISTRATION					
What are your feelings about the operation of the school?					
Nature of contact with administrators					
FACILITIES					
Appearance of building					
Maintenance of building and grounds					
Cleanliness of building					

Parents' School Report Card, Continued

Parents: Please rate our school in the categories below by checking off the appropriate box on the right.

	EXCEL-LENT	GOOD	AVERAGE	UNSATIS-FACTORY	NO OPINION
CURRICULUM & INSTRUCTION					
FOOD SERVICES					
Hot lunch					
Milk and beverage service					
BUS SERVICE					
Promptness					
Courtesy of drivers					
Safety compliance					

PARENTS' REPORT CARD, COMMENTS SECTION

Please check one response under each question.

What do you appreciate most about our school?

☐ The small class size and student-teacher ratio
☐ The course of study and special programs
☐ The care and concern shown by teachers, principal, and staff
☐ Good communication between home and school
☐ School and classroom newsletters
☐ Assemblies
☐ No opinion
☐ Other (please specify) _____

What do you believe is the most pressing problem facing our school?

☐ Overcrowding and lack of space
☐ Discipline
☐ Busing and behavior on the bus
☐ Lack of communication between school and home
☐ No opinion
☐ Other (please specify) _____

Are there areas of the school program that should receive less emphasis?

☐ Too much competition and too many competitive programs
☐ Too many contests and rewards
☐ The schoolwide discipline program
☐ Marks and grades
☐ None, it's great as it is
☐ No opinion
☐ Other (please specify) _____

Additional suggestions for improving our school:

_____

_____

_____

_____

_____
Your name (optional)

3. *The reluctant dragon.* Some parents arrive with a built-up head of steam. They are blaming everyone for their child's shortcomings. They are angry and defensive. Don't fall into this pattern. Allow parents to ventilate their feelings. When they finally simmer down, the air is usually cleared for a reasonable discussion of criticisms—which may be valid.

4. *The sweeper under the rug.* When a family is facing unemployment or a divorce, the parents often try to save face and cover up guilt feelings with statements like, "We didn't know Mary was doing poorly." Responding with, "Is there anything different in Mary's home life?" will open the floodgates, and the parent will reveal the real problem.

5. *The overly critical parent.* Some parents are incredibly critical of their child. They will eagerly tell you how terrible their child is (frequently comparing him or her to a sibling or a neighbor's child). In such cases, you begin to see why the youngster is so angry and is not performing.

At the same time, you can't play psychiatrist to every troubled family. To help your teachers avoid the many traps and potholes along the road of parent-teacher conferences, share the following guidelines with them.

Tips for Parent-Teacher Conferences

- Don't let your desk form a barricade between you and the parent. Encourage the parent to join you at a table or in two pupil chairs in a corner of your room.

- Don't confuse parents with too many suggestions at one time. Concentrate on one or two things they can do to help their child at home. Emphasize big things.

- Don't display disapproval. Any sign that you disapprove of what the parent is saying or doing may make the parent stop talking and listening.

- Don't pry or ask questions if the parent appears reluctant to discuss personal matters. As one parent told us, "I don't mind telling almost anything, but I don't like to be asked."

- Don't assume that parents want your advice. Many come to school just because they think it's their duty. If you give the impression that they need help, they will see it as disapproval and criticism.

- Don't generalize or sound vague. It helps no one if you make statements like, "Mary is having trouble with math. She needs help." What kind of difficulty is she having? Is it fractions? Does she make careless mistakes? Does she have trouble understanding the concepts? How can the parent help? Should the child get tutoring? Always try to be concrete in your suggestions and specific about the areas of weakness.

- Don't forget to leave the lines of communication open. Allow an opening for a future conference either with you or the guidance counselor. The next conference may be on the telephone or in person. Sum up and then say something like, "I think we made a good start today. We do need more time to talk again. Please call me in two weeks and we will see what kind of progress Jean has made."

There are several ways in which you can help parents prepare for the parent-teacher conference. For instance, many school systems on Long Island, New York, supply the parent with guidelines a few days before the actual conference. Most parents not only appreciate these tips but are pleased that the school cares enough to help them get the most out of the interview. These suggestions can be sent home in the form of a mimeographed notice, or they can appear in the parent newsletter

---

PARENT GUIDELINES FOR PARENT-TEACHER CONFERENCES

1. Ask your child if there is anything he or she would like you to discuss with the teacher.

2. Decide in advance the questions you want to ask the teacher. It's a good idea to write them down.

3. Take notes during the conference. Review them when you get home. Start right away on the action steps that you and the teacher have agreed on.

4. Be ready to tell the teacher a little bit about your child's home life. The school wants to know about your child's family life, hobbies, interests, habits, and feelings. Knowing these things will help the teacher understand your child's interests and needs.

5. If you are concerned about a rumor you've heard or something your child has told you about the class, teacher, lunch room, or school, ask about it at the conference. Ask the *teacher* what happened rather than another child or parent.

6. Be reasonable in what you expect the teacher to do and the amount of special attention he or she can give your child. Ask how you can help meet some of the child's needs at home.

7. This need not be your only contact with your child's teacher. You can call the teacher to set up an appointment at a time convenient for both of you. Our school values the interest and opinions of parents.

Above all, encourage your teachers to give the parents some basic information about their child's reading and math skills. We sometimes get caught up in other matters, and the parent leaves the interview without knowing how the child is doing in the basic skill areas.

7–5 INTRODUCING A NEW GRADING SYSTEM

Part of your image as an administrator is the method and success of your pupil evaluation procedures. Many schools have abandoned the traditional report card and are exploring alternative methods to number and letter grading, in the hope that these new ways will contribute to the child's learning and provide more information to parents.

If your school is considering alternative approaches or you want to take a long, hard look at your present system for reporting pupil progress to parents, explore the following tips:

- Notify parents frequently about what their child is doing that benefits his or her personal growth and academic standing. Write in the pupil's notebook and informal letters.
- Consider carefully what is to be evaluated. What we try to measure sometimes defies rating. Explain your criteria for grading (tests, home-work, class participation, etc.).
- Help youngsters learn to evaluate their own work. Children learn many skills by comparing themselves to their peers or examining their own projects.
- Exposure to a wide range of learning materials, approaches, and set-tings helps children to behave more openly, so personal and academic growth are easier to gauge.
- Using large index cards, develop a log of each student's progress. File the cards alphabetically. Record personal strengths, weaknesses, books read, new vocabulary words, writing samples, math concepts, grades, etc.
- Maintain student evaluation checklists—skills continuum sheets which provide detailed reports of a student's regular educational progress (e.g., in word recognition and reading comprehension skills).
- The most effective form of evaluation is direct observation over a long period of time. Enthusiasm, curiosity, excitement, and creativity may be nearly impossible to measure yet are among the best reflections of learning.
- The Inglewood, California, school district gives parents a choice of report cards. They may have the district's traditional report with **A,**

B, C, D rating. Or they may take part in a narrative evaluation and reporting system developed for that particular school. That system includes student self-evaluation, teacher comments, and a sheet on which parents are asked questions such as, "What is your main concern?" "How is the description different from your child's behavior at home?" If they wish, parents may indicate a convenient time and date for a conference. In one year, 75 percent of the parents chose this informal, narrative system over the conventional report card.

Follow these four steps if you want to make a new system work for you:

1. Begin with in-service faculty training.
2. Explain the system carefully to the community at large.
3. Use clear and precise language to explain a pupil's progress at parent-teacher conferences.
4. Give parents a chance to react to their child's report by asking questions.

Once a new system gets under way, most parents readily accept the more individual and personal touches it brings to their child's progress report.

7–6 MAKING THE MOST OF OPEN HOUSE

Traditionally, American Education Week in November brings parents into the school to see what purports to be a typical school day. For most parents, this is the only time they come to their child's school. For many parents this suffices, but for other parents who are tired of the same kinds of open house each year, there have been some noteworthy innovations.

For example, in addition to parents coming to see what their children do in school, the parents in one Baltimore suburb showed the students what they do for a living. The school staff felt that this would provide an insight into a variety of career choices and give parents a chance to become involved in their children's education. Some of the career glimpses included a meteorologist, hairdresser, electrician, printer, and court officer.

Another Maryland school held a Pioneer Day, which enabled parents to watch their children make bread and apple butter and display handcrafts of colonial times. This was especially appropriate since it happened near Thanksgiving. The children took their parents on a tour of the school's reading, science, social studies, and math labs. The math lab was especially interesting, showing parents the manipulative materials pupils can touch and experiment with to learn mathematical concepts.

A principal in San Bernardino, California, came up with a novel way to bring working parents into school and get them involved in the reading program. He invites parents for an evening "to hear your child's voice on tape" or "to come and see the pictures we took on our field trip." Once the parents are there, teachers explain the reading program and suggest ways parents can help their children at home.

Another way to strengthen the partnership of parents and school administrators is to engage in a common project that will aid the children. The California School Boards Association launched a statewide campaign to encourage schools and parents to protest TV and screen violence, targeting local TV stations and the major networks, sponsors, advertising agencies, the Federal Communications Commission, the National Association of Broadcasters, and motion picture companies. According to the Association's literature, "The collective voice of 20 million people in California can make an outcry that is effective." Working together on a common goal that is not specifically school centered, the parents and administrators can feel more comfortable with each other.

Most parents are only too happy to leave the job of running the school to the principal. It is only when they are turned off by a repressive or uncaring teacher or principal that they try to take control. The successful school leader of today knows how to capitalize on parent interest and turns parent involvement into a positive force in the school.

7–7 REACHING BILINGUAL STUDENTS' PARENTS

There is a great deal of emphasis today on providing bilingual education to pupils for whom English is not their native language. Such education calls for more than just a Spanish-English report card or some filmstrips with the captions in French.

Parent involvement needs to be stronger in the bilingual education movement than in many other areas of education. Here are some techniques schools are using to pull those parents into the schools and to build bridges of understanding:

- Plan special celebrations. El Dia de la Raza, the birthday of Spanish culture in the New World, is popular in many districts. Parents can prepare ethnic foods like flan, moros, or pan cubano.
- Have parent volunteers serve as interpreters. This is especially helpful if you have many admissions and discharges in a changing neighborhood and no staff member who is fluent.
- Parents can serve as tutors or help with special activities such as field trips, acting as translator.

- Have parents contact other parents who do not usually come to school or attend meetings. Many shy or troubled parents are more likely to respond to a parent of their same ethnic group than they are to a letter or a home visit by a teacher.
- Hold an ethnic read-in. Gather reading materials of minority groups not ordinarily found in the school library: *Ebony, Jet, American Indian Historian*, Spanish-language newspapers (or Japanese, Vietnamese, Arabic, etc.).
- Sponsor an international crafts fair, featuring the work of Asian Americans, Hispanics, Appalachian whites, African-Americans, etc. Use as your theme the statement, "Each has something to offer." The fair can involve community groups as well as parents.
- Use parents as after-school teachers. In Placentia, California, parents conduct after-school classes once or twice a week at each school. They teach English to Spanish-speaking students and give Spanish lessons to English-speaking students and teachers. They also try to exchange ideas between parents and teachers.

7–8 HELPING PARENTS OF AT-RISK PUPILS

Schools also can promote a positive, ongoing relationship with parents of pupils who are at risk. In some cases, counseling parents is more successful in reducing classroom behavior problems than direct counseling with the student.

Parents in Jacksonville, Florida, have been trained to work at home with other parents and their children (in grades 5 through 7) who are having problems. With help from these peer parents, the parents and student identify both behavioral or academic problems. Insights gained from working with other parents are also shared. Parents are urged to model respectful behavior toward school personnel and are asked to help pupils come to school prepared to learn. Peer parents also encourage parents to maintain good communication with the school, sometimes even setting up meetings and providing transportation for them.

Other methods of home-based reinforcement appear effective in motivating children to behave acceptably in school. Home-based reinforcement has been used successfully with children in special classes and with mainstream classrooms for a wide variety of behavioral and academic problems. Parents can administer various rewards—such as snacks, earned privileges, and verbal praise—when informed of their children's performance by daily or weekly notes from school. Individual or group instruction, and even letters, have been used to instruct parents in home-based reinforcement, and the time required of parents and teachers appears to be minimal.

Frequent feedback helps both parents and children monitor the child's performance, and it gives parents information they can use to reward performance that meets agreed-on standards of progress.

Parent education helps parents to improve communication with their children and to establish fair but firm standards of discipline. Parents who attend parent education meetings tend to experience a sense of relief and group support when they find others with at-risk children. This makes your efforts seem worthwhile.

Parents also get a great deal of support from reading fictional accounts of how other children or families have overcome their difficulties. The following five books are appropriate for upper grade pupils, their parents, or both. When both parent and child read the book, a real dialogue can take place regarding the problem and its solution.

Selected Titles for Parents of At-Risk Pupils

- Byars, Betsy. *Cracker Jackson* (New York: Viking, 1985). Cracker's babysitter seems to be in some kind of trouble. Cracker is sure his babysitter's husband is beating her. There are bruises that the babysitter can't hide.
- Greene, Constance. *The Unmaking of Rabbit* (New York: Viking, 1972). Paul's father left when Paul was two, and his mother brings him to live with his grandmother because she can't cope with him anymore.
- Greenwald, Sheila. *Will the Real Gertrude Hollings Please Stand Up?* (Boston: Little, Brown and Company, 1983). Gertrude is labeled "learning disabled." Her cousin Albert is a "superachiever." When Gertrude finds out she is going to spend three weeks with her superorganized aunt while her parents are away, she is very unhappy.
- McGraw, Eloise. *Hideaway* (New York: Atheneum, 1983). Jerry is not happy that his mother has remarried and that he will be living with the children of his new stepfather.
- Roberts, Willo. *Don't Hurt Laurie* (New York: Atheneum, 1977). Laurie has learned to stay away from her mother if she has a headache, because at those times she often hurts Laurie by hitting her with anything handy . . . once with a butcher knife.

7–9 ENCOURAGING OUTREACH PROGRAMS FOR YOUR PTA

Many principals complain that their PTA executive board members spend most of their time talking about individual teachers and tend to busy themselves with inconsequential activities. The parents have time, energy, and concern but don't seem to have any good ideas to channel their efforts. You must give them direction. The following list of ideas, from PTAs around the country, will help you.

PTA Outreach Programs

- In Anaheim, California, the PTA designates an International Week and plans parades, dinners, and programs to share information about different cultures and customs.
- In Lincolnwood, Illinois, the PTA sends a member to welcome new families, deliver information about the school and the PTA, and encourage parents to participate in their school.
- In Raleigh, North Carolina, parents and teachers as well as community members work with pupils at risk. Volunteers tutor the children once a week and make at least one other weekly contact with them.
- The District of Columbia has "student aid rooms" where needy pupils can get clothing. The PTAs hold "bundle days" to collect secondhand clothing that is still serviceable.
- A Portland, Oregon, PTA sponsored a family movie and charged admission of one can of food per person attending. This food was later distributed to needy and homeless families.

With so many worthwhile projects waiting to be launched, you can mobilize your PTA to undertake many positive endeavors.

Chapter 8

Reaching Out to Your Community

Ms. D. sees parents all day long. To her they are a necessary but unwelcome part of her job. She really doesn't enjoy interacting with them. The thought of getting involved with community members who are not parents is alien to her.

In every school district there is a neighborhood or community that offers much to enrich the school. Yet this resource is frequently overlooked.

How can Ms. D. reach out to the community without fear? This chapter offers many suggestions.

■ SAVVY PRINCIPALS REALIZE that their schools do not exist in a vacuum but rather are surrounded by communities. They must reach out to the communities and bring citizens into the school life through a variety of programs, such as reading volunteers and school events. This adds vitality to the school program and lifts the image of the school in its home community. Principals must also take the initiative and get out into the community as a speaker or active participant in its organizational life.

This chapter discusses how to get your school to become an integral member of the larger community.

8–1 BUILDING BRIDGES TO THE COMMUNITY

An excellent way to reach out to the community is to make yourself available as a speaker for civic groups, service clubs, and other organizations. Your school's image will be enhanced, as will the community's perception of you as the school's leader.

How to Make Yourself Available

1. Send press releases of special school programs to the media, including your school and home phone number.
2. Mail press releases to selected target audiences as well (e.g., International Reading Association, Federated Mothers' Clubs, Lions Club, local chamber of commerce, and local AARP chapter).
3. Look through local newspaper for announcements of newly elected officers of various community groups. Write them a note of congratulations and offer to speak to their group on a topic you think is appropriate and of interest to them (e.g., after-school programs, rezoning of the school, or new science curriculum).
4. If your community has a printed directory of speakers, ask to be included.
5. Mention your availability to speak to groups on a variety of topics (e.g., bond issues, new curriculum, sex education, reading volunteers, etc.) when talking to your own staff and to the PTA. They can refer you to other organizations.

What Can You Talk About?

1. Take a walk through your school building. Try to look at the various activities through the eyes of a stranger. You will observe many activities that are unique to your school and would be of interest to the community. Take notes on what you see.

2. Listen to new parents when they come in to register their children. What are their concerns and priorities? How can you anticipate questions of preschool and nursery school parents? Prepare a presentation on this topic.

3. List ways in which parents can help their children with homework without frustration or tears. Add a little humor and some specifics, and you have a presentation that can be adapted for a variety of groups.

4. Gather examples of outstanding pupil work (poetry, art, essays) along with some new learning materials (social studies texts, software, manipulative math materials, etc.), and you're all set for a presentation on education in the 1990s.

5. Praise some of your school's extracurricular activities. Take color slides of some activities (e.g., your school band, glee club, science fair, March of Dimes Walkathon, or clothing drive). Assemble them in a logical sequence, and you can illustrate your remarks with a slide show.

Reaching out to the community by speaking at luncheon groups and at evening meetings is an excellent public relations tool. But many principals have poorly honed speaking skills, and others, fearing embarrassment, avoid speeches altogether.

You probably have good ideas and positive programs you want to share with the community. Many principals are comfortable speaking to their staff but are in awe of outside groups and freeze up when talking to "civilians." Ordinarily fluent speakers make blunders when addressing the Lions Club, Chamber of Commerce, Block Association, or other community group.

Here are some of the worst mistakes you can make when speaking to community organizations, along with ways to prevent or overcome such problems.

Public Speaking Mistakes

1. *Being gripped by fear.* A little fear is natural. To avoid excessive fear, don't see the audience as bankers and corporate leaders but rather as a group of people anxious to support your school programs. Try to

release your fear as energy, projecting your voice more and making appropriate gestures.

2. *Ignoring your appearance.* Much of your effectiveness depends on how you look—even before you open your mouth. Good posture makes you look and feel more confident. Do *not* underdress. Your audience expects the principal to look the role (as they remember it). Dress like a business leader if you are addressing a business group.

3. *Looking over the heads of your audience.* You must make eye contact with your audience. Look one person in the eye and hold that look for a count of three. Then find someone else in a different part of the room, and do the same. This makes people more involved in what you're saying. It's also more relaxing for you because you feel like you're talking to individuals instead of a whole group.

4. *Walking in cold.* You may feel confidence about your knowledge of your school and its programs. You may feel that you can talk at a moment's notice to your staff or the PTA. But if you are invited to make a presentation to an outside group, you must prepare. Find out what your audience wants to know, and then provide that information. Be sure to summarize. When you are finished, your audience should know what you talked about.

5. *Sounding like you are in school.* Too often, principals speak to business or community groups as if they were talking to pupils in the auditorium. In school, the usual pace is slow and the presentation is simple for children's unsophisticated listening skills. When talking to a community group, remember to modulate your voice. Use inflection for a livelier sound, and pace yourself so you don't talk too slowly. Deep breathing from the diaphragm will help you project your voice without sounding as if you're scolding a class.

Compile a list of questions that you can use in preparation for your presentation. You will want to know the following:

1. Who will be in the audience? What are their expectations?
2. Who will introduce you? What would you like her or him to say?
3. What kind of aids will you need (lectern, screen, outlets)?
4. Will the audience be eating while you speak? Will anyone precede or follow you? What are their topics?
5. Do any audience members have children in your school? How much do they already know about the school?

With practice and experience, you can improve your skills in addressing community members.

Get in the habit of keeping a memo book for the purpose of improving your skills in community outreach. Small, spiral assignment notebooks work well. Every time you hear or read about a community organization that has some interest in education, youth activities, or your school neighborhood, jot down its name and the name of a contact person. Make it a point to invite these people to some of your school events.

Build a list of names and addresses of people and organizations to add to your school mailing list. Be sure to send these people your monthly school calendar, PTA Bulletin, and student newspaper or magazine.

How to Include Other Staff Members

1. Invite other staff members to accompany you when you speak. This will broaden your message and raise the staff member's morale. For example, get a school bus to take you, the band teacher, and the band to play at a dedication of a civic project, nursing home, or shopping mall at holiday time.

2. Use the assembly period or some other large-group instruction time to free one or two teachers to work with you on a school fact sheet or profile. This can be circulated among local organizations who, in turn, can request a guest speaker.

3. Enlist a staff member to take color slides of school events. Use these in presentations to outside groups (or your own students).

4. Ask a bilingual teacher to translate invitations or actually speak to non-English-speaking groups about the school's program.

5. Ask the guidance counselor or school social worker to accompany you when their expertise will be helpful in getting your message across.

6. Reward teachers who give up some of their free time to talk to community groups. Arrange to give them compensatory time or a "free period" by giving a lesson to their class.

Now that you have some ideas for reaching out to the community, how can you bring community members into your school?

A FACT SHEET ABOUT YOUR SCHOOL SHOULD INCLUDE THE FOLLOWING:

1. School name, address, phone
2. Names of administrators, special personnel (guidance counselors, resource room teachers, speech therapist, nurse, paraprofessionals, security guards, etc.)
3. Names of teachers, with grade and room number
4. Hours of operation
5. After-school programs
6. Range of reading and math scores
7. Special programs (gifted, talented, remedial)
8. Kinds of special education classes, if any
9. Percent of teachers with advanced degrees
10. Name of PTA president
11. Year school was built; dates of modernization
12. Parameters of school zone
13. Routes of buses
14. Percent of pupils receiving free lunch and/or breakfast
15. Ethnic make-up of pupil population (if appropriate).

8–2 BRINGING COMMUNITY MEMBERS INTO YOUR SCHOOL

Relations between school and community are a two-way street. In addition to reaching out to the community, it's a good idea to invite community members into your school. The benefits are twofold: Your pupils and teachers are enriched by the contributions of community members, and community members see firsthand how well your school is operating.

Here are some proven ways of encouraging the community to participate in your school life.

Some Community Participation Suggestions

- *Grandparents Day.* Hold a special assembly to which only your pupil's grandparents are invited. Entertain them with a musical program, class play, or talent show. They'll see firsthand the school's programs and act as spokespersons for your school among their peers.

- *Contests.* Invite retired experts from the neighborhood to act as impartial judges for school science fairs, spelling bees, art shows, poster contests, etc. They will share their expertise and provide the school with a fresh dimension of talent. Teachers can invite them for class demonstrations as well.

- *Crafts and skills.* Start a skill bank of community talent that the school can use. Prepare a Share-Your-Skill sheet and get parents and teachers to hand them out to neighborhood talent. Be gracious in your invitation, either in writing or by telephone. Always follow up with a thank you note.

- *School events.* Assemble a current list of community members you wish to invite to school functions, such as field day, graduation, Flag Day, etc. Keep these names, addresses, and phone numbers on a list that you update periodically. They will become your school's unpaid public relations firm. It's also a good way to reward volunteers for their time and interest by inviting them to school celebrations (Graduation, class parties).

- *Volunteers.* Encourage neighborhood people to serve as reading volunteers or homework helpers in your school. Pair them with some pupils who can benefit from the one-to-one relationship. Both the volunteer and the pupil will benefit from the experience.

An excellent way of getting volunteers into your school is to make available a Share-Your-Skill application. After you have contacted potential school volunteers either in person or on the telephone, give them a one-page application to fill out. You will be amazed at the number of people who are waiting to be asked to share an interest or talent.

The application provided here is a sample. You may want to add or subtract a few of the items to suit your situation.

You will activate some of the applications right away. You may hold onto a few of them until the right time to implement the program. For example, a neighborhood resident offers to give flute lessons. You may not have any flutes at this time, but you do anticipate getting some in two months. Let him know you appreciate his interest and that you will get back to him when the flutes you ordered arrive.

One of the most popular activities is a reading volunteer, discussed in the next section.

SHARE-YOUR-SKILL APPLICATION

We welcome members of our community who have a skill to share with our pupils. Please fill out this form and return it to the school office, either in person or by mail.

Name _____   Address _____

_____   Phone _____

1. Please check off any skill(s) you would like to share with our pupils. The following items are only suggestions; feel free to add others.

   ☐ Crafts   ☐ Computers

   ☐ Foreign language/culture   ☐ Songs/singing

   ☐ Storytelling   ☐ Playing a musical instrument

   ☐ Homework helper   ☐ Reading volunteer

   ☐ Library   ☐ Sports

   ☐ Sewing   ☐ Other: _____

   ☐ Gardening   _____

2 Can you be more specific about the skill(s) you checked? _____

   _____

   _____

   _____

3. Have you any experience teaching this skill? _____

4. Will you need any materials? (Please list them.) _____

   _____

5. Please list the days and times you can come to school: _____

   _____

   _____

6. Do you prefer working with pupils or teachers? _____

8-3 CHANNELING THE ENERGIES OF READING VOLUNTEERS

Early retirement and a concern for helping others has motivated many mature adults to turn their attention to the public schools as a place to volunteer their services.

One of the most popular avenues of service is a Reading Volunteer Program. In this program, the main job is reading, one-to-one, with pupils in need of individual help. In most districts the only requirement is a high school diploma and a medical exam that includes TB screening. In some areas the central office provides some group training. It is usually up to the individual school to provide on-site training and appropriate materials.

Experienced principals have identified specific steps that should be taken to ensure a smooth start and successful program.

Steps to Administering a Reading Volunteer Program

1. Identify a chairperson for the group (who keeps records of pupil and volunteer attendance).
2. Identify a liaison person (teacher, assistant principal) to select and schedule pupils, etc.
3. Arrange for a site where volunteers will work.
4. Provide materials and supplies.
5. Explain the program to staff and parents, alerting classroom teachers to specific criteria for referring pupils and acquainting them with the goals of program, general philosophy, and method of operation.
6. Provide teachers with referral forms (see sample provided).
7. Advise parents of pupil eligibility for participation, and secure informed consent. (A form is provided.)
8. Keep records of parental consent on file.
9. Provide a calendar of information that will affect the volunteers' program (for instance, the dates of class trips and special assemblies).
10. Facilitate communication between volunteers and classroom teachers about the children they are helping.
11. Give hints and special materials when indicated. Let volunteers feel appreciated and involved in the school program.
12. Evaluate the reading volunteer program after a few months with a committee of teachers and parents.

ANY PUBLIC SCHOOL   Jane Doe, Principal

PARENT CONSENT FOR READING HELP

I have read your notice about the Reading Volunteer Program at ANY PUBLIC SCHOOL. I understand that a trained reading volunteer will provide tutorial help to my child twice weekly during school hours.

Please call me at _____ or write me at _____

_____ so that an appointment can be set up for me to meet the reading volunteer.

I (will) (will not) be available for a Wednesday morning parent class in helping children read better at home.

My child's name is _____ Class: _____

_____
Parent's signature/date

SCHOOL READING VOLUNTEER PROGRAM
PUPIL INFORMATION SHEET
From Teacher to Reading Volunteer

_____
Date

Pupil's name _____

Age _____ Room _____ Teacher _____

Does child wear glasses? _____

How is this pupil functioning in other school subjects?

What are some of this child's strengths?

What are some of this child's interests?

Reading level—approximate _____

Pupil's main weaknesses in reading: _____

_____

_____

Any additional information which would be helpful in tutoring this pupil: _____

_____

_____

_____
Teacher

8–4 SETTING UP AN AFTER-SCHOOL PROGRAM

Perhaps you'd like to set up an after-school program that will meet the enrichment, remedial, or recreational needs of your pupils. One way to achieve this would be to request funds from the Central Office. In times of budget restraints, however, such funds are frequently difficult to obtain.

You may choose another route. When tax-levy dollars are not available, enterprising principals have set up their own programs using pupil fees to pay teachers an hourly salary and other costs such as insurance, custodial fees, etc.

By utilizing community workers whose work day goes beyond 3:00 P.M., you can save on some salaries. Librarians, recreation workers, parent volunteers, and others are likely to help out. You will need to go over the teachers' contract to make sure you are not stepping on any toes. Also, be prepared to spend several hours of administrative time setting up such a program. A parent volunteer can help you here.

Good luck! A little advance planning will really pay off. Talk to parents and pupils to see what kinds of activities they're interested in. Talk to your teachers to determine what kinds of skills they would like to offer the children.

We are including a sample letter to parents that gives you an idea of how you can set up your own self-sustaining program. If it's going to be a remedial program, try giving it an upbeat name like "Promoting Success." If you are going to have a program to meet the needs of preschool children, giving them a taste of school, use a catchy name, like "Giant Steps."

AFTER-SCHOOL PROGRAM

Dear Parents:

    Beginning February 1, we are going to have a self-sustaining after-school program at PS 3. The hours will be from 3:15 P.M. to 5:15 P.M. Parents will have to make their own arrangements for transportation.

    Each class will run for ten weeks, on Tuesday afternoons. The fee will be $45. If you would like your child to participate, please choose one course from this list. Write a number 1 beside your first choice. Please make two choices in case we cannot accommodate your child in your first choice. Some courses will be given by teachers from outside PS 3. We have identified each teacher.

    Thank you for your cooperation.

Fred Smith

Principal

------------------------------------- Detach and return to teacher -------------------------------------

_____ Arts & crafts (Mrs. Longo, PS 3)

_____ Storytelling and writing (Miss Chin, Public Library)

_____ Gymnastics (Ms. Fulgham, YWCA)

_____ Dramatics (Ms. Horne, Civic Theater)

_____ Tap dancing (Miss Rosemary, PS 3)

_____ Basketball (Ms. Flint, PS 3)

_____ Computers (Ms. Mardikos, PS 3)

_____ Cooking (Mr. Porto, PS 3)

_____	_____
Child's name	Class
_____	_____
Parent's signature	Phone

8–5 OPENING THE DOORS A LITTLE WIDER: COMMUNITY SCHOOLS

Throughout the United States, attention is increasingly focused on the community school concept. For instance, in the Thomas Jefferson School in Arlington, Virginia, the building is open from six in the morning until midnight, seven days a week. The recreation department opens the building, its canteen, club room, and gym for breakfast and recreation programs. After 3:00 P.M., recreation programs are expanded and adult education programs occupy a major portion of the space. According to the principal, "We feel that we have established a pace-setting type of cooperation in this facility. But it's just a first step. At present we're in the planning stages of a major school remodeling which will involve a public library and health services facility." Foundation grants have funded the program.

An example of how different leaders can work together with school administrators is found in Flint, Michigan. Classes extend beyond the regular school day into evenings, Saturdays, and summers. A community school director is employed in every Flint school to supervise community school activities. The community school advisory council, composed of adult and youth community members, teachers, custodian, principal, and community school director, identifies community needs and recommends programs and resources to the board of education.

Explore similar possibilities with the leaders of your school community when, and if, you think the time is right.

As an experienced school administrator, you have handled all kinds of joint efforts between pupils and teachers. However, there are some special problems you may want to look out for in considering the development of a school-community facility:

- Because of the need to coordinate activities with a variety of agencies and institutions, the planning process can be very time-consuming. Pontiac, Michigan's Human Resources Center took five years to develop. During a lengthy planning period, construction costs can rise and financing plans become increasingly complicated.
- Getting the cooperation of local agencies and institutions as well as state and federal agencies can be difficult. You must assuage local agencies' and institutions' fears of losing autonomy. Federal and state agencies must be convinced that a community education facility supports their program goals.
- The location of the facility may be controversial. School and community pride may vie with considerations of urban design, accessibility, and the racial composition of the neighborhoods in which potential sites are located.

In planning your community school, be sure to do the following:

- Begin exploring the idea with top leaders and planners. Once the general idea is accepted, then lower-level planners can develop the details.
- Get tentative agreements on operational cost sharing early in the planning process.
- Get to know the people at the agency coordinating the construction and/or operation of the facility.
- Cooperate by signing written agreements with user agencies and institutions at the proper time. This discourages disagreements later on.
- Anticipate a longer time for planning than is normally expected.
- Attempt to proceed with such a joint venture only when top-level officials are committed to its success.
- Appoint a coordinating teacher who has good community relations and who can maintain maximum community involvement in the programs and services.

Try to include the community as one of your basic school components—along with teachers, parents, pupils, and other staff members. Your school will benefit.

Chapter 9

Communicating Your School's Message

Ms. T. runs a good school. Yet this remains the best-kept secret of her Texas city. No one hears about the outstanding achievements of her pupils or the innovative programs she has introduced in her K–6 school. Even segments of the school community sometimes don't know what's going on. How can she get her school's message across?

■ As PRINCIPAL, YOU must become the catalyst for keeping information flowing throughout your school. Every segment of the school population—pupils, parents, and teachers—must be informed about those policies and practices which affect their lives. Teachers are turned off when they read about the new curriculum in a newspaper. Leaders in the student body don't want to be told about school events solely on a printed calendar. Parents want to be informed about changes in schedules before events take place.

Your role is to make certain that every school group has some input in making decisions and carrying out mutually agreed on goals and objectives. In some ways, you are a ring master who ties together the activities in each ring of the circus. Your management skills facilitate the smoothly functioning arena we call a school.

9–1 KEEPING EVERYONE INFORMED

Timing is a key factor in keeping everyone informed. If a new schedule is being prepared, be sure to make a list of all the people who will be affected by it: bus drivers, parents, custodians, pupils, school aides, teachers, lunch room workers, and district office staff. Be sure that those most involved in the change understand the reasons for it. Hold individual and group meetings so pupils and staff see the benefits that will accrue from a schedule change. Meet with PTA members and other parents and answer their questions. Weigh their objections and cooperatively work out solutions to problems that may emerge, such as dismissal coinciding with heavy traffic. In an assembly, discuss the advantages with pupils. Meet with teachers to gain their support. Be sure to inform bus drivers and lunch room aides so they understand the new time schedule before it goes into effect.

Give everyone an opportunity to air questions and comments at an early stage and in an informal atmosphere of open communication. Statements of policy seldom run afoul when staff members have free access to policy makers. Ideally, the staff members are part of the policy-making team.

Keeping people informed is more than merely "telling them nicely." They must understand the reasons for the change. Alternatives should be presented. Suggestions must be weighed. Objections should be studied. The final decision should take into account the feelings of every group. You cannot assert that you know best simply because you are the principal and impose your will on docile teachers, obedient pupils, and awestruck parents.

Five Tips for Keeping Communication a Two-Way Street

1. Place suggestion boxes in easily accessible locations throughout your school. Encourage pupils, teachers, parents, and other staff members to use these boxes to suggest improvements.
2. Eat lunch with various staff members. Follow up on luncheon suggestions promptly. Eat in the pupil lunch room occasionally. Get pupils' opinions on school activities.
3. Set up a staff advisory committee. Don't load it with friends who favor your ideas. Bring up problems in their embryo stage, thereby avoiding crises.
4. Use a questionnaire to determine how the faculty feels about the information flow. Ask for reactions to current attempts at communication and suggestions for improvement.
5. Wait in the office at dismissal time to make yourself available to teachers who have something to say.

Now let's look at some specific methods of communicating your school's message.

9–2 CREATING OPPORTUNITIES FOR COMMUNICATION

Every school administrator wants good staff morale. This depends in large measure on the effectiveness of the communication tools used in your school. In most cases, these will be written communication and face-to-face encounters.

The printed word can be enhanced if you follow these suggestions:

- Give every teacher a copy of any notice *before* it is sent to parents or pupils. Teachers must know what's going on first.
- Prepare a curriculum idea exchange newsletter with a group of teachers. Encourage the faculty to try new teaching ideas and share their successes.
- Hand out an easy-to-follow explanation of each employee's paycheck. All school workers should understand deductions and increments. Your staff will be grateful.
- Send home a map of the school, highlighting special interest areas such as the math lab or media center, for staff and parents.
- Distribute a one-page wrap-up of the school board's actions the morning after a meeting. Be factual and include only information germane to the staff.

COMMUNICATION QUESTIONNAIRE

Please complete this questionnaire and place it, unsigned, in my letter box by Friday afternoon. Your cooperation is appreciated. Each item can be answered in a few words. Use the back of the paper for more lengthy responses.

1. Have our faculty conferences met your needs? _____

2. How can they be improved? _____
_____

3. Do you feel your opinions are being considered? _____
_____

4. Have you made any suggestions this year? _____

5. Are class assignments made equitably? _____
_____

6. Does the school administration stand behind teachers? _____
_____

7. Did any positive suggestions emerge from your postobservation conference? _____
_____
_____

8. Does the school administration assist you in handling severe discipline cases? Can you suggest improvements in this area? _____
_____
_____

9. In which areas of your responsibility would you like more help? _____
_____
_____

10. Is your principal available when you want assistance? _____
_____

- Share information with parents. Send home a calendar of events early in the year, as well as a list of staff members and room numbers. Inform parents of assembly programs.

Person-to-person communication should not be just one way—over the public address system or from the auditorium platform. You must meet eyeball-to-eyeball with those you manage.

The most obvious way to accomplish this is to circulate around the building. Visiting every classroom every day should be your first priority. In some rooms your visit may be a cursory walk-through. In other rooms it may be long enough to participate in a discussion or project. Teachers and pupils must know that you "get around" and should not see you solely behind a desk or counter.

Be sure you are visible when the teachers check in in the morning. Greet them cheerfully. Yours may be the first pleasant face they have seen on a hectic morning. Brief mini-conferences may provide them with simple solutions to their questions and concerns.

It is equally important that teachers see you at the end of the day. This is a good time to compliment a teacher for something outstanding that you observed when making your classroom rounds. Don't hesitate to praise a teacher within earshot of others—but be sure to make suggestions for improvements in private.

Bulletin boards are another effective way to communicate ideas and administrative details. Have at least two bulletin boards in the general office. One large board can display notices about in-service courses, duty schedules, and district news items. A smaller "hot-line" bulletin board should be placed near the time clock or other spot that all teachers visit daily. This board should be reserved for items of immediate concern: absent teachers' names, schedule changes, reminders about due dates, etc.

Elsewhere in the building, provide bulletin boards for teachers' union announcements, social committee news, items for sale, etc. These boards should be good examples of neat, attractive displays which can be emulated by pupils and teachers. Stale, out-of-date notices should be removed promptly along with tattered items. Seasonal touches of color help enhance the general appeal.

The public address (PA) system is an efficient way to reach large groups of people at one time, but it is sometimes over-utilized or poorly utilized. The following tips will help you use the PA system to your advantage:

- Keep your announcements brief. People can't sustain interest for long periods of time, even when listening to your magnetic voice.

- Try to confine loudspeaker use to a particular time of day (morning homeroom, after lunch, prior to dismissal). Teachers will welcome not being interrupted mid-lesson. Accumulate a few short announcements and make them all at one time.

- Whenever possible, let a variety of people speak over the PA system. Club announcements should be made by pupil leaders.

9-3 IMPROVING COMMUNICATION AT FACULTY MEETINGS

As principal, you have to remember not to impose your ideas to the exclusion of others. This should extend even to setting the agenda for faculty meetings. Set up a meeting-planning committee that can make suggestions for topics of interest (testing programs, curriculum revisions, family living). By all means, however, reserve time for your own agenda items, such as improvement of instruction, report cards, and parent conference techniques.

Six Tips for Better Faculty Meetings

1. When staff members have some input in planning the faculty meetings, they are more attentive and less likely to ask for permission to be excused. A group of grade leaders meeting with you can draw up a meaningful agenda in less than one hour.
2. Encourage teachers to submit suggestions directly to their teacher leaders.
3. Carry over topics that generate lively interest from one meeting to another.
4. Encourage teachers to serve as resource persons or panel members at faculty meetings.
5. Avoid the temptation to read your meeting agenda to teachers at the beginning of the meeting. This usually discourages teacher participation.
6. Provide a folder in which teachers can keep their notes and refer to them easily.

Now let's look at how you can prepare a news release for the local newspapers or TV stations.

9-4 SURE-FIRE WAYS TO GET MEDIA ATTENTION

Here are some quick and easy ways to prepare a news release that will help make working with your local media easier and make your community more aware of your school's programs and activities:

1. The first line on the typed and double- or triple-spaced page should give your name, school address, and phone number. The second line should say FOR IMMEDIATE RELEASE. If you send your release more than a week or so in advance, specify a release date.

2. Be brief and clear. The release should be as close to one page as possible—and never more than two. Put your important information up front.

3. Send a copy of the press release to each of the local media. Newspapers, radio stations and cable and broadcast television stations will all want to know about your event. Address it to the attention of the education reporter, spelling his or her name correctly.

4. Make the local connection in the first paragraph. This way, there is no mistaking that your news is pertinent and should be printed.

5. Always double-check that you have answered the five W's—who, what, when (time and date), where, and why—early in the release, preferably in the first two or three sentences. Be objective and concise.

6. Include a contact person and both a day and evening phone number in case a member of the media has a question. A single unanswered question can keep your event from receiving the exposure you need.

7. Send a copy of the press release to the city's mayor and/or other appropriate local officials, such as school board members, with an invitation to attend your school's activity.

8. Designate a teacher, parent, or administrator to follow up with the media by telephone. This is to confirm that each media representative has received the press release and is invited to attend.

9. Adding a national connection to your release can make it seem more important. Or, if several schools in your city or county are participating in the program, the media may allow more space or airtime for the events.

10. Arrange for a photographer (perhaps a parent volunteer) to be in attendance at the festivities. You can send the resulting black and white glossy photographs to local media representatives the day after the event for possible publication. (Do make sure you have a signed release for using children's photos.)

SAMPLE OF AN ANNOUNCEMENT OR ADVANCE NEWS RELEASE

FROM: Ms. Jane Scott
        Principal, Maple Grove School
        Maple Grove, Oregon
        Day: 555-8901   Evening: 555-6123

        FOR IMMEDIATE RELEASE
        SCHOOL BAND TO PERFORM

The Maple Grove school band, under the baton of Mr. Andrew Fazio, will perform a holiday concert in the school auditorium on December 18 at 7:30 P.M. in the South Shore School, located on River Road.

The concert is open to the public. There is no charge for admission. However, refreshments will be sold during the intermission.

School administrators frequently complain that the news media are quick to publish stories about student unrest and untoward incidents but not about outstanding achievements. It is your responsibility to manage the handling and placing of news stories either directly or through others.

Here are some techniques for getting more good news into the paper:

1. Send out advance stories. If done in time, this will generate two stories—an announcement of the event and a follow-up on it. Sometimes an advance will prompt an editor to send a reporter to cover the story.

2. Time your releases. Keep alert to seasonal opportunities for a story. Many papers have a back-to-school issue that will welcome good local stories. In December or June, send papers a review of the year's important school events.

3. Write a column. Many weeklies would welcome a regular column from a school official. Contact your local newspaper editor. Keep the column to 500 words maximum, and avoid educational jargon.

4. Prepare fillers. A filler is a brief, one-paragraph item that some newspapers use to fill columns when longer stories leave gaps. Editors need many fillers daily and may welcome local items. Look for interesting tidbits about your school and write them up. Include a note to the editor.

5. Use fact sheets. Editors welcome in-depth biographical data on new faculty members, architectural details on a new wing to your school, standardized test scores, scholarship winners, and science fair and

SAMPLE NEWS RELEASE

FROM: Mr. Tom Alfonso
Principal, Taylor School
Arlo Road
Springfield, Arkansas
Day: 555-6789   Evening: 555-9012

FOR IMMEDIATE RELEASE
WHY COMMUNITY SUPPORT FOR SPRINGFIELD'S NEW SCHOOL BOND ISSUE IS VITAL

The city of Springfield was founded as a village in 1947, just one of the hundreds and hundreds of new communities that were springing up on the outskirts of larger, more established cities in the years immediately following World War II. At the end of 1948, Springfield's population was estimated at just over 1,100. The U.S. census figures tell the story of Springfield's phenomenal growth:

1950—5,057
1960—18,667
1970—31,988
1980—44,007
1990—48,430

The first public building built in Springfield was not a village hall but an elementary school. It opened its doors to over 300 children in the fall of 1948. Between 1948 and 1960, Springfield built nine more elementary schools, a middle school, and a high school. In the 1960s, three new elementary schools were built, four were expanded, a second middle school was built, and an addition was put on the high school, including more classrooms, an industrial arts wing, and a larger gym.

Today, more than half of Springfield's classrooms are at least twenty-five years old, and some are close to forty years old. Even though they have been well maintained over the years, they are simply worn out . . . (add specifics to strengthen arguments).

spelling bee finalists. Fact sheets permit journalists to write a story using their own angle.

6. Update stories. Check the papers daily for school-related news, and follow up with a fresh approach. If an article describes the opportunities for women as lawyers, send in a story about the number of your female pupils elected to the Student Council.

What about the letters you send home with your pupils? They are a communication tool, too.

9–5 SEVEN STEPS TO A SUCCESSFUL LETTER

Principals send letters home on many occasions. Some seem to be ignored, while others mobilize the reader into action. Here are seven simple steps that will ensure a positive reader response. Check your rough draft against these guidelines.

1. For maximum effectiveness, the opening paragraph in a letter should contain no more than eleven words.
2. No single paragraph should have more than seven lines of copy. If it does, break it up to simplify communication.
3. Don't assume your reader knows anything about your purpose. Tell readers what you want them to know and what you want them to do.
4. Most people look at the letterhead of a letter first, then the salutation, the signature, and the postscript before reading the body. Design your letter to take advantage of this visual flow.
5. Letters with indented paragraphs are better than those without indentations. They appear to be less formal.
6. Use a postscript to increase understanding of the main point you're trying to make.
7. Make it easy for your reader to respond. Include a "tear-off" or a reply form.

9–6 ARE YOUR NEWSLETTERS TELLING YOUR STORY?

One major newsletter of general interest to staff and parents is preferred to two separate publications. Many items are of interest to both. For example, if a committee of teachers has drafted a curriculum in sex education or family living, everyone has a stake in the news. One well-written story on the new curriculum should be of equal interest to staff and parents.

Special detailed information could follow on news sheets for a particular segment of the audience.

What kind of general news and features should be included in newsletters?

- News of upcoming events. This could be done in calendar form.
- News of what is being taught and how. Teacher-made filmstrips in social studies classes could be one feature story.
- News of policies and regulations enacted by the school board. Emphasize how they will affect pupils in your school.
- News relating to costs and financing of education. Parents and taxpayers should be apprised of how their money is being spent.
- News about people makes interesting reading. Everyone likes to know the leisure-time activities of recent appointees as well as their academic credentials.

The newsletter's design and layout must be inviting. Chances are, people won't read a messy, poorly designed newsletter. Try these suggestions:

1. Use space wisely. Type and pictures should not be crowded. Stories and pictures set off by open space will attract readers.
2. Vary article length. Don't put all long articles on one page and all small ones on another page. In particularly long articles, use subheads to break up the expanse of body type.
3. Avoid excesses. If a second color ink, especially a bright one, is used, don't splash it too heavily throughout the newsletter. Don't overindulge in boxes and rules. They can give a page a "hodgepodge" look.
4. Vary headline size. All headlines on a page should not look alike. Large heads should be used for major news stories and long features, and smaller heads should be used for less important and shorter articles.

A newsletter generally is considered a form of one-way communication—from the school to the community, staff, and students. But it need not be exclusively one way.

At least two or three times yearly, the newsletter should feature a brief questionnaire or even business reply card that can be cut out and returned to school. This should not be elaborate or detailed, but it should be well thought out. Plans must be made to publish results of the questionnaire and report on what the system will do with the results.

Readers' reactions to the newsletter should be sought as well as their suggestions for changing it. At other times, readers can be surveyed on a variety of topics and their responses sought through a questionnaire.

Distribute your newsletter widely. Remember that pupils are notorious for leaving newsletters in school or losing them on the way home. Consider mailing them. You can plan the folds of the newsletter to allow the publication to be a self-mailer.

9–7 GETTING YOUR IDEAS ACROSS IN OTHER PUBLICATIONS

There are many other ways in which you can get your ideas and programs across. Few, if any, schools need all the publications on the following list. However, every school could benefit from producing at least one.

- *Staff handbook*: This manual details school policies and procedures. It should also delineate administrative, supervisory, and organizational functions of key people.
- *Guidebook for substitutes*: This booklet is designed to help substitutes through the day. It should contain a school map, rules for pupils, homework policy, etc.
- *Student handbook*: This is a manual for students, acquainting them with the dress code, safety rules, clubs, schedules, etc.
- *Resource center brochure*: This guide apprises everyone of recent acquisitions of the library and educational media department (e.g., new audiovisual equipment). Procedures for borrowing can be included.
- *Rumor control bulletin*: This can be a one-page mimeo sheet sent to parents and key communicators in the community as needed. If you brief these people in emergency situations, rumors can be dispelled by facts.
- *School profile*: This is a pocket-sized facts and figures book. Gives readers information at a glance about the size, staff, offerings, and background of the school.

The most important segment of your school community is your staff. Yet principals do not always make themselves clear. The following section addresses that concern.

9–8 GIVING INSTRUCTIONS THAT A STAFF MEMBER CAN FOLLOW

Giving a simple order to a staff member and explaining how a job should be done should be an easy enough task, but in too many cases it becomes a difficult and frustrating experience. If you want work done properly and on time, you'll have to develop a knack for using the right approach and the right language. It all boils down to making yourself understood.

Here are the most common causes of difficulty in this sensitive area:

- *Saying too much or too little.* For example, if you go into unnecessary detail with an experienced custodian, he or she will probably get bored and stop listening; might miss an important point entirely; or may feel that you're treating him or her like a beginner and be uncooperative. On the other hand, if you don't tell beginners enough, they'll spend a lot of time stumbling around, making very little headway.

- *Not asking questions.* For example, the best way to be sure that secretaries understand is to ask them to repeat the order in their own words. Often they'll be able to repeat your words without really knowing what they're supposed to do. If you suspect that this is the case, ask questions that will test their understanding.

- *Vague or incomplete instructions.* For example, if you tell a secretary, "Be careful with this letter, we don't want to misplace it," the secretary might think, "I'm always careful," and think no more about it. But if you say, "David, we may be called on to produce this letter when the superintendent visits our school," the secretary will prepare an extra copy and put it in the file under "Superintendent."

- *Giving the wrong type of order.* In some situations, you have to give a direct order. This is particularly true in an emergency or when you must be emphatic. But if you have developed a spirit of cooperation in your group, a request is more effective because you're merely asking for help in getting a job done, not demanding blind obedience. Another effective method is to ask for suggestions so individuals are, in effect, giving themselves instructions.

- *Giving instructions at the wrong time.* In most instances, you will give instructions about an assignment when the job is delegated. But timing is most important in issuing general instructions such as those concerning school safety, maintenance, or payroll procedures. For example, if you interrupt staff members when they're busy, they won't pay much attention to what you're saying if it doesn't concern the particular job they're doing. Another poor time to issue instructions is at the end of the day. Many teachers quit thinking about the job as soon as they start to clean up, so your chances of making a lasting impression are minimal.

The preceding general rules will help you give instructions that will be effective in most situations. But to get full cooperation from the various personalities in your school, you'll frequently have to use your ingenuity.

Now let's look at how you come across when you speak to not one staff member but to a large audience of teachers or parents.

9–9 DELIVERING AN EFFECTIVE STATE-OF-THE-SCHOOL MESSAGE

Each September you are expected to fire up your teachers at the first faculty conference. In addition, the first PTA meeting of the school year usually attracts many parents who want to see you and hear about the school program.

These major speeches can fill you with dread. You may be comfortable with informal, off-the-cuff talks but insecure with the more formal format. These suggestions will help you overcome any stage fright:

1. *Remember KISS.* This stands for "Keep It Simple, Stupid." Your audience is going to come away with one or two of your main ideas, not ten or twenty. If you can't express in a sentence or two what you intend to get across, then your speech is not well focused. And if you don't have a clear idea of what you want to say, there's no way your audience will.

2. *Get organized.* No matter how long or short your speech, you've got to get your act together—how you're going to open, what major points you're going to make, and how you're going to close. Think of your last sentence first. When you know where you're headed, you can choose any route to get there. A strong close is critical: The last thing you say is what your audience will most likely remember.

3. *Keep it short.* The standard length of a vaudeville act was twelve minutes. If all those troupers singing and dancing their hearts out couldn't go on longer without boring the audience, what makes you think you can?

4. *Make contact.* In the first few moments of your speech, establish the relationship between you and your audience. Smile. Acknowledge your introducer with a nod and a thank you. Then wait. Don't begin until you have everyone's attention. Members of the audience will quickly get the idea that you are speaking *to them.* That is exactly what you want.

5. *Eye your audience.* When they've quieted, establish eye contact. Pick out three friendly faces: one left, one right, one center. By speaking first to one, then to the other, you take in the whole group.

6. *Talk, don't read.* Reading to the audience is not as good as talking, directly and from the heart. Even if it's not as smooth, it's better. We're against scripted speeches. It is smart to use notes, not a word-for-word script of your speech. Your notes will remind you of what you want to say and where you are in your speech.

7. *Use breath control.* It seems absurd that anybody should have to be reminded to breathe. But under stress we sometimes forget how to

breathe correctly. Don't take big, gulping breaths or breathe faster than usual (you'll hyperventilate). Just take easy, rhythmic breaths from your diaphragm. This will help you relax. Every public performer knows that controlled breathing is important. Look at the best basketball players. Ever notice what a professional player does on the foul line just before taking a free throw? You can learn something from that.

Public speaking is no more difficult than driving a car. The mysterious becomes simple once you know how to do it. The next time it's your turn to make a speech at a faculty conference, school board, or PTA meeting, see if these suggestions work for you.

9–10 WHAT IS YOUR CQ (COMMUNICATION QUOTIENT)?

We've discussed various kinds of communication. As a way to tie things together, take this scoring quiz to determine your CQ.

1. I provide many details about matters I think are important, regardless of whether my listeners agree with me.
   A. Frequently
   B. On occasion
   C. I've never noticed
   D. Never
2. When I speak with another person, I tend to use his or her name often.
   A. Always
   B. Sometimes
   C. I've never noticed
   D. Not at all
3. I tend to speak in run-on sentences, quickly stating connections and parallels between facts and ideas.
   A. Never
   B. Rarely
   C. On occasion
   D. Frequently
4. I say things that sound surprising simply to grab attention.
   A. Whenever necessary
   B. Rarely, if at all
   C. I've never noticed
   D. Never
5. I tell stories and illustrate my points with anecdotes.
   A. Never
   B. Rarely

C. On occasion

D. Frequently

6. When I speak with others, I often use words like *must, have to,* and *should.*

    A. Usually

    B. Sometimes

    C. I've never noticed

    D. Rarely

7. When a friend or colleague feels down, I try to be cheerful to bring the other person out of the doldrums.

    A. Usually

    B. Sometimes

    C. Depends on how I feel

    D. Hardly ever

8. If someone at work has an objection to what I say or propose, the first thing I do is restate my position.

    A. Most of the time

    B. Sounds like a good idea

    C. Sometimes

    D. Rarely

9. In listening situations, I frequently restate what I've heard with phrases such as, "as I understand it, you mean...."

    A. Most of the time

    B. On occasion

    C. Rarely

    D. Hardly ever

10. If another person in an exchange stops speaking, I immediately break the silence.

    A. Almost always

    B. Frequently

    C. On occasion

    D. Rarely

Scoring

For questions 1, 3, 5, 6, 7, 8, and 10, give yourself four points for D, three for C, two for B, and one for A. For questions 4, 2, and 9, give yourself four points for A, three for B, two for C, and one for D.

    33 and above: Excellent

    28–33: Very good

    22–27: Good

    21 or below: Study the ideal answers

Ideal Answers

1. D. Persuasive principals talk about what most interests their listeners, finding common ground to promote positive action.

2. A. If not overused, using someone's name creates rapport and is especially persuasive near the end of a letter or memo.

3. D. Linking undeniable facts or points to your own opinions and requests makes disagreement or refusal difficult.

4. A. Attention grabbing is especially useful with know-it-all types—it forces them to discern your meaning and can keep a disagreement from escalating.

5. D. People resist less when a suggestion or idea is cushioned in easy-to-understand terms.

6. D. Unless talking to children, avoid using declaratives. Ask, don't tell.

7. D. Rather than attempting to change someone's mood right off, match it; then work out of it.

8. D. Agree with resistance and objections—at first. After earning an element of trust, dismantle opposition point by point.

9. A. Restating a point will (1) validate the worthiness of another's point, (2) show your obvious interest, and (3) uncover misunderstandings.

10. D. Many people value silence as the more important part of a conversation. Most people need time to reach agreement.

9–11 GETTING STARTED TOMORROW MORNING

Would you like some favorable, free publicity? Select a story idea about your school and write down all the facts you can think of that are pertinent to that story. At this point, don't worry about writing in complete sentences or even about what order they're in. Just get down as many of the facts as you can.

After you've gotten all the facts down, go over them again and check them against the famous five W's: who, what, where, when and why. Are any of the five W's missing or incomplete?

Go over the facts again, and this time ask yourself which is the most important fact. *Why* will your story be important or of interest to the reader? Have you made absolutely clear to everyone the "gee whiz" factor in your article.

Now reorder the facts, starting with the most important fact from the reader's viewpoint and allowing the other facts to flow logically from that starting point.

Congratulations—you now have the rough draft of your first news release! Get it typed and in the mail. If you can, drop it off at the local newspaper or cable TV office.

You are now on your way to communicating your school's message effectively.

Chapter 10

Reducing the Impact of Society's Problems

Ms. S. remembers when her greatest societal concern was children playing hookey from school. Today her pupils are plagued by many of society's problems. These concerns affect the school directly: divorce, drug abuse, sexual promiscuity, crime, and so on. The list grows virtually every day.

Ms. S. knows that she can't solve these problems, but she wants to find ways of reducing the impact of societal problems, especially child and sexual abuse.

■As PRINCIPALS, WE sometimes feel that we need to act as buffers between our pupils and the cold, cruel world. Society's problems seem to grow fiercer each year: AIDS, homelessness, abuse, and more.

While there are limits on how much we can do to shield our pupils, there are steps we can take to reduce the impact of these problems.

The following sections will help you enhance your role as child advocate and protector.

10–1 HELPING CHILDREN WHOSE PARENTS DIVORCE

Husbands and wives often see divorce as the best solution to a troubled marriage. Children see divorce as the end of their family.

Too often, it becomes the school's job to pick up the pieces. It becomes our job to reassure children that parents don't get divorced from their kids—they get divorced from each other. We tell children, "Divorced parents love their kids as much as ever."

Your teachers need training in helping children understand and adjust to their parents' separation. The best way to begin is to have your teachers or counselors discuss feelings with their pupils, individually or in groups.

FEELING	REASON
Confused	over the changes that divorce brings. They don't understand their parents' reason for separation.
Lonely	because they wonder if they are still loved. Children may feel they have lost a parent.
Angry	at parents—yet they fear that, if they show anger, they will lose their parents.
Sad	that their family is changing.
Guilty	because they feel they are the reason for the divorce.
Scared	about who's going to take care of them.
Worried	about what their friends may think. They may not know what to tell their friends.

Divorce affects how your pupils behave in school. Alert your teachers to these frequent reactions to divorce:

Reaction	Reason
• Forgetting to do homework	Feeling that school isn't important compared to problems at home
• Getting angry with friends and adults	Searching for an outlet for their anger and afraid to show it at home
• Feeling bored with school	Life problems seem to eclipse school work
• Daydreaming in class	Fantasizing about life at home before divorce; dreaming about parents getting back together again

A key goal of school support programs should be to show pupils that it's not who is in your family that makes your family healthy, but how you communicate and solve problems together. An excellent resource is *Banana Splits: A School-Based Program for the Survivors of the Divorce Wars* (Interact, Box 997, Lakeside, CA 92040).

Your responsibility does not stop here, as you will see in the next section.

10-2 YOUR ROLE IN CHILD CUSTODY DECREES

A difficult issue concerns the role you should play when parents separate and there are custody tug-of-wars. The principal is frequently caught in the middle. Often, separated parents will exploit the school in an effort to achieve their own ends.

As principal, you can remain neutral and yet be of great assistance to divorced or separated parents. Focus your energies on trying to prevent custody battles and abductions rather than trying to mediate them. Do not take a parent's word about who has custody. Insist on seeing and photocopying the court order.

To remain impartial and yet be of help to parents in preventing custody problems, give the suggestions listed on the next page to parents who are considering separation or divorce or are recently divorced.

By becoming familiar with these regulations ahead of time, you may prevent misunderstandings and grief—for innocent children, confused parents, and yourself.

10-3 PREVENTING ALCOHOL AND OTHER DRUG ABUSE

There is much duplication of efforts in the way schools address substance abuse prevention. Various levels of government start programs, and after an initial publicity splash their funds are cut—but not eliminated. Another agency launches its own program, which leads to overlapping programs in some grades or schools, with a lack of services in others.

SUGGESTIONS FOR PARENTS CONSIDERING SEPARATION OR DIVORCE

1. *Family court.* To obtain a custody order, you must file legal papers in family court. It will be much simpler to do this if you get an attorney's assistance. Lists of attorneys are available from the lawyer referral service of your local bar association. Books on family law are available in many libraries, if you decide to go through the process yourself.

2. *Custody order.* Even if you are not legally married, you should obtain legal custody of your child. Many unmarried mothers feel that they are automatically entitled to custody unless there is a court order to the contrary, or that they will have custody if they have not put the father's name on the birth certificate. This is not true in every state. Be safe and get a custody order.

3. *Visitation.* To protect the rights of both parents, it is important that court orders be sufficiently specific to be enforceable. Specify exactly the beginning and ending dates and times of visitation.

4. *Restrict the removal of the child.* Think about including a clause prohibiting the removal of the child from the state without the consent of the judge or custodial parent.

5. *Post a bond.* Investigate the possibility of the judge requiring your partner to post a bond to ensure that custody and visitation rights will not be violated.

6. *Joint custody.* In cases of friction between parents with joint custody decrees, it is especially important that the custody order specify which parent is to have the child at which times.

7. *The noncustodial parent.* Visitation rights of the noncustodial parent are also enforceable under federal law. The noncustodial parent can request in the custody order a provision that (1) requires the custodial parent to get the court's approval before moving out of the state or country; (2) requires both parents to keep each other informed of the current address and telephone number of the child; and (3) requires the custodial parent to post a bond to ensure compliance with court-ordered visitation.

8. *Child support.* A parent who feels that his or her relationship to the child is threatened may be more likely to abduct. For this reason, you should treat child support and visitation as separate issues. In most areas, the refusal to pay child support is not a legal ground for denying visitation. Also, the denial of visitation is not a legal ground for failing to pay child support. The custodial parent should allow visits and at the same time go to court to collect the child support. The noncustodial parent should pay child support and at the same time go to court to enforce visitation rights.

9. *Physical abuse.* A parent suffering repeated physical abuse may be pushed to the point of fleeing to safety with the children. Similarly, a parent may flee from an abusive partner to protect the children from harm. Before leaving the state, you should consult an attorney to obtain legal custody and other emergency protection orders. If necessary, you may be able to obtain a temporary custody order in the new state. A court action for permanent custody can then be filed promptly in the original state.

To maximize your school's participation in available programs, take these steps:

1. *Seek school district approval.* Getting the approval of appropriate district-level officials is a necessary first step to establish a viable program. Without district-level understanding and support for the program, its effectiveness will be minimal. It's also a good idea to take advantage of the district's ability to publicize the program.

2. *Assume a leadership role.* You are the key to organizing a successful program. You must understand the need for and be committed to providing an appropriate program. You must provide the leadership necessary for the formation and support of your school's program.

3. *Enhance existing programs.* If the district already has a program in place, you may

   - Expand the existing elementary program.
   - Update information.
   - Address areas that were not included in the initial adoption of the alcohol and other drug prevention education program.
   - Provide supplementary materials.
   - Redefine objectives and activities that are appropriate for elementary students.

4. *Integrate the prevention program in the curriculum. Use the content areas to reinforce your prevention efforts.*

   MATH
   Solve problems regarding alcohol and other drugs. For example,

   - A man smokes one pack of cigarettes per day. If he spends $2.00 on each pack, how much money has he spent in one month?
   - Draw a graph illustrating war deaths and compare it with deaths due to alcohol-related motor vehicle accidents.

   SCIENCE AND HEALTH

   - Discuss the studies regarding nicotine and mice.
   - Compare healthy lungs and smokers' lungs.
   - Discuss drug use and AIDS.
   - Discuss the impact of alcohol and other drugs on pregnant women.

   SOCIAL STUDIES

   - Discuss different cultural and religious attitudes regarding alcohol and other drugs.

MUSIC

- Discuss how some music lyrics promote alcohol and other drugs.
- Write antidrug songs.

PHYSICAL EDUCATION

- Discuss how a healthy lifestyle precludes alcohol and other drugs.
- Address problems associated with illegal use of steroids.

LANGUAGE ARTS

- Creative writing
- Dramatizations
- Role playing
- Reading appropriate stories, plays, or novels

5. *Appoint a teacher or coordinator.* Develop a network, beginning with a committee of interested staff members. Designate (or hire) someone to serve as coordinator for the building. Involve the entire staff in the development and implementation of the school's program. All teachers need to provide input for the program. Include the support staff as well. Although the nurse, secretaries, cooks, custodians, and bus drivers do not teach in the classroom, they have frequent contact with the students and often serve as role models to students, particularly on the elementary level. Develop a consensus with the staff for program expectations that all will support. The project may become part of existing committees (i.e., staff development activities, in-service courses, curriculum development, budget, etc.).

10–4 SAYING NO TO DRUGS

It's not always easy to achieve effective communication between school personnel and pupils. This is especially true when it comes to discussing drugs. Your pupils and their teachers have different communication styles and different ways of responding in a conversation.

The following tips will help your teachers stimulate open conversations when discussing drugs with pupils.

Communication Tips

1. *Look!* Be aware of your pupil's facial expressions and body language. Is he or she nervous or uncomfortable—frowning, drumming fingers, tapping a foot, looking at the clock? Or does the pupil seem relaxed—

smiling, looking at you directly? Reading these signs will help you know how the child is feeling.

2. *Listen!* Pay attention. Don't interrupt. Don't prepare what you will say while your pupil is speaking. Reserve judgment until your pupil has finished and has asked you for a response. During the conversation, acknowledge what your pupil is saying—move your body forward if you are sitting, touch a shoulder if you are walking, or nod your head and make eye contact.

3. *Respond!* Speaking for yourself sounds thoughtful and is less likely to be considered a lecture or an automatic response. For example, "I am very concerned about . . ." or "I understand that it is sometimes difficult . . ." are better ways to respond to your pupil than beginning sentences with "You should," or "If I were you," or "When I was your age we didn't. . . ."

   If your pupil tells you something you don't want to hear, don't ignore the statement. However, don't offer advice in response to every statement he or she makes. It is better to listen carefully to what is being said and try to understand the real feelings behind the words. Make sure you understand what your pupil means. Repeat or restate what he or she says.

If a teacher suspects a child is already involved in drugs or is at risk from drug-involved parents, he or she should notify you. You must report the matter to the school nurse, guidance counselor, district drug abuse prevention personnel, or all three. You may need to refer the case to a state agency handling abuse or neglect.

There are several national toll-free 800 telephone numbers that can provide assistance to pupils at risk. Share these with your teachers, your PTA newsletter editor, and selected pupils:

1-800-356-9996	Alateen-Al-Anon (for alcohol abusers or their children)
1-800-COCAINE	Substance abuse treatment and referral
1-800-662-HELP	Information line for National Institute on Drug Abuse
1-800-729-6686	National Clearinghouse for Alcohol and Drug Information
1-800-258-2766	"Just Say No" Foundation (7 A.M. to 5 P.M. Pacific time)
1-800-835-3900	Pathfinders Alternatives (Drug, alcohol, and depression assessment and help)

As principal, you can obtain information and/or inexpensive teaching materials on drug abuse prevention and treatment from the following:

American Council for Drug Education
204 Monroe St., Suite 110, Rockville, MD 20850
1-800-488-3784 (inexpensive educational materials)

Hazeldon Education Services
P.O. Box 176, Center City, MN 55012
1-800-328-9000 (books, pamphlets, videos)

The Chemical People Newsletter
4802 Fifth Avenue, Pittsburgh, PA 15213
1-412-622-1491 (WQED newsletter service)

Chemical People Institute
1 Allegheny Square, Suite 720, Pittsburgh, PA 15212
1-412-322-0900 (brochures, literature, videos)

Parents often look to the school for help in teaching their children to say no to drugs. You can do them and their children a real service by including these suggestions in the PTA newsletter.

HELP YOUR CHILD SAY NO

Make it easier for your child to refuse an offer of alcohol and other drugs. Encourage your child to

- *Just say no.* Don't argue, don't discuss. Say no and show that you mean it.
- *Give reasons.* "I'm doing something else that night" or "The coach says drugs will hurt my game" are examples of some reasons youngsters can use. Also, don't forget the oldest reason: "My parents will kill me."
- *Suggest other things to do.* If a friend is offering alcohol or other drugs, saying no is tougher. Suggesting something else to do—going to a movie, playing a game, or working together on a project—shows that drugs are being rejected, not the friend.
- *Leave.* When all these steps have failed, get out of the situation immediately. Go home, go to class, join a group of friends, or talk to someone else.
- *Ask questions.* If unknown substances are offered, ask, "What is it?" and "Where did you get it?"

It's also important for parents to be aware of the signs of drug use. It's a good idea to include these eight questions in a PTA newsletter.

Signs of Drug Use Inventory

1. Is your child going through changes that are extreme or that last for more than a few days?
2. Does your child seem withdrawn, depressed, tired, and careless about personal grooming?
3. Has your child become hostile and uncooperative?
4. Have your child's relationships with other family members deteriorated?
5. Has your child dropped his or her old friends?
6. Is your child no longer doing well in school (grades slipping, attendance irregular)?
7. Has your child lost interest in hobbies, sports, and other favorite activities?
8. Have your child's eating or sleeping patterns changed?

These signs may also apply to a child who is not using drugs but who may be having other problems at school or in the family. If you are in doubt, get help. Have your family doctor or local clinic examine your child to rule out illness or other physical problems.

Some children are unfortunate enough to be born addicted. This increasingly prevalent tragedy is explored in the next section.

10–5 IDENTIFYING AND HELPING "CRACK BABIES"

The first wave of victims of prenatal crack exposure has reached our schools. These children have very short attention spans as well as other behavioral problems and learning difficulties. Many crack-abusing women are multiple drug users even when pregnant. Cocaine and other drugs can cause a premature baby or one that is developmentally delayed. Many of these babies are constantly distressed or lethargic and unable to bond to a caretaker.

Because they are difficult babies, so hard to console, foster parents often are unable to cope. Some of these children may have been in a number of foster care homes or institutions by the time they reach school.

Alert teachers about what to look for in identifying crack babies once they enter school:

- Language delays
- Hyperactivity
- Short attention spans

- Mood swings
- Visual perceptual problems
- Fine motor difficulties
- Spatial relations and balance problems
- Gastrointestinal problems
- Respiratory difficulties, including allergies and asthma
- Inconsistencies in learning.

These characteristics may be present in children other than crack babies, but combined with other available information they can indicate prenatal drug addiction.

Teachers of these children have found the following techniques to be helpful:

- Talking them through changes, such as leaving the classroom to go to the library
- Holding hands when moving through the halls
- Responding to tears with reassurance
- Keeping them with the same teacher for two years
- Reducing their class size, when feasible
- Forging home-school partnerships with a parent or nonaddicted relative
- Placing small footsteps on the floor to help children line up
- Structuring the classroom so the children don't have to depend on verbal directions alone. Use pictures of activities.

The National Institute on Drug Abuse (NIDA) has found that many children are now growing up in households where all the adults are drug addicts. They estimate that in Washington, D.C., Boston, Detroit, Los Angeles, and New York, 20 to 40 percent of parents of school children are currently using drugs. NIDA also estimates that one out of ten newborns in the United States is drug exposed, and in some inner-city hospitals the rate is 40 percent.

Free materials for teachers and other school personnel are available from the NIDA hot line. The telephone number is 1-800-662-HELP. The hot line is a confidential information and referral line that also directs callers to crack and cocaine abuse treatment centers in the local community.

In spite of their labels as crack babies or drug babies, these are children first—with needs and feelings. With early intervention, many can lead successful lives.

10–6 BUILDING SELF-ESTEEM IN BLACK MALES

Much attention has been focused recently on what works in the development of productive, self-assured black men. A few school districts are considering setting up special classes for African-American males to prevent drop outs in this population. Nationally, dropout rates for black males are 60 percent higher than those of whites.

You should acknowledge that racism *is* a factor in our society that continues to affect blacks, both male and female. At staff meetings, provide some sensitivity training to teachers, emphasizing how potent racism still is in our country. Demonstrate ways in which schools may unconsciously promote racism, such as through staff hiring, tracking, zoning, and Eurocentric curricula.

To induce positive thinking and invite the development of practical strategies, you must make your teachers aware of their responsibility in motivating all pupils, but especially black males, to achieve success in school. Begin by reviewing with your teachers historical background about the following:

- African and African-American heroes and leaders
- Freedom after the Civil War and migration northward
- Military service from the Revolutionary War to the Persian Gulf War
- Leadership in the Civil Rights Movement
- Political leadership in American government.

Follow up by destroying the prevalent myths that all black men are athletic, violent, irresponsible, and unemployed. Instead, present the reality of black males who are successful scholars, honor students, responsible family heads, and respected members of the community. In each curriculum area, emphasize the contributions of black men.

Invite successful black merchants and community workers, such as police and fire department employees, to speak to assembly audiences. Encourage teachers to arrange class trips to sites where boys are likely to see black men employed in middle-management and executive capacities (e.g., local hospitals, banks, etc.).

Arrange a family tree on a class bulletin board where children post photos of family members. In this way, pupils will see a variety of family configurations and will see that they are not unique.

You may want to write to the Alexandria City Public Schools, 3330 King Street, Alexandria, Virginia, 22302, and ask about their fourteen-minute videotape, "Black, Male, and Successful in America."

10–7 FOSTERING SEXUAL RESPONSIBILITY

In the age of AIDS, and with the changes in society's values and lifestyles, young people are being confronted with greater responsibility for their own sexual conduct and social behavior. The school, in cooperation with the home, must provide systematic and accurate information that will enable youngsters to make responsible decisions—decisions that will ultimately have an important impact on their lives.

Different communities have different standards for teaching sex education and/or family living. Your school board will set guidelines. This is a sensitive issue requiring both parent and community input. Set up a school advisory committee that includes a medical practitioner such as a doctor or nurse.

As with any program, you must have a clear set of goals as well as central office approval. The following goals are written in terms of pupil outcomes. They cross grade lines and can be applied to any level of pupil readiness.

Pupil Goals

1. To understand that love, responsibility, and mutual concern are basic to harmonious family life
2. To recognize the traditional values and responsibilities involved in marriage and parenthood
3. To develop a code of values that will enhance self-esteem and serve as a guide for reasoned judgments and responsible behavior
4. To build communication skills which can be applied in expressing emotions, resolving conflicts, and seeking guidance
5. To form a wholesome attitude toward human sexuality as an integral part of one's total being
6. To recognize sexual stereotyping and its consequences
7. To understand that adolescent sexual intimacy has many inherent problems
8. To acquire a body of knowledge related to human sexual growth and development and reproduction

Your advisory committee should represent a cross section of the community's population. The committee will be a great asset in starting a program and in getting support for its ongoing development.

You must determine specific functions for the advisory committee. Some examples follow.

Advisory Committee Functions

1. Determine the program's direction and scope.
2. Gather information about local needs and resources.
3. Analyze these needs and resources.
4. Facilitate liaison between school and community.
5. Involve health-service providers.
6. Act as advocates for the program.
7. Assist in evaluating the program through questionnaires and discussion groups.

Because the teacher is the single most important factor in determining the success of a family living and sex education program, it is important to select teachers who are highly motivated, properly trained or willing to be trained, and respected by colleagues, administrators, and parents. Teachers being considered for this program should also be capable of establishing rapport with students and exhibiting sensitivity to pupil concerns.

If you plan to involve all your teachers in sex education, in-service courses should present a variety of approaches and techniques, enriched subject matter, and a diversified range of teaching materials. For training to be effective, it should prepare teachers to implement a program that is responsive to pupil needs and parent concerns.

Training courses could include the following.

- The pooling of different ideas and experiences
- A discussion of varying terminology for body parts and functions
- The evaluation of lessons
- An examination of curriculum materials in family living and sex education
- The viewing of live and/or televised lessons
- The use of specialists (physicians, psychologists, social workers, family life educators, health professionals, etc.)
- Panel discussions
- Supplementary literature
- Field trips to community resources (day-care centers, museums, zoos, etc.)
- Audiovisual materials for viewing, evaluating, and adapting.

School advisory committees, which include parents, should be involved in selecting materials for family living and sex education. All instructional materials should be available for review by parents and other interested community members. Because of the sensitive nature of this instruction, only approved textbooks and audiovisuals should be used in the classroom. If teachers wish to use nonlisted instructional materials, they must consult with you and the advisory committee to determine the appropriateness of the instructional materials.

Let's look at how you can introduce a new sex education program to parents. Look at the sample letter provided. Note how carefully worded this letter is. It begins by emphasizing guidelines, philosophy, and an advisory committee. The third paragraph states, ". . . you, as parents, have the major responsibility." The next paragraph invites parents to come in to learn more. Notice the tear-off sheet at the bottom of the letter. By involving parents from the beginning, you win their cooperation.

10–8 WHAT TO DO ABOUT WEAPONS IN SCHOOL

The presence of a weapon in your school building, playground, or school bus requires immediate action because of its obvious danger to other pupils and staff. In most cases, the youngster has brought the weapon to school for one of three reasons: to impress his or her friends, to provide protection for himself or herself, or to "get even" with someone else.

In most districts, the term *weapon* is defined as including any of the following:

- Firearm, shotgun, rifle, etc.
- Switchblade or gravity knife
- Blackjack, billy club, chucka stick, and metal knuckles
- Explosive, firecracker, bomb, etc.
- Razor, stiletto, kitchen knife
- Air gun, BB gun, etc.

Possession of these weapons is totally proscribed for all staff, pupils, and school visitors. In most places it constitutes grounds for criminal arrest. A police officer should be summoned to make the arrest. School security guards are sometimes authorized to do this.

Mere possession of certain other articles should be forbidden and treated similarly. These may include any sharp, pointed instruments (such as broken glass), chains, chemicals, or imitation pistols.

Punishment for carrying weapons varies. In almost every school district, it involves immediate suspension. Punitive action alone is seldom enough. Use the checklist on page 164 to review other steps to take when a pupil brings a weapon to school.

LETTER ANNOUNCING A NEW SEX EDUCATION PROGRAM

Dear Parent/Guardian:

Our school is developing a program in sex education following the guidelines recommended by the Board of Education. Selected teachers have been trained in the program. The philosophy of the program stresses

— The awareness and importance of family, religious, and moral values in making personal decisions

— Understanding the need for consideration, love, respect, and responsibility in family life

— Recognizing responsibilities to the school, the community, and society.

An advisory committee composed of parents, teachers, and supervisors has been formed for our school. This committee will review the curriculum each year on an ongoing basis. We believe it is important that our pupils begin at an early age to develop a responsible attitude toward family life and an understanding of sexuality as it relates to wholesome living.

We also recognize that you, as parents, have the major responsibility for the formation of desirable attitudes toward family living and sex education. The role of the school is to support your efforts. We have the professional resources to create a comprehensive, sequential, and up-to-date program that will assist your child in developing these important life attitudes. The course contents, books, and audiovisuals for this program have been carefully screened. Every effort is being made to meet the varied needs and interests of our children.

We invite you to join with us in developing our school program. Our first parent workshop

has been scheduled for _____ (date) at _____ (time)

in room _____. You are invited to review our course of study and the instructional materials. You are also welcome at any time to discuss this program with me or with your child's teacher.

Your interest and cooperation, as evidenced by the result of the tear-off below, is very valuable to us. The response form also allows you the option of having your child excused from the program.

Sincerely,

Principal

--- TEAR HERE --

Please return to _____ on or before _____

☐ I would like to have my child excused from the family living/sex education program.

☐ I can ⎫
☐ I cannot ⎭ attend the parent workshop.

☐ I would like to work with the sex education committee.

I would like an appointment to speak with _____

my child's teacher _____ the principal.

Parent/guardian signature _____ Date _____

Weapons Checklist

☐ Have pupils been warned in assembly by you and by teachers about school regulations regarding weapons?

☐ Have parents been told (at PTA meetings and in newsletters) of school policy regarding a weapons incident? Have they been told of this incident? Is there a record of other contacts with this parent?

☐ Has a written report been made about this incident? Include date, time, place, and names of witnesses.

☐ Is there a statement by anyone threatened, menaced, or injured by this pupil?

☐ Does the guidance counselor, school nurse, social worker, or outside agency have any material on this youngster that is pertinent to this offense?

☐ Is the youngster in a special-ed program? Has such a referral been considered?

☐ Has the weapon been given to the police? If not, has it been labeled and stored safely in school?

☐ Have other pupils and staff been told of the resolution of the situation and thus reassured?

☐ What plans are being made for the pupil's return to school after the suspension?

☐ Have you maintained a log of incidents involving weapons, including dates, types, emerging patterns (if any), and disposition?

☐ Have you noted the incident on the pupil's permanent record?

☐ Have you considered transferring the pupil to another class or school?

10–9 HELPING PARENTS COPE WITH RUNAWAYS

Each year, an increasing number of children under age twelve become runaways.

Running away can be a frightening experience—for the child, the parents, and the school. As soon as a child leaves home, he or she becomes vulnerable to drugs, drinking, crime, sexual exploitation, child pornography, and child prostitution. Knowing this, many parents of runaways feel guilty or depressed or even paralyzed by fear.

Although the parents and police are primarily responsible for recovering the child, the school can play a role in preparing parents in case their child ever runs away.

PARENT ALERT: RUNAWAY CHILDREN

There are several ways that parents can be prepared if their child runs away. Here is valuable information to aid in the quick recovery of a runaway:

1. Keep a complete written description of your child, including hair and eye color, height, weight, date of birth, and specific physical attributes.

2. Take color photographs of your child every six months. Head and shoulder portraits from different angles, such as those taken by school photographers, are preferable.

3. Make sure your dentist prepares full dental charts on your child and updates them with each exam. If you move, get a copy of these dental records to keep in your files until you find a new dentist.

4. Find out from your doctor where your child's medical records are located. All permanent scars, birthmarks, broken bones, and medical needs should be recorded.

5. Arrange with your local police department to have your child fingerprinted. The police department will give you the fingerprint card. They will not keep a record of your child's prints.

6. If your child runs away or is missing, inform the police. This step is crucial. The police department's main mission is to find your child. They have resources and personnel that you cannot duplicate on your own. Before calling the police, you may get some support by calling the National Runaway Switchboard, 1-800-621-4000. You may also want to call the following:

1-800-I-AM-LOST	Childfind: Helps find missing children
1-800-HIT-HOME	Youth Development, Inc.: Provides services to runaways and parents
1-800-421-0353	Parents Anonymous: Helps with family problems

When your child is recovered or returns home, make sure to show love and concern for his or her safety—not anger or fear. If you react angrily, your child may feel unwanted and unloved and may run away again.

1. Promptly notify the police, state clearinghouse, or anyone else who may have assisted you.

2. If your child has been away for an extended period of time, get a complete medical examination for the child when he or she returns home, including tests for sexually transmitted diseases.

3. Try to resolve the problems in your family that prompted your child to leave home in the first place. Often, children run away because of problems or stresses in the family, such as divorce, remarriage, alcoholism, or physical or sexual abuse.

4. If you are unable to deal with the family problems effectively, seek the assistance of a trained counselor or professional. Parents can contact the local Department of Social Services, Family Services, or other public or private agencies that help families.

5. It may be necessary for your child to go to a temporary residence or runaway shelter while the family works toward resolving its problems. A trained counselor can help you make this decision.

As principal, you must use discretion in circulating an alert of this kind. Depending on your school population, you may decide to give copies of the Parent Alert from the previous page to all the parents or just to those with pupils at risk. Your guidance counselor may be of great assistance here.

10–10 REPORTING CHILD ABUSE AND NEGLECT

Child abuse is not a new problem. However, the number of reports to child protection agencies is increasing every year. In most states it is mandatory for teachers, principals, and other school personnel to report cases of suspected abuse.

Understandably, teachers are reluctant to call child abuse hot lines or write letters to report cases of maltreatment. Like so many other unpleasant tasks, reporting is passed on to the principal to handle. In many cases, the teachers are not only reluctant to get involved but also are not sure of what to look for in identifying possible indicators of child abuse and neglect.

As part of your in-service training of teachers, you must help your staff members distinguish among physical abuse, physical neglect, sexual abuse, and emotional maltreatment. The physical indicators—bruises, hunger, inadequate clothing—are fairly obvious. The following chart will help teachers recognize behavioral indicators.

BEHAVIORAL INDICATORS OF CHILD ABUSE AND NEGLECT	
Type of Child Abuse or Neglect	**Behavioral Indicators**
Physical abuse	• Wary of adult contacts • Apprehensive when other children cry • Behavioral extremes: aggressiveness or withdrawal • Frightened of parents • Afraid to go home • Reports injury by parents
Physical neglect	• Begging, stealing food • Extended stays at school (early arrival and late departure) • Constant fatigue, listlessness, or falling asleep in class • Alcohol or other drug abuse

	• Delinquency (e.g., thefts)
	• States there is no parent or caretaker at times
Emotional maltreatment	• Habit disorders (sucking, biting, rocking, etc.)
	• Conduct disorders (antisocial, destructive, etc.)
	• Neurotic traits (sleep disorders, inhibition of play)
	• Psychoneurotic reactions (hysteria, obsession, compulsion, phobias, hypochondria)
	• Behavior extremes: compliant, passive, aggressive, demanding
	• Overly adaptive behavior (inappropriate adult or inappropriately infantile)
	• Developmental lags (mental, emotional)
	• Attempted suicide
Sexual abuse	• Unwilling to change for gym or participate in physical education class
	• Withdrawal, fantasy, or infantile behavior
	• Bizarre, sophisticated, or unusual sexual behavior or knowledge
	• Poor peer relationships
	• Delinquent or runaway
	• Reports sexual assault by caretaker

The following referral form will help your staff members think through the situation and will give you the essential data for an agency referral.

POSSIBLE CHILD ABUSE/NEGLECT REFERRAL FORM

1. Child's name: _____ Class _____

Address: _____ Phone: _____

Date of birth: _____ Mother's name _____

(first and last name)

Other children in house?   Number and ages: _____

2. What concerns you about the child?

3. Any other staff members involved with pupil (guidance counselor, nurse, etc.)?

4. Amplify items below (if not mentioned in #2):

   a. General health

   b. Cleanliness

   c. Adequacy of clothing

   d. Vitality

   e. Attendance

   f. Glasses?

   g. Preparation for school (homework, materials, etc.)

   h. Other adults in home, if known

   i. Change in personality

   j. Appears depressed or withdrawn

   k. Other

5. Has child named anyone responsible for the injury or neglect?

There are times when you become aware of a pupil's problem without teacher referral. If child abuse or neglect is suspected, you must report the incident to the proper authorities. You may or may not choose to remain anonymous when you do this. In either case, it is wise to try to prepare the parent for outside help.

To overcome resistance, focus on building trust, developing a caring relationship, and getting the parents to reveal their feelings about their present state of unhappiness and concern for the child and, lastly, what they would like to see changed. Usually, you need not use provocative or judgmental words like *abuse, separation,* or *investigation.* However, in cases in which a trusting relationship is already established, you might discuss realistic consequences and confront the parents in a nonthreatening way.

School administrators often overlook the warning signs of child abuse or neglect for a variety of reasons: lack of knowledge about these signs and undeveloped intervention skills; fear of stigmatizing the parent by discussing maltreatment or "losing the parent"; being overburdened or burned out because of other work tasks; lack of knowledge about supportive community resources; or fear of being assaulted by an offended, angry parent.

It is imperative that you involve another staff member. This can be the school nurse, guidance counselor, social worker, or teacher. Do not assume sole responsibility.

10–11 HELPING PARENTS TO PREVENT SEXUAL ABUSE

You do not want to alarm parents unduly. Children should not be frightened that danger lurks at every corner or made to feel that evil adults are everywhere. However, you do have a responsibility to inform parents of what to look for and to reassure them.

From an early age, children should be taught that their bodies are theirs and theirs alone. They should be told that no one has the right to touch their body in any way that makes them feel uncomfortable or confused. Children who are taught that they have an absolute right to reject an unwanted touch or refuse unwanted displays of affection may be more prepared to resist sexual abuse directed at them. In this respect, children should be trained to follow their instincts: If they feel uncomfortable in a situation or sense that a person is potentially dangerous, they should get away, even at the risk of being thought rude or uncooperative. We have provided a sample bulletin on the next page that you may want to adapt and distribute to parents.

There are patterns of child abuse in some families. You and your guidance counselor may want to make your teachers aware of these profiles.

PARENT ALERT: SEXUAL ABUSE

It is essential that you listen closely to your children and observe them carefully. If your child says that he or she has been "touched" or "hurt," do not dismiss the statement out of hand as an impossibility or a lie. Talk to the child. Ask for details and obtain as much information as you can. Most young children are not sophisticated enough to concoct sexually explicit stories.

A sexually abused child may not volunteer what happened immediately, even if you have a close and loving relationship. For example, victims of sexual abuse may have been sworn to secrecy with promises of gifts or threatened that harm will come to someone they love if they breathe a word of the episode. Parents must watch for tell-tale signs, both physical and emotional, that may indicate sexual molestation.

Be on the lookout for physical signs such as rash, pain, infection, itching, discharge, etc. Also look for behavior signs such as the following:

- Changes in personality (from talkative to withdrawn, from reserved to hyperactive, etc.)
- Reluctance to be left alone with a particular person
- Refusal to return to school or day care
- Refraining from using the bathroom
- Not letting a parent be present while the child dresses or bathes
- Sexual knowledge that is too sophisticated
- An increase in the number and intensity of nightmares
- Insomnia or sleeping too much
- Resistance to being held or kissed
- Loss of desire to play or leave the house
- Withdrawal or depression
- Playing with new toys

Sexual abuse can happen to any child at any time. We must alert our children to the possibility gently but clearly and help them protect themselves to the extent possible.

Remember, all children need healthy, loving relationships. Do not be afraid to hold your children or to hug them. To deny such close contact would deprive them of the warmth that a loving family environment implies.

CHARACTERISTICS OF FAMILIES IN WHICH SEXUAL ABUSE OCCURS

Sexual abuse happens in all types of families, crossing all economic and social lines. The following are characteristics of families in which sexual abuse occurs:

- The families are frequently socially isolated, with poor communication and role confusion among family members.

- There may be a high incidence of alcohol or other drug use, and difficulty managing finances and work responsibilities.

- The parents usually have severe marital difficulties in which they are unable to meet each other's needs and look to the child to meet their needs.

- Family members, including the mother, frequently have difficulty consciously or unconsciously acknowledging the abuse and become "silent partners," with denial of the activity.

- The dynamics of sexual abuse are such that family participants will rarely ask for help. The outside world is perceived as hostile, and needs are met within the isolated family circle.

10–12 REACHING FAMILIES AT RISK THROUGH BOOKS

The old saying that "misery loves company" is relevant to the heartache of children and parents who are dealing with abuse, neglect, or deprivation. While reading a fictionalized version of their own trauma, young people and parents get a great deal of support from the experiences of others.

Make sure your school library has at least one copy of each of these titles. Be on the lookout for new books on this theme. Your local or school librarian can help you. As principal, you must utilize every resource to help your children and families at risk to cope and survive.

Selected Titles for Children at Risk

Anderson, Deborah, and Martha Finn, *Liza's Story: Child Neglect and the Police* (Minneapolis: Dillon Press, 1986). Liza's neglect becomes a matter for the police.

Anderson, Deborah. *Margaret's Story: Sexual Abuse and Going to Court* (Minneapolis: Dillon Press, 1986). A sexually abused girl seeks help.

Clifton, Lucille et al. *Everett Anderson's Goodbye* (Somerset, N.J.: Henry Holt & Co., 1983). Grief over dead father.

Girard, Linda. *Who Is a Stranger and What Should I Do?* (Niles, Ill.: Albert Whitman & Co., 1985). Nonscary, practical advice about dealing with strangers.

Hazen, Barbara Shook. *Tight Times* (New York: Viking Press, Inc., 1979). Mother works, father loses job.

Viorst, Judith. *Alexander and the Terrible, Horrible, No Good, Very Bad Day* (New York: Macmillan, 1976). Boy threatens to run away after an especially trying day.

Walter, Mildred Pitts. *My Mama Needs Me* (New York: Lothrop, Lee & Shepard Books, 1983). New baby gives older child new importance.

Zemach, Margot. *It Could Always Be Worse* (New York: Farrar, Straus, Giroux, Inc., 1976). Yiddish folk tale about making the best of things.

Zindel, Paul. *I Love My Mother* (New York: Harper and Row, 1975). Single mother, only child.

Zolotow, Charlotte. *If It Weren't for You* (New York: Harper and Row, 1987). Sibling jealousy.

Selected Titles for Families at Risk

Greene, Bette. *Summer of My German Soldier* (New York: Dial, 1973). Patty's father beats her.

Hamilton, Virginia. *Sweet Whispers, Brother Rush* (New York: Philomel Books, 1982). Tree struggles to forgive her mother for abusing Tree's mentally disabled brother.

Irwin, Hadley. *Abby, My Love* (New York: Atheneum, 1985). Incest is a family's ugly secret.

Newton, Suzanne. *I Will Call It Georgie's Blues* (New York: Viking Press, Inc., 1983). His father's psychological abuse drives a little boy to a mental breakdown.

Chapter 11

Meeting Your Pupils' Special Needs

The Oakdale School seems to be becoming two separate schools: one for general education in grades K through 6 and another for special education classes. The special-ed teachers feel that the general-ed teachers shun them. The special-ed pupils are rarely included in schoolwide activities. Many special-ed parents have not joined the PTA. The principal is concerned about this.

■SPECIAL EDUCATION HAS not only grown rapidly in many schools, it also appears to be changing constantly. It is hard for many principals to keep up with the latest regulations and adaptations. This is an area in which principals must be careful to protect the rights of pupils and parents. This chapter will help you in referring, mainstreaming, and evaluating special education pupils in your school.

11-1 MAKING YOUR SPECIAL EDUCATION PUPILS COMFORTABLE

As we gain insight into the unique needs of our pupils, the types and populations of special education classes grow. The very name *special ed* seems to alienate some teachers, parents, and pupils. As principal, you must prepare your staff—teachers, aides, lunch room and custodial workers—for the fact that special-ed pupils are an integral part of your school. Your pupils and their parents must be part of this orientation as well.

The following techniques will help you provide a wholesome climate in which all of your pupils and teachers can grow and interact.

- Provide general-ed teachers with speakers and literature on the specific kinds of disabilities your special-ed teachers are providing for: speech, hearing, retardation, physical impairments, language, emotional problems, etc.

- At assembly programs, point out the kinds of school activities in which both pupil populations can participate.

- In the PTA newsletter, include a column on "Special Education News."

- When special-ed pupils are newly admitted, hand their parents an invitation for membership in the PTA.

- Mainstream special-ed classes for lunch, trips, gym, and schoolwide programs, such as concerts, carnivals, book fairs, etc.

- Encourage both groups of teachers to share learning materials and audiovisual equipment and supplies.

- Invite district office personnel to train general-ed teachers in identifying pupils with special needs.

- Make both groups of teachers aware of the evaluation process that makes it possible for a general-ed pupil to become eligible for special-ed placement (testing, social history, parent conferences, etc.).

- Make all your teachers aware of the need for identifying possibly abused or neglected pupils.

- Establish a procedure for referring and reporting pupils with special needs.

- Parents of special-ed pupils should be made aware of the individual education plans (IEPs) that teachers write for their children. They are, in fact, required to attend the IEP meeting and indicate their consent by signing the IEP.

- It is imperative that material relating to child abuse and neglect be kept confidential. Only those professionals who work directly with the child should be informed.

Some teachers are not aware of the criteria for placing pupils in special-ed classes. The referral form beginning on the next page serves the dual purpose of making teachers aware of the criteria and also providing the evaluator with a picture of how the child functions in the classroom.

11–2 WORKING WITH PARENTS ON SPECIAL EDUCATION PLACEMENT

It is important to let parents know, early on, that their child is being considered for special placement. For this task, you need the help of the classroom teacher and guidance counselor. Any conference with the parent should always include the pupil's strengths, whether they be in music, art, physical activities, or social skills. Some principals find it helpful to refer to positive aspects of special education, such as small class size, more individual help, and closer supervision. Preferably, parents will agree to placement. If not, an alternative plan will have to be developed.

After the evaluation process is completed, the parents should get a letter that tells them in clear language what kind of class their child is being placed in. The placement notification letter provided on page 180 covers all the bases.

REFERRAL FOR SPECIAL EDUCATION

To the teacher:

This form is to be used by staff to refer a student for special education. The evaluation will determine whether the student has an educationally handicapping condition and if this student needs special education services. Please complete this form to the best of your ability, and attach any pertinent back-up data.

Student's name _____ DOB _____ SEX _____
　　　　　　　　　　(last)　　　　　　　　　(first)

Address _____ Apt._____

_____ Zip code _____

Student's ethnicity _____ Name of parent/legal guardian _____

Language(s) student speaks _____ Language of parent _____

Home phone _____ Business phone _____ Emergency contact _____

Emergency phone _____ Foster agency address _____

School _____ Grade _____ Class _____ Home school district _____

Check and complete when applicable:

　a) LAB scores: English _____%ile Spanish _____%ile

　b) Is student receiving bilingual education? Yes _____ No _____ Language _____

　c) Is student receiving ESL? Yes _____ No _____ Language _____

　d) Held over? Yes _____ No _____ When _____

Referred by _____ Position _____
　　　　　　(Please print your name)

　　Describe the extent of efforts made by school personnel to maintain the student in general education. Include specific actions and their outcomes (e.g., teaching strategies, guidance intervention, Chapter I Reading, drug prevention program, etc.)

Was parent contacted regarding referral? Yes _____ No _____
Indicate prior contact with parents regarding the student's educational problems (letter, telephone, conferences). Describe outcome of each contact:

Is student or family known to outside agencies? Yes ____ No ____
If yes indicate:

Name of agency	**Contact person**	**Address**	**Phone Number**

Physical Development

The answers to the following section should be based on your personal knowledge, observation, and/or documentation available to you. If you feel that any of the following areas require particular attention in the evaluation process, please indicate and describe the basis for your concern.

How long have you known this student? _____

General health _____

Vision _____

Hearing _____

Speech/language _____

Coordination _____

Mobility _____

Seizures _____

Is student taking medication? Yes ____ No ____ Describe _____

Social Development

1. *Attendance data*

    Days absent this year to date _____

    Has the student been truant within the past year?

    Yes ____ No ____ Date _____

    Was the student suspended within the last two years?

    Yes ____ No ____ Date _____

2. *Behavior:* Has the student exhibited any of the following behavior(s)? (Check all applicable areas.)

    ☐ Leadership and initiative   ☐ Fearfulness

    ☐ Persistance at tasks   ☐ Destructiveness to property

☐ Cooperative and helpful attitude to teachers

☐ Distractability, short attention span

☐ Physical abusiveness

☐ Little responsiveness to classroom activity

☐ Reluctance to attempt new tasks

☐ Frequent crying

☐ Cooperative and helpful attitude to peers

☐ Resistance to teacher's directives

☐ Little or no contact with peers

If the student exhibits inappropriate behavior, *describe* the behavior and indicate specific times of occurrence (e.g., before lunch, during math, after gym, etc.).

How does this student's behavior pattern compare with that of other students in the class or to age/grade peers?

3. *Social interaction:* Indicate the student's response(s) to management approaches. Check all applicable areas:

   a) Student works well

      ☐ on one-to-one basis

      ☐ in small groups

      ☐ in large groups

      ☐ during teacher-directed activity

      ☐ independently

      ☐ in lunch room

   b) Student interacts well with

      ☐ peers

      ☐ younger students

      ☐ adults

   c) Student responds well to

      ☐ praise

      ☐ punishment

      ☐ other (specify)

      ☐ positive reinforcements

      ☐ parent contact

      _____

      _____

4. *Family data*
Describe any events in the student's home or school life that the evaluation team should be aware of (e.g., death in the family).

Academic Development

Note: For students with limited English proficiency, include information about academic functioning in both English and the dominant language.

Current reading level

Date   Test   Result   Teacher estimate

Current math level

Date   Test   Result   Teacher estimate

I believe this student may have an educationally handicapping condition and may need special education services.

Signature of referring person   Date

PLACEMENT NOTIFICATION LETTER

Date: _____

Re: _____
(student's name)

Date of birth: _____

School: _____

Class: _____

Home district: _____

Dear Parent:

    The special education unit has placed your child in a class which reflects the program outline on his/her IEP. Your child has been placed in a class of students who have similar education needs. A description of your child's class follows:

READING RANGE: _____

MATH RANGE: _____

    Because of the range of abilities in this class, the pupils may be grouped on their functional level rather than their age or grade level.

    If you have any questions, please feel free to call me at 555-7890.

Sincerely,

Principal

NOTICE OF IEP UPDATE

Student's name _____

Date of birth _____

Date _____

Dear _____ :

  A meeting has been scheduled to discuss the educational needs of your son/daughter with his/her teacher(s) and/or the person(s) who provide related services. We would like you to join us. We will be making decisions regarding the appropriate educational program and reviewing your son's/daughter's individual education plan (IEP). It is your right to participate fully in updating his/her IEP, and we urge you to come to this meeting.

  An appointment has been scheduled for you to meet with us on:

Date: _____ Time: _____

at _____

Please return the attached form in the enclosed envelope as soon as possible. If you wish to arrange an alternative date, call _____ at _____ as soon as possible. You may bring or send any additional information or documentation. If you are unable to attend a meeting, you may call to arrange a telephone conference.

  If you do not agree with the recommendation of this conference, you have the right to request a meeting with the special education unit. You also have the right to inspect and keep copies of all school files, records, and reports about your son/daughter.

  If we do not hear from you or you choose not to attend, the meeting will take place as scheduled. If there are no substantial changes in your son's/daughter's IEP, you will receive a copy of the updated IEP and final notice of recommendations following the conference. If substantial changes are being considered, you will receive an invitation to participate in a review.

Sincerely,

_____
(Teacher's signature)

cc: School file

At each step of the placement process, parents of special education pupils should be informed and aware. A file should be maintained of all school contacts made with clinicians and teachers. The sample update notice provided will give you an example of the kinds of meetings that encourage parent understanding and cooperation.

11–3 GUIDELINES FOR MAINSTREAMING

Academic mainstreaming involves placing special education students in general education academic classes. Specific academic areas of participation are indicated on a student's IEP.

Mainstreaming is a continual process in daily school operation. Encourage mainstreaming opportunities. In many instances, mainstream teachers will be reluctant to integrate special education pupils into their activities. You must take the initiative. For example, special education pupils can be programmed with general education pupils for physical education, library, assemblies, and lunch.

Federal Law PL 94-142 requires that all students have the right to be educated in the least restrictive environment. That is, to the maximum extent appropriate, special education students must be educated with children who are not handicapped whenever their abilities make it possible.

Nonacademic Mainstreaming

All special education students must participate with general education students for the following activities: lunch, assembly, trips, physical education, and all other schoolwide activities *unless* otherwise indicated on the student's IEP. This exclusion must be accompanied by documentation.

Academic Mainstreaming

Academic mainstreaming requires that, to the extent possible, special education students participate with general education students in academic areas (e.g., reading, math, art, music, typing, computer skills, etc.). The specific subject areas of participation must be indicated on the student's IEP. The provision of all recommended services indicated on a student's IEP is mandated by Federal Law and Commissioner's Regulations.

FACTORS TO CONSIDER BEFORE MAKING MAINSTREAMING RECOMMENDATIONS

1. Student considerations

    A. Strengths and weaknesses of the student

    B. Abilities in specific academic subject areas

    C. Interests, levels of achievement, and motivation

    D. Social and emotional readiness for mainstreaming

        1. An ability to work well with others

        2. An ability to respect the feelings of others

        3. An ability to make needs known in an acceptable manner

        4. An ability to adjust to changes and transitions in the school day

        5. An ability to understand and follow classroom routines

    E. Attainment of proper work habits

        1. An ability to follow directions

        2. An ability to ask for help when appropriate

        3. An ability to begin an assignment on time

        4. An ability to demonstrate adequate attention

        5. An ability to make an effort to complete an assigned task

2. Environmental considerations

    A. Materials and procedures used in the mainstream situation, including textbooks, testing procedures, independent work, etc.

    B. Availability of support systems or ability to design systems that will structure the mainstream experience for success

11–4 IDENTIFYING PUPILS WITH LANGUAGE NEEDS

Your general-ed teachers are likely to have pupils for whom English is a second language or native-born pupils who have problems understanding and using language. The Classroom Language Checklist will help them identify those pupils who may be in need of referral.

CLASSROOM LANGUAGE CHECKLIST

Name of student: _____

Date of birth: _____ Class: _____ Date of review: _____

    Please indicate the frequency of the specified behavior in English and the language other than English by placing the appropriate letter in the corresponding column: A—Always; S—Sometimes; N—Never.

	English	Other Language
I. UNDERSTANDING LANGUAGE		
1. Understands verbal directions		
2. Understands introduction to new information		
3. Understands a story or event		
4. Understands peers		
II. USING LANGUAGE		
1. Uses single words		
2. Uses phrases		
3. Uses single sentences		
4. Uses complex sentences		
5. Answers questions		
6. Asks questions to request information		
7. Converses with teacher		
8. Converses with peers		
9. Describes pictures or experiences		
10. Retells stories		
III. OVERALL		
1. Everyday conversation and classroom discussion is fluent and effortless		
2. Conversation is halting, uses inappropriate words or terms and hesitates while searching for appropriate words		
3. Language used in stressful situations		

11–5 PLANNING SPECIAL EDUCATION MONTH BY MONTH

As principal of a school with special-ed classes, you face many responsibilities through the year. This calendar will help you structure your activities on a month-by-month basis.

Special Education Calendar for Principals

August/September

1. Meet with district placement office staff to review September organization of classes.
2. Review with special education teachers for compliance status, identification of problem areas, and determination of remedial plans.
3. Review and update with staff the school's mainstreaming plan.
4. Establish transportation and problem resolution process with appropriate bus company personnel.
5. Meet with related services personnel (speech, guidance, occupational therapist, physical therapist, etc.) to ensure that appropriate levels of service are being provided to all students mandated for such.
6. Confer with school-based support team members regarding program changes, mainstreaming planning, pending reevaluations, etc.
7. Confer with clinical staff and guidance counselors regarding the school guidance program.
8. Review with teachers:
   - Registers and class organizations
   - Instructional materials and supplies
   - Policy for lesson plans and lesson plan review schedule
   - Availability of appropriate curriculum guides
   - Staff conference plans
   - Teacher and paraprofessional training programs
   - Special programs (social studies fair, science fair, Special Arts Festival, etc.)
   - Vocational assessment project plans
   - Preobservation conference plans
   - "At risk" program with resource room teachers
9. Review the status of resource room students reading at or above grade level and initiate, as appropriate, decertification actions.

October

1. Prepare for phase 2 IEP planning and parent conferences.
2. Review classes for functional level compliance in preparation for parent notification letters.
3. Conduct Language Assessment Battery (LAB) testing of new admissions and eligible students not previously tested.
4. Conduct individual formal and informal observations (ongoing).
5. Initiate requests for teacher trainer assistance (ongoing).
6. Conduct joint visitations with clinical supervisors.

November

1. Observe Teacher Recognition Day.
2. Conduct parent-teacher conferences.
3. Review special education student records.

December

1. Discuss with teachers possible holdovers for special education students in self-contained classes.
2. Conduct joint visitations with clinical supervisors (ongoing).
3. Integrate special education classes into holiday programs.

January

1. Revise functional grouping sheets based on school reorganization.
2. Review the status to date of supervisors' goals and objectives.
3. Prepare the annual review.
4. Identify potential holdovers.

February

1. Conduct the annual review material check and training.
2. Review mainstreaming for the spring.
3. Enter IEP mastery dates and update IEPs.
4. Notify parents of potential holdovers.

March

1. The annual review is in progress.
2. Prepare projects for the Special Arts Festival.
3. Prepare for Special Games and Olympics.
4. Conduct spring LAB testing for all eligible students.
5. Inform staff of staff changes anticipated for September due to retirements, promotions, etc.

April

1. The annual review is completed.
2. Plan for the summer program.
3. Nominate personnel for "Rights of the Handicapped Month" awards.

May

1. Conduct "Rights of the Handicapped Month" activities.
2. Conduct Special Games and Olympics and the Special Arts Festival.
3. Review records for June transfer to junior high school.
4. Conduct standardized testing.
5. Conduct parent meetings on program changes as a result of test performances.
6. Plan the summer program.

June

1. Teachers prepare class profiles.
2. Transfer records to intermediate schools.
3. Plan the summer program.
4. Review performance planning including summaries of the year's performance.
5. Rating recommendations due for special education guidance counselors, speech teachers, and language coordinators.
6. Goals and objectives: End-of-year meeting with the superintendent.
7. Consult with school programming personnel to ensure appropriate mainstreaming opportunities in September based on IEP recommendations.

8. Conduct a material inventory in each classroom.

9. Review the year and plan for next year.

Many principals report that although special education students represent 10 percent of their school population, there are days when they consume 90 percent of their time. This is inevitable, but the satisfaction of seeing handicapped children learning and socializing with other children far outweighs the burden.

11–6 IDENTIFYING GIFTED STUDENTS

Many schools now have programs for gifted students (usually under the umbrella of the special education department). When deciding which pupils should be included in such a program, consider the current teacher's judgment about the pupil's giftedness in addition to standardized test scores. The classroom teacher can best report on the pupil's learning, motivation, creativity, and leadership ability.

Teachers can use the following checklist to rank these qualities. The maximum score possible is 68. Use these tallies to help arrive at proper placement. You will also find the checklist helpful in responding to parents who want to know why their child is not included in the gifted program.

GIFTED STUDENT CHECKLIST

Pupil's name: _____ Class: _____ Date: _____

Teacher: _____ Room: _____

Indicate the degree to which you have noted or observed these characteristics:
1—Never   2—Occasionally   3—Often   4—Almost always

Learning characteristics:

1.1 Has unusually advanced vocabulary

1.2 Possesses a large storehouse of information

1.3 Reads a great deal on his/her own

1.4 Has quick mastery and recall of factual information

1.5 Reasons things out; sees logical answers

Motivational characteristics

2.1 Needs little external motivation to follow through

2.2 Becomes absorbed and truly involved in certain topics

2.3 Works independently; requires little direction

2.4 Longer attention and concentration span than peers

Creativity characteristics

3.1 Displays a great deal of curiosity about many things

3.2 Generates a large number of ideas or solutions to problems

3.3 Displays a good deal of intellectual playfulness; fantasizes; imagines

3.4 Displays original thinking; offers unusual, clever, or unique responses

Leadership characteristics

4.1 Carries responsibilities well; finishes tasks

4.2 Is self-confident with peers and adults

4.3 Adapts readily to new situations; is flexible

4.4 Generally directs the activity in which he/she is involved

Total: _____

Please add any comments that you feel will give additional insight into this child's abilities:

Chapter 12

Enhancing Your School's Guidance Program

Lucille P. does not have a guidance counselor at her K–6 elementary school. But she would like to make her classroom teachers aware of what they can do to meet the needs of the pupils in this large, multicultural school. She respects the teaching ability of her staff but wants them to take a more active role in meeting the guidance needs of pupils and their parents. She'd like to get their input in referring and placing pupils. She would also like to help prepare her pupils for middle school and career choices.

■MORE THAN ANY other program, guidance varies widely from school to school. Some schools are fortunate enough to have full-time counselors as well as clinical support from social workers and school psychologists. Many schools have part-time counselors. Many more have no counselor, so the principal performs the guidance services.

This chapter provides many examples of guidance activities for you and your teachers. Using these strategies, you and your staff can provide guidance services for your pupils.

Let's begin by seeing how you can work with the classroom teacher to find out more about each pupil.

12–1 GIVING TEACHERS THE GUIDANCE INFORMATION THEY NEED

There are many guidance tools that you can make available to your classroom teachers. Most of them are already in your school, but your teachers may not be aware of them. Place this valuable guidance information at your classroom teachers' fingertips.

Guidance Information List

1. *Previous teachers.* While teachers want to draw their own conclusions, it is helpful to read the evaluations of previous teachers or the records of previous schools attended. This is often stored in the office where the current teacher can't get at it.

2. *Test scores.* Performance on standardized tests should be available to the current teacher. Offer your help in interpreting this data for use in grouping pupils and organizing for instruction.

3. *Cumulative record cards.* Give teachers help in culling information from the cumulative record cards of their pupils.

4. *Attendance patterns.* Make teachers aware of the mobility of some of their pupils among schools. Point out patterns of absence and lateness.

5. *Other siblings in school.* Make teachers aware of other siblings in the school—especially if they have another last name and may therefore escape a teacher's notice. The sharing of family information and consolidated attempts to get parents to school is one positive result of such exchanges.

6. *Principal or counselor files.* If you have a record of parent contacts, on the phone, in person, or through the mail, share it with the teacher if it is not confidential material.

7. *Past referrals.* If a pupil has been referred to an agency in the past, it may be helpful for the current teacher to have some of this information.

8. *Health or medical records.* The nurse or other health professional should share with the teacher information about illnesses, vision or hearing data, and so on.

9. *Discipline or suspense history.* If the pupil has been involved with such action in the past, the current teacher might benefit from this information, which will alert him or her for danger signs.

10. *Observations of others.* The classroom teacher will benefit from observations of other school staff—lunch room aides, bus drivers, special-ed teachers, etc. Set up a means of sharing such observations.

Now that your teachers know a little more about their pupils, let's see how they can refer pupils within the building.

12–2 INITIATING A LADDER OF REFERRAL

Teachers must have a clear idea of which guidance responsibilities you have retained and which you have delegated to the assistant principal, teacher leader, counselor, social worker, nurse, or other staff members.

A simple technique is to establish in writing a ladder of referral and distribute it to every staff member. Like any ladder, this device is made up of several rungs, or steps, in the guidance process. The ladder of referral prevents overlapping functions and minimizes duplication of services. Let's look at how it works in one school of 500 pupils where there is a part-time counselor and a part-time nurse in addition to twenty teachers and a full-time principal.

PS 3 Ladder of Referral

Step 1. All teachers complete the top portion of a simple referral form (provided) and place it in the principal's mailbox.

Step 2. Within two days, the principal reviews the referral and takes action as indicated by one of five entries on the lower portion of the referral form. A copy is given to the teacher.

Step 3. The principal may decide to see the pupil, especially if disciplinary action is indicated. The pupil may be referred to the nurse if a

REFERRAL FOR GUIDANCE

Please attach all anecdotal information.

_____   _____
Name of pupil   Class

is referred for the following:

                          _____   _____
                          Name of teacher   Date

Tear-off stub

Regarding

_____   _____
Name of pupil   Official class

whom you referred on _____, the following action
                                    (date)

has been taken:

    Pupil was interviewed on _____ by

    Pupil will be seen on _____ by

    Pupil was observed in class on _____ by

    Pupil's parents were seen on _____ by

    Additional information is needed about _____

_____

Please indicate when we can confer regarding this pupil:

_____   _____
        Date   Period

Thank you for your cooperation.

                          _____
                                    Principal/Counselor

                          _____
                                            Date

health, vision, or hearing problem is suspected. If an agency involvement is indicated or counseling is sought, the pupil will be referred to the counselor.

Step 4. The principal keeps a photocopy of the teacher's referral form and periodically checks to see if the pupil has had follow up and if the teacher has been involved.

Step 5. After being seen by one staff member, the pupil may then be referred to another. For example, after meeting with the child and parents, the principal may refer the family to the nurse for a clinic appointment. A child seen by the counselor may be referred to the principal for a possible change of class.

The value of a structured ladder of referral is that a simple, non-threatening paper trail is maintained and the teacher is involved and kept apprised of what's going on.

12–3 INVOLVING TEACHERS IN REFERRAL AND PLACEMENT

Teachers should feel free to discuss a pupil informally with you without needing to fill out a form first. Just being able to talk to another professional about a pupil may give the teacher needed support and insight.

At other times it may be necessary to have some information on paper so you (or counselor, if available) can study the pupil and make a recommendation. There are times when the youngster will do things in class that the teacher feels are disruptive or give other clues to the pupil's lack of adjustment. The "Referral for Guidance" form provided in the previous section of this chapter works well for this. It does not take the teacher a great deal of time to complete it, but it gives you or a counselor some factual material.

Frequently, a teacher will note a series of incidents that form a pattern. Instead of ignoring them or trying to commit them to memory, recording incidents on an "Anecdotal Record Form" (provided) will help the teacher focus on a particular child's behaviors. Each entry will take only a minute to record. However, when several entries are made and studied, a significant pattern may be revealed.

After the referral is made and the pupil is being seen by the counselor, principal, social worker, or outside agency, there is still a need for periodic teacher input. We have included a "Classroom Teacher's Report on Pupil Progress" that helps provide an ongoing dialogue between the classroom teacher and you or a counselor.

Give the classroom teacher a role in placing pupils within the school. Of course, you should interview all new entrants. If you are aware that a pupil with special needs is entering the school, make every effort to inter-

ANECDOTAL RECORD FORM

Pupil: _____ Class: _____ Teacher: _____ School year: _____

Date	Time	Class activity	Description of incident	Teacher comment	Initials

CLASSROOM TEACHER'S REPORT ON PUPIL PROGRESS

Pupil's name: _____ Class: _____ Date: _____

Parents' name: _____ Teacher's name: _____

Date of last report: _____

Since the last report, how has the pupil performed?

	Better	Same	Worse	Comments
Attendance				
Homework				
Lateness				
Class work				
Attitude				
Appearance				
Class tests				
Conduct				

Describe any home contact that has been made:

Describe any other staff contact that has been made:

What areas would you like to see explored with the pupil?

What areas would you like to see explored with the parent(s)?

Additional comments:

_____
Initials

view the parent and pupil before placement. It's also a good idea to confer with the pupil's prospective teacher. Consider the personality of the teacher and the type of class before placing the child. Seek the teacher's input.

Consult with the teachers concerned when class transfers are indicated. The teachers' knowledge of each class's group dynamics, organization, and specific children equips them to make recommendations regarding appropriate placement.

There are times when a school loses the services of its counselor for budgetary reasons, or it may never have had one. In these cases, you may want to establish a guidance committee of experienced teachers from different grade levels. These people will not have as much time available as a full-time counselor, but they can advise you on guidance matters. You will have to perform many of the functions of a counselor yourself.

If you assume counseling duties, you can use all the help you can get. Sometimes a teacher will send a child to your office without giving you much information about the pupil. Trying to get the pupil to speak can be difficult without some kind of "ice breaker." A Denver principal uses a "Feeling Checklist" (provided here) for the pupil to work on at their first meeting. When completed, this checklist gives the principal a springboard for talking things over with the youngster.

12–4 HELPING TEACHERS GET THE MOST OUT OF PARENT CONTACTS

Whether or not your school has a guidance counselor, encourage your classroom teachers to initiate contacts with parents. We use the term *contact* because this communication can take many forms:

- An actual parent-teacher conference in school. This may be at a formalized Open School Week or on an as-needed basis before or after school or during the teacher's unassigned time.

- A phone call home. In some instances, the teacher may give a parent his or her phone number and encourage the parent to call.

- Notes home with a request that the parent acknowledge receipt of the note and return with a reply or request for an appointment.

- Use of the pupil's notebook as a vehicle for short messages back and forth between teacher and parent.

In some cases, the contact will be hard to establish. The parent may not have a telephone, may be reluctant to talk to the teacher, or may appear defensive. Encourage your teachers to pursue these hard-to-reach parents. Frequently they are the ones for whom it is most important that a home-school dialogue be established.

FEELINGS CHECKLIST

Name _____ Class _____ Date _____

	Yes	No	Sometimes
1. I wish I had more friends.			
2. I worry about the way I look.			
3. I get tired easily.			
4. I often feel lonely when I am with people.			
5. I never get angry.			
6. It is hard for me to keep my mind on anything.			
7. My feelings are easily hurt.			
8. I often say things I shouldn't.			
9. I become nervous when someone watches me work.			
10. It is hard for me to keep my mind on anything.			
11. I am secretly afraid of many things.			
12. I have trouble making up my mind.			
13. I feel I have to be the best in everything.			
14. I like everyone I know.			
15. I worry about how I am doing in school.			
16. At times I feel like shouting.			
17. I get angry very easily.			
18. Other children are happier than I.			
19. I wish I could be very far from here.			
20. I get nervous when things don't go the right way for me.			
21. I worry a lot.			
22. I feel that others don't like the way I do things.			
23. I worry about what my parents will say to me.			
24. I am always good to others.			
25. I always am well behaved.			
26. I worry about doing the right things.			
27. It's hard for me to fall asleep at night.			
28. I often do things I wish I had never done.			
29. I get headaches frequently.			
30. I often worry about what could happen to my parents.			

You can show your teachers how important such contacts are by taking the lead and calling a hard-to-reach parent at work or by calling another family member and leaving a message. Once you have made the initial contact, it's best that you let the teacher handle the follow-up. Some principals get to school early so they can call parents before they leave for work.

Train your teachers to be active listeners. Point out the importance of observing parents and not just listening to their words. Help teachers read between the lines by making mental notes of their general impressions as the parents speak.

Listening With the Inner Ear

1. What is the parents' attitude toward the school?
2. How much, if any, pressure is placed on the child to do well?
3. Is there a close or remote family relationship?
4. What is the emotional tone of the home?
5. What are the parents' values toward cultural matters?
6. What is regarded as good and bad behavior?

Encourage your teachers to keep these points in mind as they listen to and observe parents. Also emphasize the two most important points when interviewing a parent, in person or on the phone: starting with a positive statement and closing when both parties begin to repeat themselves.

There is a definite positive correlation between teachers who make frequent contact with parents and teachers who are successful with their pupils.

Now let's see how your teachers can integrate guidance into their daily teaching.

12–5 USING THE CURRICULUM AS A GUIDANCE TOOL

You should recognize the teacher as the most important member of the guidance team. It is the teacher who sees the child every day, sees the child as a member of the total class constellation, and has access to the parents most frequently.

If there is a counselor assigned to your school, teachers should view him or her as a coworker assigned to provide services rather than an outside expert or member of the administration. The counselor must be aware of the teacher's contribution to the overall guidance program.

You can accomplish this by involving the classroom teacher in these ways:

1. Share with the classroom teacher as much information as possible (for example, family changes, agency involvement, former school experiences).
2. Notify teachers promptly about action taken in cases they have referred, such as testing for special education placement.
3. Invite teachers to be part of case conferences with parents and clinical personnel. Utilize their perceptions of the child's functioning in the classroom.
4. Involve teachers in curriculum activities that have a guidance component. They frequently provide insight and clues about pupils' feelings and concerns.

The following inventory of classroom guidance activities contains six examples of teacher-directed or counselor-directed activities that your teachers can adapt and use. Many teachers already use them as part of their curriculum, but they should be aware of the opportunities each presents for learning about each child's guidance needs.

Inventory of Classroom Guidance Activities

1. Art

Materials: Markers, crayons, paints, clay

Rationale: Work with manipulative or representational materials gives the pupil an opportunity for emotional release, fosters creativity, furnishes feelings of satisfaction, and gives the teacher and counselor a base for deeper verbal exploration.

2. Puppetry

Materials: A variety of pupil-made or commercial puppets. These can be finger puppets or stick figures.

Rationale: Puppetry is a form of dramatic play that is ideally suited for the shy, withdrawn pupil, the language-limited pupil, and for pupils with low self-esteem who are fearful of exposing their own attitudes and emotions. The pupil feels safe in acting out a variety of feelings.

3. Autobiography

Materials: Biographical material on well-known personalities as well as original stories based on the lives of pupils

Rationale: Reading each other's stories helps pupils recognize the similarities and differences among classmates. It may serve as an introduction to new class members. It provides the teacher with each child's perception of self, family, and outside world.

4. Play activities

Materials: Family figures, dolls, blocks, toys, musical instruments

Rationale: Play activities allow the pupil to express feelings and relationships in an accepting atmosphere. Pupils express their feelings and explore their own role in their world.

5. Poetry

Materials: Poems (published and original)

Rationale: Poetry provides a socially acceptable outlet for expressing deep feelings and ideas. It enhances self-expression. Pupils delight in its sounds and rhythms as well as its imagery and the emotions it arouses.

6. Sentence completion

Materials: Duplicated sheets that include sentence starters, such as

I feel happy when . . .

I am sad when . . .

I wish I could . . .

Someday I want to . . .

My best time was when . . .

The worst day in my life was when . . .

I often dream about . . .

Rationale: This device strengthens teacher/counselor insights regarding pupils. Through spontaneous completion of sentences, pupils express their innermost thoughts and feelings.

12–6 SMOOTHING THE TRANSITION OUT OF ELEMENTARY SCHOOL

You are a key factor in making the transitions between grades and schools smooth and free of tension. The information which the elementary school transmits to the middle school or junior high school will aid in determining class placement that will develop pupils' talents and potential and overcome any weaknesses. The "Profile Sheet" (sample provided) can help this process.

Beyond merely transmitting record cards, there is much you can do to defuse the fears of pupils and parents concerning the middle school or junior high school. Some typical student fears include the following:

- Getting lost while traveling to school or not being able to find their way in school buildings

- Finding themselves in unfamiliar surroundings—traveling far from home, being separated from friends, and having classmates from different communities

- Having to enter into new social and personal relationships—not knowing any adults in the school who can help them, feeling dwarfed next to upper-grade students, having to compete with pupils from other schools, and having to relate to teachers or supervisors who do not know them

- Having to learn new rules related to behavior in the halls, staircases, assembly, and lunch room

- Not knowing the school staff or to whom to turn for particular problems

- Overcoming anxiety about increased homework assignments and the varied requirements of different teachers.

Parents also may feel apprehensive when their children are ready to enter the middle school or junior high. It was easy to know their children's teachers in the elementary school, but the new school is so much larger, and there are so many more teachers. Parents may feel that they and their children will be lost in this strange, new environment.

In addition to dealing with these concerns, there is much you can do to smooth the transition. The following suggestions will prove helpful.

Practical Suggestions for School Transition

1. Arrange for the fifth (or sixth) grade to visit the middle school (or junior high). Suggest that the school have pupil guides who can usher small groups around the building. Encourage the school counselor to

PROFILE SHEET

© 1992 by Prentice Hall, Inc.

CONFIDENTIAL (FOR TEACHERS' USE ONLY)		Class	Room	Date	NAME OF SCHOOL TEACHER							CLASS DATA FORM
NAME				Date of birth	READING		ARITHMETIC		ESL	Days absent	Eye-glasses	REMARKS Health data, talents, personality data, speech improvement, etc.
Last	First				Score	Date	Score	Date				

greet the prospective pupils and distribute sample materials, such as school newspapers, literary magazines, and school handbooks, for additional insight.

2. Set up a visit of student representatives from the middle school or junior high to visit and speak to the pupils and parents in the elementary school. Encourage them to bring color slides or a videotape of school events and activities.

3. Suggest that the parents of the final elementary school grade be invited for an evening meeting in the middle school or junior high.

4. Prepare a profile sheet with the help of the final grade teachers for use by the middle school or junior high in programming. Encourage the teachers to write a remark for each pupil. This data and additional comments will be helpful to the new school and teachers.

5. Include a confidential file on those pupils whom you have targeted as needing additional help. These can be pupils you have seen individually, potential school dropouts, truants, suspected substance abusers, children from addicted families, underachievers, gifted and talented pupils, etc. Hand deliver these materials to the counselor.

6. On the "Profile Sheet," include a place for elementary school teachers to indicate which pupils are new to the country or need additional language help because they are non-English-speaking. We have labeled that column "ESL." Also, let the new school know which pupils should wear glasses or in some other way have special needs.

12–7 PREPARING PUPILS FOR THE WORLD OF WORK

You have a responsibility to develop a career education program. Information on the working world increases a pupil's feeling of security, encourages inborn curiosity, and broadens occupational horizons. Knowledge of careers helps pupils develop wholesome attitudes toward all useful work and realize the importance of completing their education.

Some schools sponsor a career day in which members of the community come to the school to discuss their chosen occupation. Whenever possible, parents of pupils are encouraged to participate. This event requires a great deal of preparation on your part: setting the date and place, inviting the career models, scheduling the classes, etc. The classroom teachers must prepare the pupils to participate in this kind of activity. They must discuss with pupils the kinds of questions to ask and the requirements of each career, and they must plan follow-up activities.

A less formal approach to careers is the field trip. Field trips provide an opportunity for students to see people at work in various kinds of public and private enterprises, to learn specific job information, to build occupational awareness, to broaden interests and experiences, to raise aspirational levels, and to meet successful role models.

Before the trip, discuss with teachers and pupils appropriate dress and behavior, trace the route to be traveled, and decide what they want to see and what they want to learn. In cooperation with the trip sponsor, allow time after the tour for pupils to question a representative of the company or agency.

After the trip, evaluate the experience with pupils. You might ask them to complete a questionnaire such as the one provided. Focus your discussion on pupil observations and reactions to types of jobs, working conditions, number and kind of people employed, and general atmosphere of the place.

You or the teacher can ask pupils to make use of the information they learned and the materials they received on the trip in the following ways:

- Prepare a bulletin board.
- Set up a library display.
- Start an occupational scrapbook.
- Draw a chart showing interconnecting jobs.
- Prepare an assembly program.
- Write an account of the trip for the school newspaper.
- Report to their classmates.
- Examine the high school directory for courses that prepare for the occupations seen.
- Examine college catalogues to find programs related to occupations seen.
- Role-play interviews for jobs seen.

As a result of studying occupations, pupils should understand why people work, the interdependence of workers, the changing role of women in society, and the relationship of personal qualifications to job requirements.

12–8 EVALUATING YOUR GUIDANCE PROGRAM

Unlike reading or math achievement levels, there is no objective tool for evaluating your guidance program. Yet because of the time and energy invested in guidance services, you must make an effort to determine if you and your staff are meeting your goals and objectives. The following questionnaire will help you do this.

FIELD TRIP QUESTION SHEET

Name _____ Class _____ Date _____

1. Where did we go? _____

2. How did we get there? _____

3. What were we looking for? _____

   _____

4. What did we do when we got there? _____

   _____

   _____

5. What did we see? _____

   _____

6. What did you find most interesting? _____

   _____

   _____

7. What were the people doing? _____

   _____

8. List the different jobs you saw people doing. _____

   _____

   _____

9. Which job did you find the most interesting? _____

   _____

10. How could you prepare for such a job? _____

    _____

    _____

11. How could this trip have been more interesting? _____

    _____

    _____

12. Where would you want to go next time? _____

    _____

Classroom Teacher Questionnaire

1. How do we identify children with special needs?
2. Are at-risk children identified early enough?
3. How are we accommodating these needs?
4. To what extent are we utilizing the classroom teacher in the guidance process?
5. Which areas of our program need revision?
6. Have parents been informed of the purposes of our guidance program?
7. To what extent has the program been shaped by parental views?
8. Have any potential problems been prevented through guidance?
9. How are we making guidance a team approach?
10. What in-service training has been made available to staff members in the area of guidance?
11. How is guidance in evidence in the curriculum?
12. What evidence do we have, if any, that our pupils are becoming more self-directed?

Your staff's candid opinions in response to these questions, and others you may include, will greatly affect the outcome of your guidance program. For example, in response to question 4, some teachers may indicate that they have not been sufficiently involved. If so, make efforts to include these teachers more directly. In light of responses to question 10, you may want to include more staff development programs in the area of guidance.

The overall state of the school climate, including pupil attendance, behavior, attentiveness, involvement, and parent interest, serves as a barometer of the success of your total guidance program.

If you are lucky enough to have a full-time counselor, you will be able to delegate many guidance responsibilities to the counselor. If the counselor works only part time, or if there is no counselor, you will have to handle the activities outlined in this chapter yourself. But principals have always had to assume a guidance function providing for pupils' personal, social, educational, and vocational needs. Your guidance counselor will be looking to you for a sense of priorities. You are the head of the guidance program in your school. Assume the role with the same professional spirit that characterizes all you do.

Chapter 13

Improving Scheduling and Time Management

Phillip G. has been a principal for seven years. He maintains a "tight ship"—his teachers and pupils respect his leadership and recognize his authority. The parents are grateful to Mr. G. for "turning their school around" by improving pupil attendance and reducing pupil misbehavior.

The major problem that perplexes Phillip is his inability to get things done on time. Whenever you ask him how he is doing, he answers, "Busy, busy, busy. Got to run." He always has a piece of paper in his hand, and it appears that he's accomplishing quite a bit. But he's really running around doing a lot of small chores, all easy and nonthreatening. The teacher evaluation report that was due yesterday is still sitting under a stack of phone messages.

Phillip would like to improve his time management skills.

■WE ALL HAVE the same number of hours in the day, yet some of us seem to get so much more done. One of the major frustrations of principals who have learned to manage their own time well is that their staff members don't seem concerned about scheduling themselves.

13–1 DEALING WITH PROCRASTINATING TEACHERS

Every school has at least one Scarlett O'Hara who says of her problems, "I won't think about it now . . . I'll think about it tomorrow." You're fortunate if you have only one such teacher. Occasional procrastination or ignoring a schedule might have little effect, but when you multiply this by many teachers or by a few teachers on many occasions, havoc will reign.

To discourage procrastination, you have to start with yourself and lead by example. Assuming you've taken steps to eliminate such behavior in yourself, what can you do to get your teachers and other staff members moving?

Some Common Solutions for Procrastination Problems

1. *Define the problem.* For example, let teachers know why they must forward end-term records to the new teacher by a certain date. Point out the consequences of their delay. Be specific in requesting promptness.

2. *List priorities and goals.* Spell these out at staff meetings and provide them in written form as conference notes. Cooperatively arrive at goals and objectives for the school. Point out to teachers the order of importance of each task assigned.

3. *Set reasonable deadlines.* Don't encourage teachers to throw up their hands in disbelief by setting an impossible schedule. Keep in mind the amount of time realistically needed, anticipating possible crises and obstacles. Give them the deadline in writing.

4. *Divide work into manageable units.* Sometimes teachers procrastinate because a task is so large that it appears overwhelming. Break a reading improvement project into pieces, and treat each piece as a smaller part of a larger project (e.g., determining the goals of phonics instruction as part of the total reading program, instead of designing all of it at once).

5. *Offer assistance.* If a teacher seems bogged down by a particular aspect of the total project, you may have to offer some back-up help. For instance, a teacher who has not been able to get pupils to select books for their book reports may need the help of the school librarian.

6. *Get feedback.* During a major undertaking, such as the selection of textbooks, keep in touch with the committee. These exchanges can reinforce the importance of the project and allow you to foresee and possibly forestall potential mishaps.

7. *Meet privately.* If a teacher chronically procrastinates, hold a heart-to-heart discussion. Perhaps there are family or personal problems. Some advice from you or an appropriate referral may bring about an improvement. If the teacher is bored or unchallenged, a change of grade next year or some added responsibility may help.

8. *Praise and reward sincerely.* When a project is completed or a deadline is met, write a note thanking the teachers who brought it about. Praise them publicly as well. Reward exceptional workers with some free time. This will help motivate the sloths for next time.

13–2 ACHIEVING YOUR OBJECTIVES—ON TIME

Why is it that some principals seem to accomplish more than others? Do they have some deep, dark secret or elusive talents that enable them to get things done and to follow objectives through to successful conclusion? Not at all. The more effective principals have learned how to use a few basic steps to help them get things done.

The starting point of achieving objectives is knowing what you want to accomplish before you do anything. Not thinking a problem through at the beginning leads to false starts and wasted effort. Before you take any action, you should have

- A clear understanding of the end result you want to accomplish (e.g., improved problem-solving math skills)
- An outline of the steps you'll have to take to achieve this result (e.g., ordering materials, teacher meetings, testing)
- A realistic timetable for completion of the task (e.g., September—ordering, October—staff training, May—evaluation)

Steps to Improve Time Management

1. Return phone calls the same day you receive them. Make this a priority. Set aside a time period each afternoon for answering phone calls.

2. Do disagreeable chores first. Get them out of the way so you can savor and enjoy the activities of the day that you do enjoy.

3. Talk through with others some of the reports you have to write. By talking things over and getting a teacher's or other staff member's thoughts on the subject, you reduce the size and complexity of the undertaking.

4. Keep a single index card in your pocket or handbag that lists steps toward your objective. Cross off each step as you accomplish it. This will give you a sense of satisfaction and will remind you of steps that still have to be taken. "Forgetting" to take a step is the ultimate in procrastination.

5. Keep a monthly calendar of reports and projects that are called for at the same time each year. Anticipating the annual science fair a few weeks ahead of time is better than scrambling around the last minute to run one hastily so you can supply the central office with the name of a winner.

The opposite of procrastination is initiative. An important factor in initiative is imagination. Don't be afraid to let your mind wander into strange places and keep it open to ideas not generally accepted. No better system or method will ever be invented unless you have enough imagination to realize the problem, see that a better way is possible, and devise a new method. Then get going on it and see it through to completion.

13–3 MANAGING YOUR TIME BETTER

How often have you said to yourself, "I don't know where the time goes"? The first step in effectively managing time is to find the answer to that question—just how am I spending my time? Until you make an effort to find out how you spend your time, there's little likelihood that you will disturb yourself sufficiently to take corrective action. As in the solving of any other problem, you must first have the facts.

It takes time to save time. But it is worth the effort to determine how you are spending the hours of your day. This must be done before you can help those you supervise to save their time. The "Personal Time Analysis" chart (provided here) can make this task easier. A precise time study isn't necessary. But by using a check mark for each ten minutes, you can get a fairly accurate picture of how you spend most of your time.

For example, if you spent a full hour between 9:00 A.M. and 10:00 A.M. at a meeting, in each of the 9:00 and 9:30 squares under "Meetings" you would put three check marks, one for each ten-minute interval. It takes only about a minute to mark the sheet for the previous hour or two. You will have to estimate how much time you spend on the phone or talking to pupils, of course. No one else will ever see the analysis unless you choose to show it. The same sheet can be used for the entire week, or individual

PERSONAL TIME ANALYSIS

TIME	Meetings	Personal contact	Scheduling	Checking building	Planning	Paperwork	Visiting classrooms	Parent interviews	PTA	Pupil interviews	With secretary	District office	Community contacts	Guidance/ psychologist	Miscellaneous
8:30															
9:00															
9:30															
10:00															
10:30															
11:00															
11:30															
12:00															
12:30															
1:00															
1:30															
2:00															
2:30															
3:00															
3:30															
4:00															

sheets can be used each day. Generally, one sheet for the full week carries a greater impact at week's end.

The column headings are for purposes of illustration only. You will have to determine which best cover your own activities. After a day or two, you might want to modify the headings. For example, if your job involves large amounts of time in personal contact, you might want to break that down into types of contacts—personal problems, grievances, discipline cases, etc.

By the end of two weeks, you will have a good idea of where your time is going. Many principals, for example, find that they spend literally no time in planning.

Case Study

Mrs. S. is a very energetic person. She spent just three years in the classroom before being assigned principal of an elementary school in a small city. She likes to get around her building and spends a minimum amount of time in her office. This is good since her predecessor was completely deskbound and never visited classrooms that were not on the main floor.

Mrs. S. is proud that she does not go directly to her office when she reports to work in the morning. Usually she tours the quiet building, checking halls and classrooms, and then goes to the school yard to supervise the line-up of pupils as they get off the buses. Some mornings she goes directly to the lunch room to see what the cook is preparing for breakfast and lunch. After the nine o'clock bell, she again visits every classroom to be sure that each class has gotten off to a smooth start. Discipline problems have greatly diminished. The halls are quiet, and teachers are on their toes. Any requests for supplies or books are filled immediately. Any problems with pupils or parents are solved on the spot.

The curriculum has remained unchanged. Teachers' lesson plans are not reviewed. Mrs. S. prefers to drop in unannounced to see lessons being taught. Telephone messages are seldom read, and calls frequently are not returned. Teachers follow the textbooks they are using, page by page. There are no plans for adapting materials to meet the needs of individual pupils or the school as a whole. Goals and objectives have not been set. There are no specific strategies or tasks for special personnel to follow. Every day moves from one minor crisis to another.

The "Personal Time Analysis" did help this Michigan principal—she actually told us so. Mrs. S. began to look at the columns that had few, if any, checks. This brought some of her weaknesses to her attention, and she began to remediate them. By answering her phone messages and devoting time to planning and scheduling, she found less time for unannounced classroom visits. Her teachers appreciated this and applauded the "new" Mrs. S

Actually, Mrs. S. later developed a refinement of this plan, which she shared with us. She found that each Friday afternoon, after everyone had left, was an ideal time to look at the next week. She developed another form to project some of the tasks that she wanted to accomplish—jobs that until now she had put off until she had more time. Her chart, the "Personal Planning Sheet" (provided here), left a wide column for comments. Some sample entries: help Teacher A. with class play, prepare for American Education Week, call a grade 4 conference on social studies. As she listed each activity, she put an X in the appropriate column—Monday A.M., Wednesday P.M., etc. Rather than trying to do everything tomorrow, she would force herself to evaluate activities, set priorities, and schedule each activity when it wouldn't be crowded by a dozen others. During the week, as she completed a job, she put a circle around the X. If she didn't get to it, she used the "Comments" column to give the reason and to reschedule the job.

The advantage of this kind of planning is that the explanations or alibis for not accomplishing the job are made only to oneself. When you get tired of explaining, you usually discipline yourself to get the job done by setting aside less important things.

Benefit from the experiences of Mrs. S. Put the time analysis and planning sheets to work for you. If you try it for two weeks, we're sure you will see a much better utilization of your time and energy—two precious commodities.

PERSONAL PLANNING SHEET

Week of _____

Activity	Mon. A.M./P.M.	Tues. A.M./P.M.	Wed. A.M./P.M.	Thurs. A.M./P.M.	Fri. A.M./P.M.	Comments

13–4 DO'S AND DON'TS FOR SCHEDULING MEETINGS

"Next Monday is the November staff meeting . . . I can hardly wait." That was the sarcastic remark of a fifth-grade teacher who was not looking forward to another after-school faculty meeting.

There are so many central office directives and other memoranda that you want to share with your teachers. You also have so many things you would like to tell them. Monthly staff or faculty meetings seem like the best way to do this. Perhaps after-school meetings *are* the best way. But before you schedule another meeting of any kind, look over the following guidelines.

Do's and Don'ts for Scheduling Meetings

1. *Do* call a meeting when a meeting is the best way to achieve your objective. Consider your alternatives: sending a memo to each teacher, conferring with small groups of teachers, or posting central office directives on the faculty bulletin board.

2. *Do* have an objective in mind when you call a meeting. Write out your goal in one sentence. If you can't reduce it to a simple sentence, you probably won't be able to convey it to your staff at the meeting. What will your role be at the meeting? What do you want to achieve as a result of the meeting? How can you tell if you achieved your objective?

3. *Don't* hold meetings on a routine basis. They become tedious and wasteful. Often you are forced to create situations to discuss after routine matters are concluded.

4. *Do* include others in the presentation. The teachers do not want to hear you lecture them for forty-five minutes. Include staff members in writing the agenda and in presenting it to the staff.

5. *Do* prepare for the meeting. In addition to knowing what you are going to say, prepare by asking and answering these questions: Who is likely to favor your objective? Why? Who is likely to oppose it? Why? How did we do this in the past? How should we do it now? Is a change necessary?

6. *Don't* have all meetings at the same time. Consider having a staff meeting before the school day begins. Try having a lunch-time meeting for which teachers bring their lunch and you supply a beverage or dessert.

Try these scheduling suggestions and you will find that your teachers look forward to rather than dread staff meetings. Getting them involved in the planning is essential.

13–5 USING TIME LINES AS A PLANNING TOOL

After you have established goals and objectives with your staff, you can help ensure reaching these goals by setting up "time lines."

A time line is nothing more than a calendar of activities that lead to a specific goal. It becomes a planning tool when it sets up visually what has to be done and who will do each piece of the total project. The visual aspect of a time line shows you clearly what has to happen in step 1 before you go on to step 2, etc.

A large sheet of paper—the kind that comes on a chart roll—works best. Have a column for each month from now to the time the objective is to be met. In rows, list those people or groups who are likely to participate.

Sample: Time Line

Assume as your objective: By May, every class will be aware of good health practices, improved nutrition, disease prevention (including AIDS), and life-long good health routines.

Methodology: A series of ten lessons will be taught by the classroom teacher on the appropriate grade level.

Staff: Decide on the staff members and others you want to include: teachers, school nurse, dietician, gym teacher, community center director, health clinic personnel, PTA, student council.

Meet with representatives of these constituent groups for a brainstorming session. Go over some of the sensitive topics, get parent and teacher feedback, and determine the degree of teacher commitment. You are now ready to begin filling in your time line. Look at this sample:

HEALTH CURRICULUM TIME LINE

Teachers	Sept	Oct	Nov	Dec	Jan	Feb	Mar	Apr	May
Nurse									
Dietician									
Gym teacher									
Community center director									
Health clinic personnel									
PTA									
Student council									
Others									

Begin filling in your time line. You will see not only chronological sequence but also the sharing of responsibility.

When you have filled in different responsibilities in pencil, show the time line to the affected people. When you achieve agreement, write responsibilities in ink.

Now that it is complete, post the time line in a conspicuous place, like the teachers' lounge, with a copy in your office. Revise the time line as needed. Don't hesitate to add new features as they come up. Specify dates for meetings as they are decided on. Place a check next to items that are completed. Use the time line to plan agenda for staff meetings. (Make your boxes large enough to accommodate these notations.)

You now have a road map that will take you to your goals!

13–6 EIGHT IMPORTANT TRADE SECRETS OF EFFICIENCY EXPERTS

Joe D. gets to school an hour before the teachers are due. He is always the last one to leave the building at the end of the day. Yet he can't seem to get things done in an orderly manner. Much of the time he goes around in circles, duplicating effort and running behind schedule.

We've consulted some efficiency experts to see how we can help Joe D. and others with similar problems. We've gleaned a great many strategies, which we have reduced to the following trade secrets:

1. *Develop a system.* Organize your day with some kind of "to do" list. Use a desk or pocket calendar, a lined yellow pad, or simply a 3″ × 5″ index card. Jot down the tasks you want to accomplish that day— and every day. You will derive a keen satisfaction from crossing out tasks as they are completed. Stick to this plan every school day.

   EXAMPLE:

   Call to Mrs. Kay regarding Jodi's behavior in Class 3-2.

   Check payroll matter for Jim Wang.

   Speak to custodian about broken yard fence.

   Meet with lunch workers about low-fat milk.

   Ask secretary to locate fire drill records of last year.

   Observe Ms. Lester teach science lesson.

   Talk to bus dispatcher about late-arriving Bus #4.

   Invite PTA executive board to Spring Band Concert.

   Look in on rehearsal for Dance Festival.

2. *Set aside reaction time.* Schedule some free time in the late morning and again in the afternoon. This will give you a chance to return phone

calls and see teachers who were looking for you earlier. You need this time to react, because most of the time you initiate activity. At these times you can scan the mail, phone messages, or list of office visitors.

3. *Prepare for brush fires.* Prepare yourself emotionally and intellectually for the likelihood that little emergencies will take place that will throw off your daily schedule. An angry parent may come to the office insisting that he or she see you immediately. A pupil may have an accident running in the school yard and require an ambulance. A teacher may become ill and request permission to go home in the middle of the day. Be flexible enough to extinguish the brush fire and get back to your list. Too many principals put out the fire but then spend the rest of the day talking about the emergency.

4. *Gain mastery over the telephone.* Limit your phone conversations to five minutes or less, no matter who it is. The long-winded parent or book salesperson can be helped in five minutes or not at all. If necessary, suggest a call-back. If you can't resolve a problem in five minutes, it's unlikely you'll be able to do so in fifty minutes. Before making or accepting a call, put your hand on the receiver and pause for a few seconds before picking up. This lets you collect your thoughts and decide what you want to accomplish in the conversation.

5. *Limit chitchat.* Irrelevant conversations are insidious time consumers. You do want to make yourself available to teachers and others—just be aware of the passing of time and make these encounters brief.

6. *Decide quickly on minor matters.* Most problems that cross your desk are so routine that they have "autopilot" solutions. If matters are minor, a quick yes or no enables you to dispose of a query without having to return to it later. Try to handle each piece of mail or other communication only once. Make marginal notes and pass it on.

7. *Set up a "talk to" file.* Set up a manila file for each of the staff members with whom you have regular contact (e.g., custodian, teacher union leader, dietician, nurse, speech teacher, or guidance counselor). Toss any letter or note for that person in the appropriate file. The next time you see that person, pull out the file, and your note will be right on top. When that staff member leaves your office, jot down a summary of how you left things, and include the date. You'd be surprised how much time this saves. Next time you won't have to wonder where things were left—it will be in your "talk to" file.

8. *Maximize your leisure time.* Don't underestimate the restorative powers of a relaxing weekend or an afternoon of exercise. Plan your relaxation time and stick to it. If you don't, your time is like an empty desk drawer—it just fills up.

Now let's see if we can recap some of the ideas we have discussed.

13–7 PRINCIPAL'S TIME-SAVER CHECKLIST

None of us is perfect. You should not be disappointed if you are not planning your work and working your plan every minute of the day. However, if you read this chapter carefully, you got some helpful hints for managing your time. Review the following checklist to see how you can improve your use of time.

Time-Saver Checklist

☐ **1.** I carry blank 3″ × 5″ index cards in my pocket to jot down notes and ideas as well as my "to do" list.

☐ **2.** I keep my long-term goals in mind even while doing the smallest task.

☐ **3.** I always plan first thing in the morning and set priorities for the day.

☐ **4.** I keep a list of specific items to be done each day, arrange them in priority order, and then do my best to get the important ones done as soon as possible.

☐ **5.** I ask myself, "Would anything terrible happen if I didn't do this item?" If the answer is no, I don't do it.

☐ **6.** If I seem to procrastinate, I ask myself, "What am I avoiding?"—and then I try to confront that thing headon.

☐ **7.** I focus my efforts on items that will have the best long-term benefits.

☐ **8.** I do much of my thinking on paper.

☐ **9.** I try to do my creative work in the morning and use the afternoons for meetings. (This seems to work for most people.)

☐ **10.** I set deadlines for myself and others.

☐ **11.** I have someone screen my mail and phone calls and handle all routine items. If my secretary is absent, I utilize a school aide.

☐ **12.** I generate as little paperwork as possible and throw away anything I possibly can.

☐ **13.** I write replies to most letters right on the letter itself. My secretary types and makes a photocopy of my response and attaches it to the original letter before filing.

☐ **14.** I recognize that inevitably some of my time will be spent on activities outside my control, and I don't fret about it.

☐ **15.** I continually ask myself, "What is the best use of my time right now?"

Can you honestly answer yes to eight of these items? Try to master a dozen and see the difference it will make in the way you run your school—your scheduling and time management will improve dramatically.

Chapter 14

Getting the Most out of the School Budget

It's time for voting on the school bond issue again.
This is a stressful time for Mr. B., an Illinois principal.
The central office has asked his help in "getting out
the vote." Mr. B. feels that the role of drum beater for
the bond issue compromises his role as educator.
Besides, he is confused by many details of his school
budget. He is also annoyed at comments by some
teachers and parents that this school is not getting its
fair share of central office funds because Mr. B.
doesn't know how to ask for a larger slice of the
district pie.

■THE DISTRICT SCHOOL budget is often clouded by mysterious terms, numbers, and details that make the average principal want to delegate all its ramifications to the central office business manager. But the successful principal cannot afford this luxury. You must understand what the budget is and make sure that your school is getting its fair share of the district's resources.

Simply stated, the school budget is a blueprint of what the educational program will be and what it will cost. A sound budget is more than a document; it is an apparatus for moving your school program.

Your district will be involved in three types of school budgets:

1. *The annual budget* covers a fiscal year and includes the current operating expenses along with annual capital outlay and any debt service payments due.

2. *The capital expenditure budget* includes expenditures for site purchases, building construction, and large-scale renovations. These are usually financed by a bond issue and extend over several years.

3. *Long-range financial planning* is a forecast of combined annual and capital needs projected over an extended period of time, usually five years.

Budgeting appropriations are the starting point for all expenditures. They identify the amount and kind of purchasing that may be undertaken. These allowances identify the kind and numbers of staff to be employed. The budget also indicates the salary rates to be paid to all staff members. In most states there is a law that restricts school district expenditures to the budgetary total, unless an emergency arises.

14–1 LOBBYING EFFECTIVELY FOR YOUR SCHOOL

Your superintendent has many schools vying for the limited resources of the central or district school budget. In most cases, the superintendent is aware of the various problems and needs of each school in the district. However, in the real world there are political and other pressures that supercede purely educational reasons for the allocation of funds to each school.

As principal, one of the many hats you wear is that of lobbyist for your school. You have to be the chief spokesperson for your school's personnel and budgetary needs. You may have the support and assistance of the parents' association and teacher representatives, but you must be ready with the facts and figures at your fingertips.

School board members and the superintendent will listen to parent and teacher groups as well as community representatives, but they won't commit themselves until they hear what you have to say on the subject.

You must assume that your school's needs are pressing and urgent. You may be sympathetic to the needs of other schools in the district, but you must be prepared to tell the central office people why your school needs the extra teacher, computer allocation, or modernization of the lunch room. Your reasons should be so compelling and cogent that they will assign you a high-priority status.

The following guidelines will help ensure that your school gets its fair share of central office money and maybe a little extra.

DO's and DON'Ts for Convincing the Central Office of Your School's Needs

1. *Don't* in any way disparage the needs of another school. Merely emphasize the urgency of your school's needs.
2. *Don't* ask for additional personnel to relieve you of nonessential duties or make your teachers' jobs easier.
3. *Do* emphasize how the extra position will ensure pupil safety, increase pupil attendance, or provide an enhanced learning environment for gifted and talented pupils.
4. *Do* have handy some easy-to-grasp statistics, such as pupil-teacher ratios in a special education class or the increased enrollment since the construction of a housing development in your school zone.
5. *Do* become familiar with the specific aims or objectives of the superintendent. Pinpoint how your request for additional textbook money or a school aide position will foster better interaction of ethnic groups, improved reading scores, greater parent satisfaction and participation, etc.
6. *Don't* go above the superintendent by appealing to one or more board members in the hope that they will put pressure on the superintendent on your behalf.
7. *Do* keep all board members informed of the special programs, activities, and needs of your school. Use newsletters, invitations, and publicity to accomplish this.
8. *Do* accent the positive ways in which you utilized last year's budget to achieve higher test scores, increased parent involvement, or improved school safety and discipline.

9. *Do* invite central office staff, board members, and community leaders into your school to speak to pupils, judge contests, and watch performances.

10. *Do* involve your school and its staff in school board and community activities. Volunteer your services as a committee member to standing committees on curriculum, personnel, budget, or education. Encourage your teachers to participate in professional and cocurricular activities.

11. *Do* emphasize the positive things taking place at your school (e.g., pupil awards, teacher recognition, and grants received). Don't come across as a whiner or complainer who foresees only disaster and decline in the year ahead.

12. *Do* be persistent. If your request for an assistant principal or new gym falls on deaf ears this year, renew your request next year and the next, until you get it. Just approach your request from a slightly different angle each time.

14–2 WHAT SHOULD YOUR BUDGET DOCUMENT LOOK LIKE?

In many districts, the principal is involved in preparing an official budget request for his or her school. If this is a new request, however, you may be nonplussed and unsure of where to begin.

We contacted several principals who are involved in this process and have distilled their collective thinking into simple steps for budget design.

Budget Document Design

1. *Letter of transmittal.* Introduce the budget with a brief explanation of major increases or decreases in pupil population, funding requests, grant money, etc.

2. *Accounts.* Present a detailed breakdown of various accounts at the school: personnel services, equipment, supplies, textbooks, etc.

3. *Graphics.* Include pictures of pupils engaged in worthwhile activities, especially if you want extra money for specific enrichment, such as more computers, new uniforms, and additional library books.

4. *Changes.* Include a column showing increases or decreases in different accounts and specific requests for the new year.

5. *Summary.* Include a complete summary of expenses and a complete listing of income sources. Include names of teachers and parents who were consulted.

SAMPLE BUDGET SUMMARY, 19___

	Expenditures Last Year	Budget This Year	Increase (Decrease)	Totals
Personnel services				
Equipment				
Supplies				
Textbooks				
Plant operation				
Plant maintenance				
Fixed charges				
Auxiliary agencies				
General control				
TOTAL CURRENT EXPENSES				
Debt service				
Capital outlay				
TOTAL CAPITAL EXPENDITURES				
TOTAL EXPENDITURES				
State aid				
Miscellaneous receipts				
TOTAL RECEIPTS				

NET AMOUNT TO BE RAISED BY TAXES:

For added impact, attach a timetable of how you plan to implement your new programs if you get the additional money. Include plans and specifications.

14–3 BOND ISSUES AND THE PRINCIPAL

It is becoming more difficult to get public support for floating school bonds and tax overrides. The politicization of school financial support issues is commonplace.

School districts frequently marshal their own people in the power play which accompanies public resistance. Your central office may call on you to help in "getting out the vote." For many principals this is the worst part of the job. They dislike "begging" for more money. They resent the few who see them as self-serving.

Get the Sting out of Asking for Votes

1. Show parents how public issues that concern the school have a direct effect on their child. This will bring home the importance of their support.

2. Convey information about school financing elections in the same way you would convey any other appropriate information.

3. Continue to gain the respect of parents by being helpful, direct, honest, and open. This will help parents accept your suggestions on school financial matters.

4. Hold meetings on special topics throughout the year. Make the budget just another urgent topic that you want to bring to parents' attention.

5. Build an attitude of parents-as-partners throughout the school year. When parents are willing to help the school, they will be more likely to extend their help into the voting booth.

14–4 PROVIDING EFFECTIVE FISCAL SAFEGUARDS

Every taxpayer is familiar with money management problems, especially those of elected and appointed officials. Because it is taxpayers' money, they rightfully expect and demand that the administrator of school funds be scrupulously honest, prudent, and held completely accountable for every cent of school budget money—from minor expenditures to larger sums.

You must be careful to keep accurate records and give occasional reports on all funds. Follow these suggestions and you will have nothing to worry about.

Blueprint for Fiscal Integrity

1. Involve others in accounting for monies. Have at least one teacher and a school aide or secretary work with you in handling money.

2. Set up suitable accounting records and controls. Insist on petty cash receipts for all purchases. Reconcile checking account statements promptly. Require two signatures for all school account checks.

3. Have teachers in charge of school activity accounts or extracurricular funds keep their own records subject to your inspection.

4. Do not keep large amounts of cash in school. Avoid having collections on a Friday in case a bank deposit is not possible and money would have to be safeguarded all weekend.

5. Keep money separate for different activities. Class trip, school lunch, and book fair money should not be lumped together.

6. Set up file folders for each activity. Keep all receipts and deposit slips available. Get an electric adding machine that produces a tape so you can make notes alongside entries.

7. Keep all PTA financial activities separate and apart from the school fund.

8. Set up a school finance committee consisting of your secretary, two teachers, and two parents. This committee will oversee fund-raising plans, budget projections, expenditures, and periodic balance sheets of assets and liabilities.

9. Publicize all fund-raising activities. For example, let parents know how the school picture sale went. Tell them how much money was raised and how it will be spent.

10. Keep a careful inventory of all equipment purchases including serial numbers, price, vendor, sale date, etc.

11. Put a ceiling on petty cash disbursements. Attach a photocopy or original receipt to the petty cash voucher plus a photocopy of the cancelled check.

12. In June of each year, post on the bulletin board a listing of monies spent during the year and the activities that raised the money.

13. Keep people informed. The key to trust in financial matters is good communication. Don't let citizens, teachers, or parents wonder where certain sums have gone—*tell* them. Show them in black and white the school's balance sheet (in the PTA newsletter, the bulletin board, and elsewhere). This is one show-and-tell activity that will earn you high marks for openness.

14-5 REACHING OUT TO THE BUSINESS COMMUNITY

In recent years, private businesses have increased their support for education. For example, local pizza parlors are rewarding classes who achieve their goal of reading a certain number of books, and the Exxon Corporation is funding grants to teachers who want to improve the teaching of math in grades K through 3.

Yet individual principals are left on their own to try to cultivate business and education partnerships. We discussed this problem with dozens of elementary school principals who had succeeded in linking with businesses. We then contacted the businesses to see if they would welcome communication from other principals seeking a partnership. We present some successful strategies here along with the addresses for more information. (Please note, however, that this information may go out of date as time passes.)

Success by Six™ began in Minneapolis, Minnesota, in 1988 with the leadership and support of the Minneapolis area United Way, chaired by Dr. James Renier, CEO of Honeywell, Inc. It was a communitywide initiative to address children's early childhood development needs. The goals of Success by Six™ are to work through community partnerships to raise public awareness about the importance of healthy early childhood development and to make health and social services accessible to the children and families who need them. United Way of America has launched a national initiative to help communities across the country replicate Success by Six™. For more information, contact

> Honeywell, Inc.
> Att: Laurie Ryan
> United Way of America
> MN125300
> P.O. Box 524
> Minneapolis, MN 55440
>
> (612)870-6845

A Hartford elementary school principal was concerned about the growing number of children who are developmentally unprepared to enter the first grade. This led to the Hartford Early Learning Partnership with The Travelers Insurance Company. For more information, contact

> The Travelers Companies
> National and Community Affairs
> HELP Program
> One Tower Square 6SHS
> Hartford, CT 06183-1060

The principal and parents of the 600 pupils at Newark's Miller Street School were concerned about improving parent-school communication. This led to Partners in Education, which has been replicated in hundreds of schools. For more information, contact

> Mr. Steve Gould
> Education Relations Consultant
> New Jersey Bell
> 540 Broad Street
> Newark, NJ 07101

The children at Chicago's Cabrini Green housing projects needed tutoring help. There were few adults available to help. When contacted, Montgomery Ward furnished employee volunteers working after hours and during lunch time to plan, develop, and administer an extensive tutoring program in grades 2 through 6. Local Montgomery Ward stores will offer similar help. For more information, contact

> Mr. Daniel Bassill
> Cabrini Green Tutoring Program
> 844 Larrabee
> Chicago, IL 60610

In the Houston, New Orleans, and District of Columbia public schools, the Shell Oil Company Foundation is helping develop math and science skills of minority and female students, and plans to expand its program each year to other areas. It also sponsors family math centers and workshops. For more information, contact

> Ms. Paula Saizon
> Two Shell Plaza
> P.O. Box 2099
> Houston, TX 77252

Use these ideas as springboards for your own mini-grants or funded programs. Incidentally, if you're interested in Exxon's math program (mentioned in the first paragraph of this section), contact

> Mr. Michael Dooley
> Exxon Education Foundation
> 225 Carpenter Freeway
> Irving, TX 75062-2298
> (214)444-1104

If you are interested in free pizza reading programs, you may want to contact your neighborhood pizza parlor. For a more structured reading incentive program, contact

> BOOK IT!
> Pizza Hut, Inc.
> 9111 E. Douglas Ave.
> Wichita, KS 67207

Good luck, and let us know (through the publisher) of any ideas that worked for you so we can share them with others.

14–6 CATCHING ON TO SCHOOL-BASED OPTIONS

One aspect of the shared decision-making approach to school management is the idea of school-based options. It works this way: Using the existing resources of the school (space, money, supplies), the teachers, together with a group of parents and the school administration, work out options or variations of the regular program that meet pupils' needs. This is a popular technique because it stays within the existing budget.

For example, say a school has an allotment of twenty-three teachers. When assigned in the usual way, each teacher has a class of twenty-five pupils. There is no allocation for a reading or resource room teacher. The central office has no funds for such a position this year. The school-based options committee is made up of three teachers (primary, intermediate, and upper grades), three parents, and the principal. The committee feels strongly that a resource room teacher is sorely needed. It came up with the idea that one of the alloted twenty-three teachers will become a resource room teacher. The other twenty-two teachers will then have slightly more pupils per class (an average of one and a fraction). Instead of twenty-five pupils, most will have twenty-six and three will have twenty-seven. The committee agrees this will be best for the pupils. It also points out that while the teacher will have twenty-six or twenty-seven pupils, those most in need of help will be with the resource room teacher.

This may be a great idea, but it may not be easy to achieve. Let's look at this scenario more closely.

Ground Plan for School-Based Options

1. The staff, at a meeting, must vote if it would be in favor of developing an option. They must select teacher members of the committee. They must also decide the kind of majority (simple, 66 percent, 75 percent) needed to implement a future suggestion or option.

2. The principal must agree to consider options that the committee develops. It is understood that agreement must be arrived at by all three groups: teachers, principal, parents. It is further understood that no additional money will be available to fund the option.

3. If the principal agrees, then approval must be obtained from the central office.

4. At a PTA meeting, the idea of school-based options must be explained. Parent members should then be selected by the PTA.

5. A convenient meeting time and place must be agreed on. In most schools, the first few meetings are usually at lunch time.

6. All teachers and parents should feel free to suggest options.

7. The basic rule for considering an option is that it does not violate any contract with staff members, any district or federal mandates, or any pupil's or teacher's civil rights. Also, it must operate within the existing budget.

8. Copies of the printed option should be furnished to all voting members prior to the vote. Changes in language or intent may be made before the vote as long as consensus among the three components remains (principal, teachers, parents).

When this is done, and central or district office approval is obtained, the school-based option goes into effect. There should be a provision for evaluation and follow-up. The usual procedure is to implement an option for one year. If it works to the satisfaction of the majority, it can be renewed annually.

This is the format started in Dade County, Florida, and replicated in New York and Kentucky. You can adapt it to meet your own needs.

14–7 FUND-RAISERS: PROCEED WITH CAUTION

Opening your mail on an average day will yield one or two fund-raising solicitations to help school principals supplement their tax levy budget. Usually students and parents do the actual fund-raising, and the school keeps 30 or 40 percent of the money raised as its profit.

Reading the mailed literature or talking to the salesperson who calls makes it all seem so simple, safe, and lucrative. We would like to point out some of the caveats so you will be more aware of this double-edged sword before you sign on the dotted line. First, let's look at some popular fund-raisers:

- School pictures of pupils (individual and class pictures)
- Book Fairs at which new paperback books are sold for between $1 to $4 each

- Candy and cookie sales (pupils sell to adults)
- Stationery, note paper, Christmas and general greeting cards (pupils sell to adults)
- Pencil and pen sales (plain or with the school name printed on pencils; for pupil use)
- School spirit items: T-shirts, baseball caps, team or school jackets, pennants (parents buy these items for pupils and themselves)
- Costume jewelry items (popular around Mother's Day)
- Seed or plant sales (wide range of prices)
- School supplies: notebooks and binders, rulers, glossy folders with school data printed on them, book covers
- Food items sold in lunch room: pretzels, cookies, potato chips, ice cream, other snack items (for pupil consumption after lunch).

While each of these items is popular with different groups of pupils and parents, you will have to select the item that best meets your school's needs. Meet with parents, teachers, and one or two pupils before you make your choice. Then consider these questions.

Choosing a Fund-Raiser

1. Who will earn the profit from the sales? The PTA or the school directly?
2. Who will be responsible for getting parent volunteers? A PTA committee or the school administration?
3. Will the profits be earmarked for a particular item or a general fund?
4. Will there be prizes for outstanding pupil sales, grade prizes, etc.?
5. Will there be a pep talk in the auditorium to launch the campaign? Can it include rules for polite sales pitches?
6. Is the product one with universal acceptance, or will some parents find it objectionable? Some parents may not support sales of candy or costume jewelry.
7. Is the timing right? Photographs should be back in time for holiday giving. Chocolate items should not be distributed in warm weather. Some items are ideal for Mother's Day.
8. Is the sales company reliable and trustworthy? Call other schools in your area who have used them before you sign up.
9. How will the gift items come to your school? Some companies will fill individual orders; others will ship in bulk.
10. Is it going to be worth the effort? Take time to project the hours of work necessary compared to the projected amount to be raised.

Potential Trouble Spots

1. Will pupils be collecting money or ringing doorbells? This is fraught with danger. Have students call on only people they know. Insist that all payment be made in the form of a check. The check can be made out to the school or the sales company. Work this out with the vendor ahead of time.

2. Is this going to be a schoolwide project, or will it become a fierce competition among a dozen kids to see who can raise the most money and win the ten-speed bike or other first-place prize that the sales company offers? You must walk the line between an enthusiastic fund-raiser and a cut-throat competition for prizes.

3. Who will decide how the money will be spent? You will be depending on parents to help make the fund-raiser a success. It's natural for them to want a say in how the money is spent. Be sure you and the parents agree on how the bulk of the fund-raiser profits will be spent. Parents resent spending money for items such as textbooks, workbooks, or other instructional material that they feel the board of education should supply. They will put forth a great deal of effort for enrichment items that exceed the basic tax levy expenditures. Computers, copy machines, team uniforms, and athletic equipment are possibilities.

4. Is the item sold worth its price? You don't want to compete with local merchants. If your pupils can get the T-shirts, school supplies, or snack items for less, then you have a problem. You want quality items, attractively presented, at a fair price. Avoid tacky, easily broken items that can cause injury.

5. Has this item been sold at your school before? Parents of more than one pupil resent having to buy potholders every year from each of their children. Present a variety of items depicted in colorful folders that your pupils distribute at home.

Parents will be glad to help out as long as you make it a cooperative effort and tell them what a good job they are doing.

14–8 DEVELOPING A SCHOOL PROFILE

There will be many occasions when you will want a thumbnail sketch of your school—a short, accurate statistical picture of your school and its occupants.

We can all describe our school in words (that is, give a narrative description). But that tends to get subjective. If you apply for a grant or want additional funding of any kind, it will be helpful if you can pass along a one- or two-page school profile. This will enhance your chances of getting some extra money for your school.

Preparing a school profile is time-consuming at first, but subsequent annual updates will be easy. Think of it as a resume for your school.

School Profile Sample Format

1. Name, address, and phone of school
2. Year built, year of modernization
3. Number of classrooms, special rooms (library, computer) and special areas (gym, lunch room, auditorium)
4. Community: type of homes, commercial areas, neighboring parochial or private schools
5. Pupils: Number, grades; reading and math scores (percent on or above grade level, by grade)
6. Ethnic composition of pupils, teachers and other staff
7. Pupil transportation: school bus, parent vehicle, and walkers
8. School lunch: percent bringing lunch from home, percent paying for school lunch, percent receiving free lunch.
9. Special programs:
   Gifted and talented
   Remedial
   Resource room
   Speech and/or hearing
   Special education
   Before and after school
   Breakfast
10. Building and plant needs
11. Average length of teaching service for teachers
12. Instructional program
    Names of reading and math series
    How classes are formed
    How needs of bright or slow pupils are met
    Number and type of specialized teachers (art, music, computer)
    Any foreign language instruction
13. Parent involvement
    Parent association president (name and phone), number of paid memberships
    Nature and time of meetings
    Committees involved with school

14. Annual events, such as spelling bee, field day, earth day, senior trip

15. Awards won by pupils or school

An up-to-date school profile is ideal for appending to grant requests, sending to newspaper editors at bond vote occasions, and forwarding to the central office when requests for added funding are made.

In this chapter, we have given you pointers for getting the kind of funding you need from the board of education, private organizations, and your own fund-raising abilities. Good luck!

Chapter 15

Supervising and Evaluating Your Staff

Ms. G., a principal of a suburban school outside Atlanta, is seeing signs of apathy and burnout among several of her teachers and other staff members, for no apparent reason. Ms. G. feels that perhaps she has been too easy on her staff. She is so concerned about the new teachers and the large numbers of poorly prepared pupils transferring into her school that she has not really supervised or evaluated the senior staff members. Their discontent and lackadaisical attitude can have a ripple effect that spreads dissatisfaction throughout the school. She feels she can't afford to let that happen. She wants to get a handle on supervising her staff directly and regularly.

■As HEAD OF the school, you have a responsibility for supervising your teachers and other staff members. Many principals are so bogged down with administrative details that they seldom get around to observing teachers and others on a regular basis. This is a dangerous trap. Your teachers, secretaries, and custodial workers need direction and evaluation from you.

15–1 WHAT IS SUPERVISION IN A SCHOOL SETTING?

Evaluating teachers is a stressful activity for both the supervisor and the teacher. It's a common practice for principals to observe new or probationary teachers and to stay away from senior teachers. The assumption is that the experienced teachers are doing a good job and don't need any help.

This practice assumes that there is no room for improvement and/or that the principal has nothing worthwhile to suggest to senior staff members. Both are incorrect.

You can improve the level of instruction by regularly supervising your teachers. This ongoing evaluation can take the following forms:

- Collecting and reading lesson plans on a regular basis
- Visiting classrooms informally on a daily or nearly daily basis
- Conducting formal observations of teachers at least once each school year
- Reviewing with the teacher before the lesson what you will be looking for in the lesson
- Meeting with the teacher after the formal observation to review the strengths and weaknesses of the lesson
- Collecting pupil test papers, creative writing, or projects on a regular basis to see how they are progressing and how closely the teacher is following the course of study.

There is much you can do to ease the stress of the evaluation process.

Taking the Sting Out of Supervision

1. Refer to observation of lessons or written evaluations as a positive tool for growth, for both the teacher and you. Emphasize that it is not something you take lightly or use as a weapon.

2. Visit classrooms on a regular, informal basis. Do not limit visits to special, formal occasions such as evaluations. Pupils as well as teachers should be accustomed to your presence in the classroom.

3. Present the evaluation as part of your role in helping teachers improve. Describe it as a natural follow-up to providing materials, conducting training, assessing needs, etc.

4. Become a partner in your teachers' ongoing growth. Listen to their complaints, assist with discipline problems, provide resources, and work through problems.

5. Clarify when and how you will provide feedback after the observation. Don't let too many days pass between the lesson and the feedback or postobservation conference.

6. Give teachers some leeway for when the observation of the lesson will take place. Respect their request for day of week or time of day.

In addition to observing lessons, both informally and formally, there are other ways you can improve the effectiveness of teachers regardless of their experience level.

Two Dozen Ways to Make Every Teacher a Better Teacher

1. Take specific steps to help improve discipline in the classroom.
2. Encourage interclass visitations among teachers.
3. Involve teachers in the selection of learning materials.
4. Use team teaching as a catalyst for change and improvement.
5. Promote an aggressive program of staff development and in-service training.
6. Use aides and student teachers so teachers can work with small groups of pupils or act as mentors for new teachers.
7. Encourage cross-grade-level teacher exchange programs.
8. Develop learning contracts for teachers to use with pupils.
9. Compile and distribute a list of sound practices that have worked for some teachers.
10. Distribute up-to-date, easy-to-follow scope and sequence guides in all major subject areas.
11. Spend some of your time in demonstration teaching, sharing curriculum expertise or other aspects of instructional leadership.
12. Foster use of community resources by giving each teacher a directory of available volunteers and class trip destinations.

13. Initiate grade-level meetings to discuss matters of mutual concern.

14. Publicly recognize excellence in all areas of teaching.

15. Make computers available to all grade levels. Encourage teacher training in this area.

16. Make available videotape equipment so teachers can record their performance in the classroom and view and critique it privately.

17. Provide opportunities for teachers to become technologically comfortable with camcorders, computers, cable TV, CD-ROM, etc. (Compact Disc-Read Only Memory) (stores computer data rather than music.)

18. Start a process for teachers to nominate colleagues who will share successful strategies at staff meetings.

19. Help teachers arrange intergenerational experiences for pupils with grandparents or other senior citizens.

20. Conduct an annual competition for the best teaching ideas and innovations. Offer prizes.

21. Develop daily schedules that accommodate grade-level or team planning.

22. Start a voluntary program of lesson-plan review and comment by peers on an anonymous basis.

23. Provide teachers with an attractive, well-equipped lounge where they can prepare lessons, photocopy materials, inspect sample textbooks, and relax with peers.

24. Set up a teacher center in your school offering a wide range of supplemental and enrichment materials, games, and project ideas available for checkout. Get your librarian or media specialist to help, or try to free a senior teacher for an hour each week to do this.

15–2 MAKING TEACHER OBSERVATIONS EFFECTIVE

Your teachers want to know what you are looking for when you observe them. Less experienced teachers may not know what components a good lesson should include.

Assume you have met with Mrs. Senior and together you have selected a date for the lesson and the subject area. The next step is to send her a letter detailing this.

After you have observed the lesson and read your notes, you want to prepare for the feedback to the teacher. If this is a formal observation, and perhaps the only evaluation for the year, you will want to hold a postobservation conference with the teacher, at which you can discuss the lesson. This is a good time for each of you to clarify various points before the written report is typed.

Before meeting to discuss the lesson, it's a good idea to give the teacher a list of what you will be looking for in the lesson. This will provide your conference with a structure that you can both refer to.

Use this list of fifteen questions to make the evaluation process easier and more comprehensive.

Questions for Evaluating a Lesson

1. What was the aim of your lesson? To what extent is it worthy? Definite? Specific with regard to this class? Attainable?

2. To what extent did the students share in proposing the aim? To what extent do they comprehend and adopt the aim?

3. What was the appropriateness of the activity used to achieve the aim?

4. How suitable was the plan for achieving the desired objectives?

5. Was your preparation adequate? How is preparation or lack of preparation evidenced in the lesson?

6. What assignment has been made? To what extent does it conform to the criteria for good assignments? How effective is it when judged by the responses of the students?

7. How were pupils' preparation and past learnings or experiences used in the lesson?

8. How did the students behave, as demonstrated by good manners and respect?

9. What related learnings did you encourage and direct?

10. How suitable were the materials used in the lesson? How well were they managed and used?

11. To what extent was the aim of the lesson carried through and achieved?

12. What were the outcomes in terms of knowledge, concepts, skills, and attitudes? What evidence was there that the lesson was learned?

13. What provisions were made for summaries of the learning?

14. What provisions were made for individual differences in interest, needs, special aptitudes, and ability?

15. How much participation was there by the students? In planning? In active contributions? In activities? In evaluation?

There will be occasions when a much less detailed process of discussing a lesson will suffice. The sample letter provided will give you an idea of this simpler process, which merely asks for a summary of the lesson and discussion of what was good about it and what improvement is needed.

November, XXX

Dear Mrs. Senior:

I plan to observe you teaching a science lesson on November 10.
In evaluating your lessons, I will be looking for the following items.
Please let me have a written lesson plan the day before the actual lesson.

1. Objective or aim of the lesson
2. Materials used
3. Motivation
4. Reference to syllabus
5. Questioning techniques
6. Development of the lesson
7. Individualization of instruction
8. Appearance of classroom
9. Class routines
10. Pupil behavior
11. Variety of activities
12. Teacher's voice and manner.

At a mutually convenient time, we will hold a postobservation conference.

Sincerely,

M. Hoyt
Principal

15–3 THE NUTS AND BOLTS OF EVALUATING A TEACHER

Each year, or twice a year in some districts, you are asked to rate your staff. For probationary teachers, this rating can spell the difference between keeping their job and losing it. For more experienced or tenured personnel, it becomes a somewhat perfunctory exercise.

In many school districts with a strong teachers' union, there are contractual regulations in addition to the customary district regulations for

REPORT OF LESSON OBSERVED

Mrs. Morris   Class 3-112

Dear Mrs. Morris:

Please read this report of your lesson given on October 17.

If you wish to discuss this report before signing it, let me know. A copy will be placed in your file.

Sincerely,

_____

L. Newman, Principal

Lesson summary _____

_____

_____

_____

_____

Commendable features _____

_____

_____

_____

_____

Suggestions for improvement _____

_____

_____

_____

_____

I have read and received a copy
of this lesson observation.

_____

Teacher's signature

_____

Date

staff evaluations. In many cases, principals are constrained to rate teachers as either satisfactory or unsatisfactory.

While each school district has different rules and regulations, we include here a summary of some common rules. They serve as a guide to some of the pitfalls to avoid

Don't delay in giving your teachers their rating. One district advises, "In the case of a teacher whose assignment is terminated before the end of the school year, but who has served for at least twenty days during this time, the individual rating report must be given to him or her not later than four school days following the last day of service."

You needn't neglect the exceptional teacher: "Special reports for exceptional services of a teacher may be submitted by the principal. If approved by the district superintendent, such reports are placed in the teacher's file." This appears in an increasing number of district manuals.

Some teachers appear to be neither satisfactory nor unsatisfactory: "A rating of doubtful may be used for a teacher on probation where the probationary period will extend more than one year. A rating of doubtful or unsatisfactory must be accompanied by a statement giving general reasons such as lack of control of class, lack of or improper preparation of lessons, irregularity in attendance, lack of punctuality." You will find a variation of this quote in many district manuals.

If you are going to rate one of your teachers as unsatisfactory, you should be aware of the following rules that exist in most districts:

1. All evidence submitted must be based on occurrences within the rating year.
2. No evidence with respect to events which occurred in any previous year may be introduced unless the teacher chooses to do so. In such cases, you may offer the relevant data.
3. You should make enough supervisory observation to warrant your conclusions.
4. It is advisable to hold a conference with the teacher following each supervisory visit.
5. Prepare a copy of the report of the visit and send it to the teacher promptly. This report should indicate the areas in which the teacher was unsatisfactory and the supervisory help that was given.
6. If your assistant principal is the immediate supervisor of this teacher, you should make at least three visits during the rating year.
7. The teacher should be given a copy of every item placed in his or her official file.
8. Notify the district superintendent when contemplating marking the teacher unsatisfactory, so the superintendent may make a visit.

9. When submitting the documentation of an unsatisfactory rating, be sure that the report is factual. Generalizations should be avoided, and opinions stated should be supported with concrete examples.

10. If you rate a teacher as unsatisfactory, it is not necessary to prove him or her unsatisfactory in all respects. For example, a teacher may be satisfactory in a number of aspects of teaching but may be so lacking in class control that an unsatisfactory rating is warranted.

When should you rate a teacher as unsatisfactory? It is usually your duty to report immediately to the district superintendent a teacher or other staff member who has been unduly absent; negligent, insubordinate, incompetent, or inefficient in respect to instruction, discipline, or supervision; guilty of conduct unbecoming a teacher; guilty of conduct prejudicial to the good order, efficiency, or discipline of the school; or displaying a mental or physical condition that renders him or her unfit for service.

An unsatisfactory rating may be given at any time during the school year. Give the teacher a statement of the reasons for the rating. Send a report of the rating, and the accompanying supporting data, to the superintendent of schools. There have been many court cases that could have been avoided if the principal had followed the district's regulations.

There are ways in which a teacher can appeal an administrator's evaluation or rating. Be aware of these rights, which are usually similar to the following (from a large school district):

1. A notice of appeal must be filed in letter form to the district superintendent within three weeks of the rating.

2. The three-week period does not include summer vacation.

3. The appellant must receive from the principal a written statement of reasons, facts, and conditions on which the unsatisfactory rating was based.

4. The statement of reasons for the unsatisfactory rating must be filed within three weeks after the receipt of the notice of appeal, excluding summer vacation.

5. Upon receipt of the statement of reasons, the teacher has three weeks in which to file a written answer to the statement of reasons.

6. Following the submission of the appeal, the reasons for the unsatisfactory rating, and the rebuttal, the superintendent designates a committee to hear an oral argument on the teacher's appeal.

7. The teacher will request to review his or her official file. The teacher will be advised that he or she will need documentary evidence if she feels any items are not factual.

8. The teacher will gather copies of all documents, favorable and unfavorable, that appear in her official file. She will want to duplicate all documents contained in her file.

9. The teacher is authorized to be accompanied to the hearings by a person of his or her choosing. The person may be an employee of the board of education or the teachers' union, but cannot be an attorney.

10. The teacher can be expected to present documentary evidence contradicting the statements of the principal. The teacher may present ratings given by former principals or former supervisors and may present letters received from the principal, parents, or colleagues.

As we mentioned earlier, you are expected to make enough supervisory visits. These observations of a teacher in front of a class are a necessity. Your management ability rides on how you handle this function. The extent to which your visits will result in improved instruction depends on the feeling of mutual respect and confidence between you and the teacher. The frequency of supervisory observations and visits will vary. The pattern may consist of brief visits, planned or informal, or classroom visits for observation of a complete lesson. For satisfactory teachers who are on permanent license, one visit per year is sufficient. For probationary teachers having three years' experience or less in your school, two visits per year are recommended. If the probationary teacher appears weak, more than two observations may be appropriate. For the teacher who may be rated unsatisfactory or doubtful, supervisory visits once monthly with a complete write-up may be necessary.

In all situations, use your discretion regarding the frequency and duration of visits. Be mindful that excessive classroom visits may be viewed as teacher harrassment.

What should you do if you suspect that one of your new teachers may turn out to be a lemon? For this teacher and for any teacher that you observe, we recommend a written report form. Give a brief description of the lesson, commendatory practices, and recommendations for improvement. This should contain the conclusion that you and the teacher reached jointly during the postobservation conference. The report form may be a letter to the teacher stating that the observation has been made and the conference held. A detailed report is needed for the teacher who may receive a negative rating. Specific recommendations for improvement discussed at the conference should be included in the written report.

Be sure that the teacher receives the original and that a copy is filed in your office. You may want to note on the report when the teacher receives it. The teacher may be unwilling to sign a copy of the report. In such a case, have your secretary deliver a copy of the report. If the teacher refuses to sign the report, then the secretary attests to this in writing on the file copy.

Now let's look at some ways in which you can help a weak teacher overcome his or her shortcomings and become a better teacher.

15–4 GETTING TEACHERS TO MAKE OR ACCEPT CHANGES

There are times when you will be disappointed in a teacher's lesson. You may feel that there were special circumstances that prevented the teacher from doing a good job. Rather than write up a report on a poor lesson, you can offer the teacher a second chance. Even more important, offer the teacher a list of weaknesses that you observed.

The sample letter provided on the next page gives you several weaknesses to choose from. There may be others.

Some changes are difficult to bring about. Teachers' egos sometimes create an impenetrable barrier to change. Many teachers are afraid of losing status due to a new staffing arrangement. They don't want to see some of their duties taken over by a school aide. Others dislike seeing younger teachers move out of the classroom into other positions. Countless emotional reactions make it difficult to implement change. We all need to feel important. That need is frustrated when people are not consulted on changes concerning their jobs.

It is easier to carry out a job if there is a specific plan. When major changes are to be installed, careful planning and preparation are necessary for success.

Here is a case study that illustrates two different approaches to getting teachers to accept change in their professional lives.

Case Study

Two principals leave the district office after a conference with the district superintendent. Both are determined to get back to their schools and implement the new district policy regarding teacher observations. Both principals are enthusiastic about the new procedures. Mr. X. decides that there is no time to waste and calls an emergency meeting of his staff at three o'clock that same day. Ms. Y. plans to talk the new policy over with her staff members informally during the course of the next week. Mr. X. is able to sustain his enthusiasm throughout the half-hour meeting with his staff. He tries to condense the two-hour meeting with the superintendent into thirty minutes. To avoid wasting time, he asks teachers to hold their questions until the end of his talk. The question period gets out of hand, and some teachers with other obligations leave before their questions are answered. A few teachers catch the enthusiasm of their principal, while most of the others are dazed and threatened by the new plan.

Principal Y. decides to feel out some of her more experienced teachers over lunch. She tells of the superintendent's plan without giving her own

CHECKLIST OF LESSON WEAKNESSES

TO: Mr. Mistretta, Class 5A
RE: Observed Lesson Weaknesses

Your lesson contained several weaknesses. I do not want to write a formal observation on this lesson. I'm sure you can do better, and I would like to reschedule at a mutually convenient time. In planning your next lesson, please pay special attention to the weaknesses I have checked.

Examples of Weaknesses:

☐ The aim did not become clear until the middle of the lesson.

☐ The pupils, working in groups, did not seem to know the purpose of their activities.

☐ There was no way of determining whether the aim had been achieved.

☐ Most pupils were inactive during the lesson.

☐ Pupils often answered in concert or called out answers.

☐ Some pupils could not answer the teacher's questions.

☐ The teacher repeated pupil answers.

☐ The teacher took too long to distribute the materials.

☐ The demonstration was not visible in the rear of the room.

☐ The bell rang for lunch before the lesson could be completed.

☐ The content was too simple for the brighter pupils.

☐ In general, pupils gave one-word or two-word answers.

☐ The teacher talked too much.

☐ The pupils were orderly but passive.

☐ Pupil reports sounded as if they had been copied from a book.

☐ The teacher wrote extensive material on the chalkboard which pupils copied without comment in their notebooks.

_____
Principal

opinion. She seeks the opinion of her teachers. She then talks to other staff members informally, and lets the new plan "percolate" throughout the school. Teachers have time to think about it before their regularly scheduled faculty conference. At that time, Ms. Y. details the new program and asks for questions. The staff has had time to think of questions, and the principal has had time to anticipate their questions. Much ventilation takes place, and there is room for understanding.

As you know from your own experience as a school administrator, teachers respond best to instructions that are clear, concise, and understandable. They can easily become confused if you overstate your case by giving too many details too quickly. Let them do some of the thinking themselves. That way, you can emphasize results (not methods) and work (not rules). Getting staff members to think for themselves, to use their imagination and initiative, will lead to a better way of doing things.

15–5 THE SECRET TO GETTING TEACHERS TO DO THEIR BEST

Staff members will do their best for you when they know exactly what their jobs are and precisely what you want them to do. They often fail to do a job properly simply because they didn't understand what you wanted done in the first place. Vagueness, indecisiveness, ambiguity, and incompleteness of instructions are often to blame for disorder and chaos in a school. It's up to you to tell your staff what you expect, when and where you expect it, and then to supervise to make sure the job gets done. Train your assistants to do this, too. You'll be rewarded with a well-run, well-respected school. Your teachers will do the best they know how for you. Make sure you involve your teachers in setting the expectations, however. For example, if you plan to introduce an individualized reading program, be sure to include the teachers, as well as the school librarian, in book selection. Include the teachers in planning the evaluation of the program as well as in informing the parents.

You will also have more time for long-range planning when your staff does things right the first time. Principals often complain that there is not enough time in the day. When you make sure the job is understood in the beginning, you won't lose time by repeating the same instructions over and over again.

People respond much faster and you'll get far better results from orders phrased as suggestions. Make sure your staff understands the reason for the request. If you want teachers to escort their pupils into the lunch room as a class to cut down on unrest, tell the teachers *why* you are insisting that this be done. Don't let them guess. Assume that no one knows about the situation until you tell them.

As an experienced principal, you know that you must have a clear idea of what you want before you can ask your teachers to do something. If you aren't sure of the results you want, you're not yet ready to get your teachers to respond appropriately.

To help you establish the results you are seeking, follow these simple guidelines:

1. What exactly is it that I want to accomplish?
2. Who is the best person to do this job?
3. When does this job have to be done?
4. Why do I want this job accomplished?
5. Where is the best place to carry out this task?
6. How can this best be done?

Get in the habit of asking yourself these questions *before* you issue a directive or ask your teachers to do anything. By doing so, you will ensure that the job is understood, supervised, and accomplished.

15–6 RECOGNIZING THE VALUE OF SCHOOL SECRETARIES

Most school staffs include more than one secretary. This presents two potential challenges: assigning responsibilities, and the human relations of two or more people working closely together. It is a good practice to assign specific duties to the secretaries. Mr. F. may be concerned with pupil personnel matters: transfers, attendance, records, referrals, admissions, and discharges. Ms. K. may be responsible for teacher and other staff matters: payroll, increments, absence reserves, arranging for substitute teachers, etc. Secretaries may share some general responsibilities concerning reception, telephone, dictation, opening mail, distributing teachers' mail, and duplication of spirit master and mimeo materials. You will find that things go much more smoothly if you follow these suggestions:

1. State in writing the specific responsibilities of each secretary. Discuss these duties with them first. Make sure they understand why they are being asked to perform these duties.
2. Stagger their hours. Have one secretary arrive early to take calls from teachers and parents who have a problem. Be sure that at least one secretary stays late to take calls about delayed buses and calls from the district office and to handle any typing of yours that wasn't finished during instructional hours because of interruptions.
3. Be sure that each secretary understands the work of the other secretary or secretaries. There is always the possibility that one secretary will

quit, and no one will know the job. In addition, rotate the responsibilities after a few years. In this way, no one becomes entrenched.

4. Show respect. This will encourage your teachers to be respectful to the secretarial staff. The greatest morale problem facing school secretaries is that the teaching staff treats them as second-class citizens.

5. Whenever possible, avoid last-minute rush jobs. If you have two weeks in which to prepare a report, don't keep it on your desk for ten days and then give it to your secretary to get out on the final due date.

6. Caution your secretaries about playing favorites. They should be courteous to all the teachers and parents with whom they come in contact. People shouldn't feel that they can't get the information or service they require because they do not have an "in" with the secretary.

7. Emphasize the importance of reception. The first impression that callers get on the telephone or in person can frequently influence their opinion of the entire school and its program.

8. Encourage your secretaries to refine their skills and improve their performance by taking courses. Give them some time off if you think this will encourage them. Spend some money on upgraded equipment and the supplies they request.

It is often the little things that you do that endear you to the secretarial staff. Remember National Secretary Week and bring in a little memento. If you take a trip during the summer, bring back a souvenir for your secretary. Is your PTA running a plant sale? Buy a few plants and present one to each secretary for his or her desk. That single act will boost the plant sale, encourage an attractive-looking office, and flatter your secretaries.

The skill with which your office staff does things is a reflection of your priorities. For example, if you place too much value on speed, you may lose in accuracy or morale.

5–7 SUPERVISING THE CUSTODIAL STAFF

Your pupils and teachers are entitled to a clean, comfortable, and attractive school building. Although everything is your responsibility, more specifically building maintenance is the function of the school custodians. In some school districts, custodians are school employees; in others, they are contractors who provide a variety of maintenance and custodial services for a fee based on the size and use of the school building.

In either case, set appropriate standards and insist that they be met. The sample standards and cleaning schedule included in this chapter can be adapted to your own school and used to make your expectations perfectly clear.

The custodial staff includes a variety of employees with various job titles: cleaner, firefighter, sweeper, groundskeeper. Whether these people report directly to the head custodian or whether they are on the school payroll, your primary dealings are with the head custodian, who, in turn, gives the orders necessary to meet your requests. It is a mistake if you go directly to the cleaner each time you want the rest room floor mopped or a paper dispenser refilled.

It is also good practice to train your teachers to send you a note if they want some special cleaning, maintenance, or repair work done. This is better than having each teacher contact the custodial staff. It gives you some idea of the kinds and number of requests each teacher is making. You can also make a spot check to see how long it takes one of these requests to be completed. Another advantage is that it avoids the favoritism that is inevitable when each teacher contacts the custodial staff. Written requests to you are fast, dated, and more effective.

Insist that your teachers and other staff members cooperate with the custodial staff. Before the winter, spring, and summer vacations, send out a notice with simple items that the pupils and teacher can do to help in the clean-up: remove material from the bulletin boards, store books, and stack chairs. This will improve efficiency and raise the morale of the custodial staff.

Take frequent walks with your head custodian through the halls, into public areas (cafeteria, auditorium, gymnasium), and outside the building. This gives you an opportunity to point out areas where some preventive maintenance is called for. It also helps you improve the safety program of the school because you see how children are using or abusing the school building and grounds.

Custodians, cafeteria workers, and other nonteaching staff should be aware that you are also interested in them and their work. Remind them in word and deed that they are an integral part of the educational program. One method is to hold some staff meetings with your entire staff (teachers, nurse, maintenance workers, etc.). Another is to praise the custodial staff when an especially thorough clean-up was completed during a school holiday. Words of sincere gratitude and praise serve as a tremendous morale booster and are powerful reminders that you're on the same team. Remember what Mark Twain said: "I can live for two months on a good compliment."

MINIMUM CUSTODIAL STANDARDS FOR CLASSROOMS

Items to be cleaned	CUSTODIAL DUTY							
	Sweep	Mop	Scrub	Wax	Seal	Wash	Dust	Clean
Soft floors	Daily		3×/yr					
Wood floors	Daily	4×/yr	2×/yr	3×/yr	2×/yr			
Furniture						1×/yr	Weekly	
Chalkboard								Weekly
Chalk troughs								Monthly
Upper windows						2×/yr		
Lower windows						4×/yr		
Upper walls							3×/yr	
Lower walls						1×/yr	3×/yr	
Woodwork						2×/yr	Monthly	
Sinks								Daily
Lavatories								Daily
Cork board					1×/yr			

DAILY CUSTODIAL SCHEDULE—TAYLOR SCHOOL

Assignment for Daytime Custodial Worker

Morning	Types of Duties
7:30–8:30	Getting school ready for opening
8:30–9:30	Sweeping entrances, policing grounds, doing preventive maintenance
9:30–12:00	Duties related to corridors, rest rooms, grounds

Afternoon	
12:00–12:30	Lunch
12:30–1:30	Duties related to cafeteria, corridors, special rooms, rest rooms
1:30–2:15	Cafeteria cleaning
2:15–4:00	Cleaning of classrooms and care of grounds

Assignment for Evening Custodial Worker

Evening	
3:30–6:30	Duties related to sweeping classrooms, special rooms, and care of grounds
6:30–7:00	Supper
7:00–11:00	Periodic cleaning, scrubbing, waxing; providing building services for evening activities, including heating

SUMMER CLEANING STANDARDS

Items to be cleaned	CUSTODIAL DUTY					
	Scrub	Seal	Wax	Wash	Clean	Refinish
Floors:						
Wood	Yes	1 coat	1 coat			
Asphalt tile	Yes		2 coats			
Cork	Yes	1 coat	2 coats			
Terrazzo	Yes	1 coat	No			
Concrete	Yes	1 coat	No			
Vitrous tile	Yes	No	No			
Ceramic tile	Yes	1 coat	No			
Light fixtures					Yes	
Glass				Yes		
Walls				Yes		
Woodwork				Yes		
Screens				Yes		
Chalkboard				Yes		
Shades/blinds				Yes	Yes	
Furniture				Yes		As needed
Plumbing fixtures					Yes	
Floor drains					Yes	
Dry wells					Yes	

15-8 FINAL WORDS ON EVALUATION

You can conduct meaningful employee evaluations (instructional, secretarial, custodial) if you do the following:

1. Develop a sincere approach that permits adjustments to individuals and situations.
2. Develop your own outline of points to discuss to supplement the required forms.
3. Maintain a proper balance between positive and negative elements.
4. Avoid a false formality by being natural in manner and conversation.
5. Set realistic and specific objectives that the employee can accept as attainable.
6. Avoid using lip-service praise that precedes and follows strong criticism.
7. Permit the employee to participate in setting a positive objective.

Granted, there is no one best plan for every administrator—any plan that requires you to pause long enough to evaluate the employee's progress is desirable as long as you do it fairly and not in anger or pique.

Finally, don't be especially critical in evaluating your own performance. Too many administrators remember to protect the ego of their staff members but are unduly harsh in rating themselves. You have one of the most difficult jobs of this century. Everyone knows what is wrong with the schools. Everyone seems to be writing a book criticizing the American educational scene. While teachers are protected by their contracts and pupils are protected by their parents, the school supervisor is open game for pot shots. Be armed with a sound philosophy and enforce it with strategies and tactics that have proven successful.

Chapter 16

Working with the Power Structure

Michael G. has been the principal at John Adams Elementary School for three years. He's amazed at the many extras his neighboring schools are receiving from the central office: a remodeled lunch room, several additional computers, and an allocation for a guidance counselor. His school seems to be passed over. He would like to know what he can do to work within the power structure to enhance the services and materials at his school.

■MANY PRINCIPALS, GIVEN their choice, would like to run their schools and have little or no contact with the central or district office. But in the real world, principals do not have that luxury. In addition to parents and community leaders, we must build bridges to the central office staff as well as members of the community school board.

There are many pitfalls you can avoid and strategies you can use that will put your school in a more favorable light.

16-1 RELATING POSITIVELY TO THE CENTRAL OFFICE STAFF

The staff at the central office must relate to every head of school. They view certain principals as professional leaders and others as pests or cry babies. There are those principals who call the office daily about the most trivial items. Some call to complain or whine. Others call or come in only when asked to.

At every central office there are some untapped resources that can help you run your school better. Too often, principals keep their distance or don't know how to go about getting the extra services that are available.

Use these guidelines to help you relate positively to the central office staff.

Guidelines for Mining the Central Office's Resources

1. *Identify your best sources.* Every district office has a handful of movers and shakers who can ease a project to completion or stall it forever. Get to know who's who. Make sure you know who does what job. Whom do you call if you need another school aide? What's the procedure for getting additional pupil furniture? Find out who to contact *before* you need their services.

2. *Cultivate your relationships with key people.* Begin small, with just one supportive person, if necessary, and build slowly to a full network. Start with the superintendent's secretary. If he or she doesn't like you and doesn't perceive you as important to the district, you're often dead in the water as far as the district office is concerned. Find out about the secretary's family or hobbies and chat for a moment whenever you call, in person or on the telephone.

3. *Become informed.* Read everything that goes out from the district office. Keep a file of names and phone numbers. Read copies of speeches made by the superintendent. Get to know about pet projects or district goals. Make your projects and goals consistent with them.

4. *Get involved in outside groups and organizations.* The key members of the central office undoubtedly belong to civic, fraternal, and educational organizations. Get involved in these groups. Ask questions and express yourself. Volunteer to serve on committees. Circulate among those you know, speaking up with phrases such as

"Is there any way I can help?"

"I like the way you handled that problem."

"I'd welcome a chance to work with you on. . . ."

5. *Learn to network.* Make additional contacts wherever you go. Talk to the attendant who fills your car's gas tank. Let him or her know who you are. Try to use merchants in your school community. These people may know others who can be of assistance to your school in some way. Trade business cards and referrals with other professionals.

6. *Recognize significant events.* Invest a few dollars in birthday and other greeting cards. Read the local newspaper regularly. Send an anniversary or condolence card to central office staff whenever an item appears in the newspaper or district publication. Inquire about grandchildren or ailing parents. Don't forget to include all those you deal with in the district office on your Christmas card list.

7. *Avoid taking sides.* Politics is frequently a daily sport in district or central offices. There are bound to be factions and school board member favorites. It is essential that you avoid the temptation of taking sides or joining in political ploys. The smart principal gets along well with everyone and remains independent. Be smart and master the art of being savvy but apolitical.

16–2 WINNING YOUR SUPERINTENDENT'S SUPPORT

Just being a good principal in the eyes of parents, pupils, and teachers is not enough. To get your full share of the central office's budget allocations and cooperation, you must win your superintendent's support.

There are six techniques you can use to impress your superintendent with the good job you are doing.

Six Techniques for Winning Your Superintendent's Support

1. *Keep him or her informed.* Superintendents don't want to hear from board members or others about problems, programs, or special needs you may have at your school. Be sure to send the superintendent all

the memoranda you are handing out to parents and community members. If something the least bit controversial is being considered, such as a sex education program, be sure to touch base with the superintendent to get his or her views and caveats on the subject.

2. *Seek the superintendent's advice.* Before you launch a new program, such as an after-school latchkey program, seek out his or her advice. You will usually get support because you have made the superintendent a partner in your project.

3. *Know what you're talking about.* You must know your subject inside-out. Don't waste the superintendent's time and yours by not being able to anticipate his or her questions.

4. *Have recommendations ready.* Many superintendents will listen to your problem or proposal carefully and then, after a pause, will ask you what you think. Be prepared to make decisions concerning your school when your boss asks for your recommendation. Don't sit back and ask him or her to make your decisions for you. Make recommendations that your boss can support.

5. *Put your proposal in writing.* Make your presentation brief and easy to follow. Give the superintendent only the basic points unless he or she asks for more information. Have your idea outlined in writing so the superintendent can review it later. A written outline of your plan will also help if the superintendent wants to present your idea to the school board.

6. *Remain open minded.* Adopt a "nothing sacred" attitude about your proposal. Don't act as if your idea is etched in stone and thus immune from criticism. Your superintendent may want to make modifications that reflect his or her personality or philosophy. Be flexible enough to go along.

Practice these six techniques when dealing with your superintendent and you'll be amazed at how supportive he or she will become.

16–3 GETTING SCHOOL BOARD MEMBERS TO HELP

There are over 16,000 school boards in this country, and they all share the same basic mission: to represent the wishes of the people and to exercise lay control of the education of the children in the district. Boards follow the universal practice and requirement of employing a chief administrative officer, the school superintendent, who is your boss.

In theory, the board members formulate policy for the school district while the superintendent and his or her staff, along with the principals, carry out or implement the policy. In reality, the edges get a little fuzzy in some districts when board members try to implement policy as well as make it.

You must tread carefully and avoid upsetting the superintendent by going directly to board members in seeking additional funds or services. In fact, many superintendents forbid principals from writing directly to school board members. Instead, they insist that principals write to the superintendent and send a copy of the letter to any or all board members.

Yet there is much you can accomplish by cultivating members of the school board. Here are some valuable hints on getting help from school board members:

1. *Adopt one particular board member as your liaison to the school board.* This can be a member who lives in your school neighborhood or has a business there. Perhaps his or her child attends or formerly attended your school. Routinely send this member school newsletters, bulletins, and schedules of upcoming events. This board member will now be well informed of what's going on at your school and will champion your cause at board meetings.

2. *Become aware of the various responsibilities of the different board members.* Get to know who makes policy in the area of personnel, school lunches, transportation, etc. Knowing which member has the expertise to help your school is an important first step.

3. *Involve school board members in the events of your school.* Invite them to science fairs, art shows, band concerts, graduations, and so on. Take them on a tour of your building when they are there for one of these events. When a board agenda item comes up regarding the proposed replacement of your leaking roof or installation of accoustical tiles in the lunch room, board members can say they were on site and can attest for the need for the item.

4. *Get to know which functions are primarily the superintendent's and which are shared with board members.* In addition, review these degrees of authority as they affect your central office:

   - The superintendent has complete authority to decide and act within limits of law, board policy, propriety, and common sense.
   - The superintendent has complete authority to act but must inform the board about decisions or action.
   - The superintendent must obtain prior approval from the board before taking action.
   - The school board makes the final decision but may permit or require a recommendation from the superintendent.

5. *Take advantage of sunshine laws,* which require school boards to conduct most of their meetings in public. In most places, executive or

closed sessions are exempt from open meeting laws. Attend as many open meetings as you can. This practice will make you aware of what's going on in the district and identify you as a concerned principal.

6. *Make yourself available to board members who are close to your school.* School board members are usually involved in many organizations. For example, if a board member has been pivotal in getting your gymnasium refurbished, you can show your personal gratitude by volunteering at the March of Dimes Walkathon if the member is deeply involved in that project.

The important thing is to see each board member as a potential friend of your school rather than as some remote figure that you'd best avoid.

16–4 GAINING SUPPORT FROM ELECTED OFFICIALS

Schools do not exist in a political vacuum. You should mount strategies to establish good school-community ties. This is usually labeled public relations. Actually, it also involves political action. The political structure of the community is the suprastructure of the central office leadership and of the school. While many principals view political leaders as insincere deal makers, this stereotype is not true today, if it ever was.

When viewed in its proper role, politics is the democratic process of making significant decisions concerning public policy, including educational policy. For this reason, you must use your knowledge and expertise to make sure that education in general, and your school in particular, gets its share of the tax dollar and community resources.

You will not have as much direct contact as the superintendent with the most powerful leaders of the school district, but you will interact with some of them. These elected and appointed leaders can be very helpful in the development of good community and school relations.

The support of leaders in the community power structure is a critical variable in a school's success. A whisper from them about the school has greater influence on public opinion than a shout from the rooftop by the administrator.

The following guidelines will help gain—or at least not lose—the support of elected officials.

1. *Do* identify who the elected officials are in your school district. Keep an up-to-date list of their names, titles, addresses, and phone numbers. Maintain folders of their newsletters and your correspondence with them. Save newspaper clippings of their comments and doings on the educational scene.

2. *Do* mail the political representative of your school's attendance district news of contest winners, pupil awards, PTA bulletins, and other material that lists the positive achievements of the school and its pupils.

3. *Do* notify local elected officials of accomplishments of your staff members, such as advanced degrees, published materials, fellowships and grants, etc.

4. *Don't* get involved in political campaigns, partisan fund-raisers, or the distribution of party literature.

5. *Do* invite elected officials to speak at graduations, install PTA officers, and attend significant school events.

6. *Do* keep abreast of political change in the community and within the area of the school. Observe and note nonschool issues that may affect your school, such as the construction of a homeless shelter, the closing of a defense installation, or changing demographics.

7. *Do* join groups of nonschool leaders in your school community, such as service clubs, neighborhood and block associations, and your local chamber of commerce. Keep these people informed about your school's needs.

8. *Do* attend town hall meetings and other open forums where community problems are discussed and elected officials are likely to be present.

9. *Don't* ever insinuate that your school is in greater need than a neighboring school of funds or other resources. Avoid comparing schools or making disparaging remarks about other schools or school leaders. These will come back to haunt you.

10. *Do* make yourself available to help write position papers on the need for enhanced funding for education, more state aid for schools, or a greater slice of the federal education budget.

Never succumb to political behavior that compromises principles of professional ethics or moral behavior.

16–5 HELPING YOUR SUPERINTENDENT RATE YOUR PERFORMANCE

Performance appraisal is one of the most onerous tasks of the school superintendent. Oddly enough, it is more difficult to write up a good principal than it is to document a poor one. In the case of the unsatisfactory principal, there is already a file of parent complaints, teacher grievances, pupil misbehavior, low test scores, and other specific materials.

In the case of the principal who is doing a good job, the superintendent frequently relies on a gut reaction based on what he or she saw when visiting the school and the teachers' and parents' general feelings of satisfaction. In many cases, the superintendent has just vague, positive feelings about the satisfactory principal at rating time.

You can come to the superintendent's assistance, and yours, by keeping your file in the central office full of positive material all year long. This will help your superintendent rate your performance with greater accuracy and ease.

Some strategies for doing this include the following:

- Send your superintendent a letter early in the school year in which you list your goals for the school. Follow up in February with a mid-year appraisal of how you are reaching these goals. In May, summarize your progress.

- Each month, mail the superintendent a list of awards and prizes won by your pupils in school, district, and city or statewide contests that involved essays, posters, science experiments, music performances, sports, or other competitions.

- Whenever you receive a complimentary letter from a satisfied parent or community resident, send a photocopy along with a cover letter to the superintendent.

- Invite the superintendent to significant school events, such as student council installation of officers, Honor Society induction, band concerts, art shows, science fairs, Flag Day exercises, kindergarten graduation, and so on. If the superintendent does not appear, mail him or her a printed program (with his or her name and title printed above yours).

- Share any minutes or handouts you have prepared for teacher training sessions at your school. The superintendent may choose to use them with a less creative principal.

- Have your secretary help you draw up a graph or chart that shows an improvement in some area for your pupils. This could be in school attendance, reading or math scores, reduction in fights, or participation in reading programs, such as Book-It or Read-a-thon. Send it along with your May letter.

- Document improved parent-teacher relations at your school. In a letter, tell the superintendent about teachers' increased attendance at evening PTA meetings or the number of parents who came out for Open School Night.

- Summarize the comments the superintendent made during his or her visit to your school. Cite the superintendent's suggestions for improvement and tell how you plan to achieve this. Follow up a month later with a progress report.

These strategies will help you see the progress you are making and assist the superintendent in rating your performance.

16–6 STAYING IN TOUCH WITH ALL YOUR PUBLICS

The power structure extends beyond the school board and district office. You must answer to, or may choose to interface with, several "publics," or groups of people. None of these groups likes to be ignored. Whether you are announcing a major curriculum change or have invited a minor league ball player to talk to your fourth-grade assembly, you would do well to inform your various publics.

By keeping everyone informed, you are building a positive image of your school and its principal. You are also preventing the spread of rumors by supplying factual data. Send messages that either enhance knowledge or anticipate questions.

Sit down and make two lists of people and organizations you want to keep informed, on a regular basis, of school happenings. Label as List A those groups or individuals that should get every major communication. Label as List B those who are less directly tied to your school but with whom you want to keep the channels of communication open.

After taking this first step, the rest is easy. Whenever you have a written announcement (e.g., new staff member, dance program, change in bus schedule, etc.), label it either A or B, or A and B, and give it to your secretary. This will be his or her signal to send a copy to everyone on the appropriate list.

You can easily develop a list of the components of your public by referring to the following sample lists. Feel free to move some items from one list to another.

List A

School staff (including part-time and itinerant teachers)

PTA (via monthly newsletter or directly to president)

Superintendent (including selected staff members)

Middle school principal

Pupils (via loudspeaker, assembly, student council)

Ancillary personnel (custodial, kitchen, security, bus)

List B

> Local newspaper
> Civic organizations
> Neighborhood improvement groups
> City council
> Chamber of commerce
> Minority organizations
> Religious groups
> Recreation organizations
> Other agencies (police, fire, health)
> Appropriate unions

There will be times when you will want to make modifications. For example, you may hand your secretary a memo with the notation: "List A, *plus* local newspaper." Or, you may request distribution to "List B, *minus* recreational organizations."

The lists keep you from neglecting any one of your publics. This reduces hurt feelings and improves communication. Today's principal must remember to keep the public aware of what is going on in the school. This will improve the image of the school and its leader.

Chapter 17

Growing as a Leader

Marie A. has been a principal for ten years—
seven of them at the Maple Shade School. She is well
organized, and each school year seems to progress
much like the one before.

She has earned the respect of her teachers,
parents, and pupils. Yet Marie would like to derive a
little more satisfaction from her job. She'd like to
refine her leadership techniques and utilize her staff
and her talents more effectively.

Her leadership style seems to be growing stale,
her relationships with staff members are becoming
static, and she appears to be burying herself under a
mountain of paperwork.

Marie remembers her first few years on the job
when things were fresh and exciting. She'd love to put
the joy back into her job.

■EVERY SCHOOL DAY is different from the day before, and yet, over the years, a sameness about the principal's job seems to develop.

The alternative to this impending burnout is to take specific steps toward refining your skills and growing as a leader. These seven sections will take you through the process step by step.

17–1 DEVELOPING YOUR LEADERSHIP STYLE

You will find yourself in different situations that require you to wear different hats at different times. The key is knowing when to do what and how to do it. You begin by deciding which hat to wear from your collection. This will help you assume different roles in a variety of situations and with different people.

Before you can decide on which leadership style to adopt, you'll need to stay alert to the needs of the people around you. To make the right choice of style or hat, you'll need to know the six leadership hats in the elementary school.

1. *A director's hat.* This is for giving specific instructions and supervising teachers and staff. This is good with first-year teachers, who need lots of structure and supervision.

2. *A coach's hat.* This is for explaining every decision and asking for suggestions from teachers. This works well with nontenured teachers, who are in the second or third year on the job. They're gaining confidence, but they still need a lot of encouragement.

3. *A backer's hat.* This is for making decisions together with staff members and backing or supporting their efforts toward performing tasks. This works well with creative teachers, backing them up and helping them reach their goals.

4. *The delegator's hat.* This is for turning over responsibility to experienced, capable teachers. This is good with staff members who have been successful in the past. Giving them a little latitude usually brings excellent results.

5. *The influencer's hat.* This is for handing over decisions and the responsibility for implementing them to staff members. This is a good style to use with teachers who regularly go above and beyond their basic duties. Putting a teacher in charge of the lunch room would be

a good example. You would influence the teacher on basic routines and leave the decisions and responsibility to him or her.

6. *The owner's hat.* This is a hat you share with teachers, staff, and parents. In so doing, you convey a sense of ownership in a project before it begins. They buy into the project by planning with you and assuming certain responsibilities. This puts everyone at ease as long as you understand you may have to give up your own ideas when they aren't working.

This list gives you ideas and examples of the appropriate leadership style you should use at different times and places.

Keep in mind that the leadership style that works with one teacher may fail you when you use it the next time if the situation is different. For example, an ordinarily competent teacher working outside his or her field of expertise may need direct supervision. You must reevaluate each staff member every time; when people need change, your approach must change, too.

Keeping your leadership style flexible will keep you in tune to your staff's needs and is a basic component of the successful school principal.

17–2 DELEGATING RESPONSIBILITY EFFECTIVELY

We all know principals who pride themselves on being indispensible to their school. They're hardly ever absent and handle virtually everything themselves. By not training anyone to take their place on occasion, and by not delegating any responsibility to others, they limit their own chances for advancement. If no one has been trained to take over, districts would be loathe to promote these principals for fear the schools would flounder without them. Even more importantly, these principals miss the opportunity to capitalize on the strengths other staff members possess and are willing to share.

Here are five proven techniques you can use to provide on-the-job training to an assistant principal or an ambitious teacher who wants to move ahead:

1. *Give a total picture.* See to it that your assistant has all information necessary to fulfill the mission. If the teacher is to improve the science program, for example, provide a clear, complete list of available equipment, the course of study, and what outcomes you hope he or she can accomplish. Let the teacher know at what level the pupils are.

2. *Tell what you are doing.* If your assistant is to do a good job consistent with your philosophy, you will want to keep him or her advised at all

times about what you are doing. If you want to improve pupil behavior, for example, tell your assistant about your plans for a discipline code, the reasons for your decisions on pupil suspensions, etc.

3. *Add responsibility gradually.* Don't scare your assistant away by loading up at once. Let him or her get the feel of the job in stages. If your assistant is to work on school routines, start with the line-up area and the movement of classes in the morning. When this improves, your assistant can go on to another facet of the school program. Your staff will gradually learn to accept and respect the second in command.

4. *Don't strangle.* Some administrators keep such a tight rein on their assistants that the subordinates feel harassed. Keeping your finger on each and every tiny detail of your assistant's improved science program will actually diminish his or her efficiency.

5. *Give authority.* If you're going to hold your assistant responsible for the math program, then you must give him or her the authority to propose changes. Encourage your assistant to bring problems to you only when something is wrong (e.g., if the new math books have not arrived).

By using these techniques, you will have the satisfaction of delegating some of your work to people who can do the job. Your assistants will have the joy of knowing they are being utilized properly and that their true potential is being fulfilled.

17–3 PUTTING YOUR LISTENING SKILLS TO WORK

All principals have received formal training in reading and writing, and most have studied speaking—but few, if any, have been taught to listen. Many principals listen poorly, even though research and studies by communication experts have shown that people spend more time listening than reading, writing, or talking.

Because you are in the communication business and listening is one part of verbal communication (but not a means of communication itself), good listening ability is what separates the superior principal from the ordinary one.

Knowing how and when to listen can provide you with an excellent tool with which to analyze parents, pupils, and staff members and give you feedback into what they are thinking as well as what they are saying. Your good listening skills will also make teachers more receptive to a different viewpoint. People are more likely to listen to you if you have listened to them and understand their views.

You may not know how well tuned your listening skills are until you measure yourself against the following list.

The Twelve Most Common Listening Mistakes

1. Asking a teacher or parent a question and only half-listening to their reply
2. Pretending to listen while concentrating on your own thoughts
3. Letting your eyes wander around the room while someone is talking to you
4. Parting your lips while you anxiously await others to finish so that you can start talking yourself
5. Paying attention merely to the words and ignoring the speaker's message or not catching his or her feelings
6. Jumping to conclusions before the speaker has finished
7. Offering advice when the speaker merely wants you to listen and doesn't want any advice
8. Being preoccupied with your own problems and showing no patience with the concerns of parents and staff
9. Misinterpreting what the parent or teacher is saying because of your preconceived ideas and prejudices
10. Deciding immediately that you can't help the speaker
11. Judging the speaker's words on delivery rather than content
12. Engaging in passive rather than active listening (Involve your mind as well as your ear!)

Do any of these common mistakes seem to apply to you? Do you see how easy it is to succumb to these pitfalls?

The sense of when to listen and when to speak is a verbal communication skill that develops with practice. While you're honing and refining it, you'll do well to lean more toward keeping quiet. Spend more time listening to others before you respond. This is especially true when dealing with difficult people—complaining parents, upset teachers, and misbehaving pupils.

With a little effort, you can add good listening to your arsenal of people skills. Start by mastering these four skills.

Four Listening Skills

1. Make a note of the key words people use while speaking. These will be the action words that pinpoint an area of meaning in their message. Focus on these words so you can use them in your response. This will ensure that you have grasped the speaker's true meaning.

2. Try to filter out emotion, bias, mannerisms, or accent while listening. If someone has a facial tic or accent, many people focus on that and don't hear what the person has said. By screening out these distractions, you can target the key words and true content. Make an effort to mentally underline the speaker's key words.

3. Develop the ability to separate the speaker's content into primary and secondary points. If he or she makes two points, the second one is usually what is primary on his or her mind. The first point is usually just a warm-up or introduction to the main event.

4. Become sensitive for what is left unsaid and for the inner feelings words often mask. An excellent book on this subject is by Robert L. Montgomery, *Listening Made Easy* (New York: American Management Association, 1981).

There are several things you can do or say while listening that will assure the speaker of your concern and will help you get the true message:

1. Look right at the nose of the speaker. This will keep you from distractions. This is better than looking into the speaker's eyes, which may unnerve him or her.

2. Move your head up and down in a nodding gesture to offer agreement or concern when you don't want to interrupt the speaker's flow and yet want to communicate support.

3. Use phrases such as "I see," "of course," or "That must have been awful" when you want to offer support.

4. Catch the speaker's name and use it in your conversation. This assures connection and dignifies the speaker.

5. Ask questions to see if your interpretation of what the speaker has said is correct.

6. Follow up with, "Tell me more about . . ." or "When did this happen?" or "Who else was there at the time?" when you want to get more facts about an alleged incident.

7. Don't commit yourself before you have investigated a situation. Conclude the conversation with phrases like, "I'll get back to you tomorrow. Will you be home in the morning?" or "You'll hear from me as soon as I speak to the teacher."

The philosopher and prolific author Dr. Mortimer Adler sums this up well in "Are You Listening?" (American Express cardmembers' *Newsletter*, June 1983). He writes, "To agree before you understand what the other person has said is inane. To disagree before you understand is impertinent."

17–4 CREATING A LOYAL SCHOOL STAFF

There is no escaping it—it's important to be liked rather than disliked by those on whom you depend to carry out your decisions. It makes your job much easier and allows you to spend your energy on productive school matters rather than on trying to figure out why teachers—or bus drivers, aides, lunch workers, etc.—are so uncooperative.

In talking to principals selected by their superintendents for retraining because of their weaknesses, one flaw led all the rest. Insensitivity to others was the chief reason these principals failed to get staff loyalty.

If you sometimes wonder why you are surrounded by disgruntled, disloyal, oversensitive people who seem bent on ignoring your leadership or the needs of your school, here's what you might consider to remedy the situation:

Five Ways to Lift the Level of Staff Loyalty

1. *Recognize staff members' egos.* Your staff members' egos are large—as large as, or possibly larger than, your own. If you ignore them when they need to be recognized, criticize them when they are hoping for praise, or demean them when they want support, they will perceive your behavior as a threat to their self-esteem. If you don't foresee this, or fail to regard it as natural and legitimate, then you might be in for some unpleasant surprises.

2. *Become aware of your staff members' sore spots.* Teachers' sensitivities are extensive, and it's important to do as much mental cataloguing of them as possible. Find out what they are and be aware of them in your dealings and face-to-face encounters. This will endear you to your staff, and they will respect your leadership. Get to know who is fearful of classroom visitors, who needs repeated recognition for their attractive classroom, who is challenged by an acting-out student, and who is repelled by wimpy cry babies. Try to accommodate them, and watch the benefits.

3. *Understand that relationships are not static.* Sometimes they are only as good as your last conversation. It can be dangerous to assume that your relationship with a teacher is so fine that you no longer have to think about it. It is at this point, usually, that you find yourself stepping on toes, disregarding sensitivities, and incurring resentment. You have to work at building loyalty continuously. The attitude of many staff members is, "What have you done for me lately?"

4. *Watch your language.* Your words can be upsetting unless you take pains to avoid angering those who are affected by them. For example,

if you are about to criticize a teacher in response to a parent's legitimate complaint, it's better to prepare the teacher with, "I'd like to talk to you about something that I think needs some improvement." You may encounter disagreement, but you lessen the chances that the other person will feel victimized.

5. *Keep negative feelings from escalating.* Don't wait too long to take ameliorative action after you have made a staff member angry by some thoughtless remark. It doesn't have to be an apology, but it should at the least open the door to a better understanding: "You're angry with me, aren't you?" That way, your initial mistake won't turn into a feud.

Loyalties are built when teachers and other staff members feel that you are aware of their feelings. We're not suggesting that you pander to your staff's emotional needs. But sensitivities are often trampled when you insist on a course of action without consulting those who will be most affected. Allowing others to change your mind about what you're going to do is not a sign of weakness. Neither is consulting others. Recognizing staff members' egos is the best way to keep yours from being bruised. Listening to their voices in school matters is a must in today's environment. This kind of sharing is also good management, because it tends to dissolve resentment and build loyalty.

17–5 USING COMPUTERS TO EASE YOUR WORKLOAD

There are many reasons why you should use computers: to serve as a role model for teachers and pupils, to individualize instruction, and to be on the cutting edge of a revolution in education.

An even more immediate reason is that using a computer can greatly reduce your paperwork and make you infinitely more efficient. It is now accepted practice for top administrators in any organization to use computers. Executives who would never have been caught using a typewriter find it perfectly acceptable to use a computer. And so it is with top principals.

There are many applications for computer use that you can put to work as soon as you are plugged in:

- *Increased learning opportunities for pupils.* You can provide your teachers with valuable information on their pupils by retrieving stored information from the microcomputer and printing it for teachers when making a decision about class placement. Data on test scores, past performance, attitude ratings, and family history can all be accessed by the computer in seconds.

- *File creation and management.* The computer stores information electronically just as information is stored in file cabinets—except that it is much more easily stored and retrieved by the computer and occupies less space. The usual information kept on pupils, such as name, address, date of birth, phone, attendance, test scores, grades, behavior, etc., can be extracted at will. For example, you can generate an attendance list of pupils absent ten or more days without going to every pupil's file.

- *Scheduling pupils and teachers.* This was one of the earliest uses for computers in school administration. The computer can do in minutes what formerly took hours to do by hand. Class lists, room utilization, teacher preparation periods, departmental programs, and so on can all be enhanced by the computer.

- *Attendance reports and records.* Shortly after the teachers take attendance in the morning, the computer can generate an absentee list, by class, complete with phone numbers. The secretary or school aide can call home on the same day of a suspicious absence.

- *Grade reporting on report cards and records.* There are several excellent grade-reporting software packages on the market. They provide capabilities for reporting letter grades, number grades, honor roles, teacher comments, and much more.

- *Internal bookkeeping of the school.* Records of internal finances can be managed by computer. Payroll, supply money, textbook expenditures, petty cash, postage, etc. can be satisfactorily maintained on a ledger produced by a spreadsheet program.

Computers are no longer a luxury but a necessity in the modern school office. Getting your school "on line" is well worth the money and initial effort.

17–6 MANAGING BY PRESENCE

If we were asked for the one single trait that separates the outstanding principal from among the ordinary, it would be the ability to manage by presence. By that we mean the principal who circulates around the building every day, ideally being seen in the lineup areas, lunch room, bus loading area, wherever pupils and teachers gather.

Management by presence is not easy. It takes time and courage. It exposes you: Your ability to listen is exposed. Your knowledge of what's going on is exposed. You are scrutinized by the toughest watchers of all—your teachers and pupils. You can placate an angry parent on the phone or cover up a judgment error in a letter to the central office. But if you are walking around the school every day, you can't fool the pupils or teachers.

The advantages are legion. You can prevent problems before they emerge, you gain the respect of the pupils who see you everywhere, your teachers remain on their toes, and parents see you as having greater credibility. You're not giving them some public relations line, but you're talking from your hands-on experience.

Once you establish the habit (and that's what it needs to be), you will make it a regular part of your routine. You will be able to nip problems in the bud and you will have made observations at close range that will make your job easier when you do return to your office. Having been in and out of the classrooms, halls, lunch room, etc., you know what's happening and can do a better job of requesting repairs, ordering books, evaluating staff, making interclass transfers, and so on.

Just as the involved teacher is constantly moving around the classroom and the noninvolved teacher is most often perched behind a desk, the involved principal is all over the building, not deskbound.

Exceptional principals who make it their business to visit classrooms and roam the halls and stairwells have the same clamoring constituencies. What makes them different is their determination to manage by presence. From daily life experience, we know that wandering around, staying in touch, and keeping out of the office is the mark of the superb hospital administrator, mayor, plant manager, and, obviously, the school leader. Make this part of your daily routine, and you will grow as a school leader.

17–7 PUTTING JOY BACK IN THE JOB

More and more is being asked of today's principal. We must now focus on cooperation with teachers, parents, and even pupils. Our new role casts us as a facilitator who encourages ideas, experimentation, and collegiality.

Fending off the central office and making sure the buses run on time is no longer enough. Principals are now expected to share power over the curriculum and school management with their teachers. In the future, principal certification will examine not just theory but applied skills in actual decision-making situations. A few states—including Georgia and New Jersey—already require such performance assessments. Several also require school-based internships for their aspiring principals.

While some senior principals gnash their teeth at the many changes taking place, not all of the changes are bad. Most make a lot of sense, as long as they are put into place on the school level and not merely mandated from above.

School administration theory and responsibility have changed throughout the years. What has not changed is the fun part of the job.

Draw up a list of the things you enjoy doing and make it your business to do at least one of them each day. After talking to hundreds of principals across the country, we have come up with some sample items of activities they enjoy. We're sure you can add several more. We'd love to hear from you about what gives *you* joy in *your* job.

- "Walking into a classroom and talking to the kids."
- "Helping a promising new teacher get started."
- "Working with a small group of teachers on a school project."
- "Helping parents hone their parenting skills."
- "Coaching kids on a team."
- "Putting out a school newspaper."
- "Observing teachers in the classroom and seeing them grow in ability."
- "Working with teachers in putting on a school program."
- "Counseling parents who need someone to talk to."
- "Reviewing new textbooks and other learning materials for possible adoption."
- "Organizing a student council."
- "Planning graduation exercises."

Of course, there are frustrations—but take the time to put the joy back into the job.

Good luck!

Index